FamilyCircle®
Quick & Easy Recipes

FamilyCircle®
Quick & Easy
Recipes

More than 300 tasty,
easy-to-make recipes plus 75 photos

From the editors of Family Circle

BROADWAY BOOKS New York

Published by Broadway Books
A division of Random House, Inc.
1540 Broadway, New York, New York 10036

BROADWAY BOOKS and its logo, a letter B bisected on the diagonal, are trademarks of
Broadway Books, a division of Random House, Inc.

A Roundtable Press Book

Printed in China
First Edition March 2001

Library of Congress Cataloging-in-Publication Data

    Family circle quick & easy recipes from the editors of Family circle.--1st ed.
       p. cm.
     ISBN 0-7679-0605-5
      1. Quick and easy cookery. I. Title: Family circle quick and easy recipes. II. Title:
    Quick & easy recipes from the editors of Family circle. III. Family circle (New York, N.Y.)

    TX833.5. F33 2001
    641.5'55--dc21

                           00-039738

FOR ROUNDTABLE PRESS, INC.:

DIRECTORS: Marsha Melnick,
Julie Merberg, Susan E. Meyer
SENIOR EDITOR: Carol Spier
BOOK DESIGN: Vertigo Design, NYC
ILLUSTRATIONS: Kathryn Adams
LAYOUT: Smythtype
EDITORIAL ASSISTANT: Carrie Glidden
PRODUCTION: Bill Rose

COVER DESIGN: Amy C. King, Broadway Books

FOR FAMILY CIRCLE MAGAZINE:

EDITOR-IN-CHIEF: Susan Kelliher Ungaro
CREATIVE DIRECTOR: Diane Lamphron
EXECUTIVE EDITOR: Barbara Winkler
FOOD DIRECTOR: Peggy Katalinich
SENIOR FOOD EDITOR: Diane Mogelever
ASSOCIATE FOOD EDITOR: Julie Miltenberger
EDITORIAL ASSISTANT: Keri Linas
TEST KITCHEN ASSISTANT: Keisha Davis
RECIPE EDITOR: David Ricketts
NUTRITIONIST: Patty Santelli
TEST KITCHEN: JoAnn Brett, Lauren Huber,
Michael Tyrrell, Robert Yamarone

FOR G+J PUBLISHING:

BOOKS & LICENSING MANAGER:
Tammy Palazzo
BOOKS & LICENSING COORDINATOR:
Sabeena Lalwani
BOOKS & LICENSING ASSISTANTS:
Tana McPherson, Carla Clark

Cover photographs: front, Alan Richardson (left) and Brian Hagiwara (top right and bottom right); spine, Ellen Silverman; back, Brian
Hagiwara (top and bottom); inside back flap, Jeff Weiner.

All other photography credits are found on page 240 and constitute an extension of this copyright page.

The recipe for Grilled Tenderloin with Caper Mayonnaise (shown on page 2, left) appears on page 142. The recipe for Tomato Tart (shown
on page 2, right) appears on page 175. The recipe for Basil Stuffed Eggplant (shown on page 3, top) appears on page 167. The recipe for
Blackberry Jelly Roll (shown on page 3, bottom) appears on page 207. The recipe for Key Lime Pie (shown on page 6) appears on page 191.
The recipe for Lemon-Pepper Chicken Breasts (shown on page 7, left) appears on page 95. The recipe for Cavatelli Arrabbiata (shown on
page 7, top) appears on page 39. The recipe for Peanutty Chocolate Chip Cookies (shown on page 7, bottom) appears on page 216.

Foreword

On weekdays, I arrive home about 7 o'clock. Last night, before I could even kick off my shoes, my 6-year-old daughter, Christina, was begging me to let her raid my jewelry box. My 18-year-old son, Ryan, gave me a nod as he looked up from his homework. My husband, Colin, was at our 13-year-old son Matthew's basketball game. They were due home at eight. So that was my deadline for supper. I had 45 minutes to change into something more comfortable, play with Christina, set the table and whip up a nice meal.

Whew!

That's why I'm a huge fan of the quick and easy dinner. And that's why I think our newest cookbook is a must-have for busy women. Give us a fast and tasty recipe and we're forever grateful. As you can imagine, I owe a lot of thanks to the food editors who create the recipes for *Family Circle* magazine. I especially love the way we've organized *Quick & Easy Recipes* into categories to suit every culinary desire.

So what did I make for supper last night? Our new family favorite is stir-fry. As my daughter "juggled" the mushrooms (I let her safely cut a few with an egg slicer), I put on the rice, sliced the steak and chopped the peppers. Everything was ready to "stir" at eight. Both Matthew and Ryan like taking turns at the wok. It really felt like quality time until Christina started throwing the rice! My solution? I pacified her with ice cream while we enjoyed our meal. Necessity (or desperation) is still the mother of invention.

Tomorrow night's menu?

Easy! I'll select a new favorite from the inspiringly speedy recipes in this cookbook.

Susan Kelliher Ungaro, Editor-in-Chief

Contents

Introduction

WHEN IT COMES TO DINNER, I suspect beating the clock is the order of the day for most of us. My kids don't even wait for me to get home—they call me at work to ask, "Mom, what are we having?" (Nothing like a little added stress at the end of the day!) But it doesn't matter whether you're a stay-at-home mom or employed full-time elsewhere, if you've got kids or not: time has become the ultimate luxury.

Making the most of your time is the mission of this book. In the *Family Circle* test kitchen, we're constantly working to create the best-tasting yet easiest-ever dinners and desserts, and this collection is a compilation of the best of the easiest. Through surveys and feedback from our most valuable resource—our readers— we've been able to identify the most helpful techniques for getting in and out of the kitchen fast. Each and every recipe had to fit into one of six categories before making the grade for this book.

Our six clever symbols tell you what's what at a glance—for instance, recipes that cook up in just 🍲 **one POT** (easy cleanup). When you really don't have time to stand and chop or to watch the stove closely, look for 🥄 **quick PREP** or 🧤 **quick COOK**—you'll spend no more than 10 minutes prepping or cooking, and often both aspects are extra quick. Hungry for recipes with only 🧺 **5 ingredients** or that make it from cupboard to table in 🕐 **30-minutes MAX**? For the ultimate convenience, choose 🥄 **no COOK** recipes, which don't require turning on the stove at all. We've got them all. Plus, an added bonus: **FAST FIX** boxes with superfast recipe tips and tricks—no-fuss potato salads, last-minute glazes for grilled chicken, ways to jazz up purchased pound cake and more. Throughout, we use convenience products whenever the substitution delivers the same "from scratch" flavor in a fraction of the time, ingredients such as veggie slaw mixes, prebaked bread shells, prepared pesto or marinara sauce. For our list of don't-ever-be-without-these pantry items, check out the appendix, page 230.

However, speed means nothing if the recipe doesn't pass the ultimate test— great taste. I'm sure you'll find that Teriyaki Chicken, Smothered Steak, Tomatoes with Grilled Mozzarella and Key Lime Pie are destined to become part of your permanent repertoire, not just because they are quick and easy, but also because they're delicious!

The *Family Circle* Food Department's Kitchen Commandments

▶ Start a pot of water boiling the minute you walk into the house. This way, there's minimal delay if you decide it's a pasta night.

▶ Make double batches of easy-to-freeze dishes, such as taco filling or sloppy Joes. On a night when you're feeling weary, all you'll need to do is stop and pick up tortillas or buns to complete a nearly instant meal.

▶ Freeze chicken breasts, pork chops, even strips of bacon individually so that you can pull them out as needed rather than have to thaw one solid mass.

▶ Try to prep for several meals at a time—cutting up peppers, for instance, can be time-consuming, but they last several days. Prep ahead when you know you'll be really pressed on an upcoming night.

▶ Cook a big item like a pork roast on the weekends if you have a little time, then recycle it through the week.

▶ Check out your supermarket meat counter for some of the new fully cooked products. Items like a pot roast that microwaves in less than 10 minutes or precooked shredded barbecue pork may work—and save work—for you.

▶ Keep staples in stock. The fastest recipes in the world are no good if you have to make repeat supermarket trips for basics.

▶ Get your whole family involved—it's no fun when the burden falls on just one person. If you can't get them to cook, remind them that cleanup is within everyone's ability.

▶ Organize your kitchen; there's nothing more frustrating (and time-consuming) than digging around for a measuring cup or the right spatula. A corollary to this tip: Invest in the best knives, pots and pans you can afford. Ultimately, they will reward you with quality cooking.

▶ Relax. It is, after all, only dinner. The most important thing is to enjoy your time with family and friends. Don't feel guilty if the centerpiece is take-out pizza.

Peggy Katalinich, Food Director

Soups & Salads

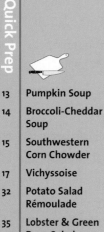

Beef & Barley Soup

5 ingredients or LESS

MAKES 4 servings

PREP 5 minutes

COOK 20 minutes

PER SERVING
430 calories, 40 g protein,
13 g fat, 38 g carbohydrate,
512 mg sodium,
96 mg cholesterol.

1 tablespoon vegetable oil

1¼ pounds boneless sirloin steak, cut into ¾-inch cubes

1 can (13¾ ounces) beef broth

¾ cup quick-cooking barley

1 package (10 ounces) frozen mixed vegetables

1. Heat oil in a large saucepan over medium-high heat. Working in batches, add beef; sauté until browned, about 4 minutes per batch. As beef browns, transfer it to a pie plate or bowl.

2. Return all beef to saucepan. Stir in broth, barley and 5 cups water. Bring to boiling. Cover; simmer 10 minutes or until barley is tender.

3. Stir in frozen mixed vegetables; gently heat through, about 5 minutes.

Beef & Barley Soup

Italian Minestrone

MAKES 8 servings
PREP 10 minutes
COOK 30 minutes

PER SERVING
203 calories, 7 g protein,
7 g fat, 28 g carbohydrate,
860 mg sodium,
1 mg cholesterol.

1 cup small pasta shells
2 tablespoons olive oil
1 onion, chopped
2 large cloves garlic, finely chopped
2 cans (14½ ounces each) beef broth
⅓ pound green beans, trimmed and cut into ¾-inch pieces
1 medium-size zucchini, quartered lengthwise and cut
   into ¼-inch-thick slices
1 large tomato, seeded and diced
1 cup prepared marinara sauce
2 teaspoons prepared or homemade pesto
   (recipe, page 231)
¼ teaspoon black pepper

1. Cook shells in a large pot of lightly salted boiling water until al dente, firm but tender. Drain well.

2. Meanwhile, heat oil in a large nonstick saucepan. Add onion and garlic; sauté over low heat 12 minutes, until onion is softened.

3. Add broth; bring to boiling. Add green beans; simmer 8 minutes.

4. Add zucchini; simmer 5 minutes.

5. Add tomato, marinara sauce, pesto, pepper and cooked pasta shells. Heat through, 3 minutes.

Fast Fix

Meal in a Bowl

ADD A LOAF OF CRUSTY BREAD and a green salad to these quick soups and dinner's on the table in minutes.

Black Bean Soup

▶ Puree 1 can (19 ounces) undrained black beans in a food processor or blender.

▶ Heat 1 tablespoon olive oil in a medium-size saucepan. Add 1 small onion, finely chopped, and 1 clove garlic, finely chopped; sauté over medium heat until softened.

▶ Add ½ cup chicken broth and the bean puree. Bring to boiling.

▶ Serve soup with a dollop of sour cream.

▶ Makes about 4 servings.

Speedy Tortellini in Broth

▶ Simmer 1 package (9 ounces) fresh tortellini in 6 cups chicken broth until cooked.

▶ Add 5 dried tomatoes, chopped, and 1 cup frozen peas; heat through.

▶ Sprinkle with grated Parmesan cheese.

▶ Makes about 4 servings.

Pumpkin Soup

quick PREP

MAKES 6 servings

PREP 10 minutes

COOK 25 minutes

PER SERVING
145 calories, 8 g protein,
7 g fat, 14 g carbohydrate,
835 mg sodium,
18 mg cholesterol.

1 tablespoon butter

1 large onion, chopped

1½ teaspoons curry powder

⅛ teaspoon red-pepper flakes

2 Granny Smith apples, peeled, cored and diced

1½ cups canned solid-pack pumpkin

2 cans (13¾ ounces each) chicken broth

½ cup water

⅔ cup half-and-half or heavy cream

1. Heat butter in a large saucepan over medium heat. Add onion and sauté 5 minutes or until softened but not browned.

2. Stir in curry powder and red-pepper flakes. Add apples and continue cooking 10 minutes longer.

3. Add pumpkin, broth and water; stir to combine. Cook 5 minutes. Remove from heat.

4. Puree pumpkin mixture in a food processor or blender until smooth, working in batches.

5. Return pumpkin to saucepan. Bring to boiling and immediately lower heat. Simmer 2 to 3 minutes to blend flavors. Just before serving, stir in half-and-half.

Carrot Soup

5 ingredients or LESS

MAKES 4 servings

PREP 5 minutes

MICROWAVE 10 minutes

PER SERVING
104 calories, 2 g protein,
7 g fat, 10 g carbohydrate,
1,087 mg sodium,
10 mg cholesterol.

1 pound baby carrots

3 cups chicken broth

½ teaspoon salt

¼ teaspoon ground ginger

¼ cup sour cream

1. Place carrots and 1 tablespoon water in a microwave-safe pie plate. Cover with plastic wrap; vent one corner. Microwave at 100% power 10 minutes.

2. Transfer carrots to a food processor or blender. Add broth, salt and ginger. Blend until smooth.

3. Ladle soup into soup bowls. Place a dollop of sour cream on each serving.

Broccoli-Cheddar Soup

MAKES 8 cups

PREP 10 minutes

COOK 25 minutes

───────

PER SERVING
224 calories, 13 g protein,
12 g fat, 18 g carbohydrate,
543 mg sodium,
38 mg cholesterol.

5 cups water

1 head broccoli (about 1½ pounds), tough ends trimmed
   and stems peeled

2 onions, chopped

⅓ cup long-grain white rice

2 cups milk, plus another 1 cup if a thinner soup is
   desired

1 teaspoon salt

¼ teaspoon black pepper

2 cups shredded cheddar cheese

2 tablespoons spicy brown mustard

1. Bring water to boiling in a large saucepan.

2. Cut 6 flowerets from broccoli head and cut each into quarters. Cook in boiling water for about 4 minutes. Remove with a slotted spoon and reserve for garnish.

3. Coarsely chop remaining broccoli and add to water in saucepan with onions, rice, milk, salt and pepper. Simmer until vegetables are tender, about 20 minutes.

4. Working in batches, transfer vegetables with some liquid to a food processor or blender. Add cheese and mustard. Whirl until smooth, 2 to 3 minutes.

5. Return soup to saucepan. Add more milk if desired. Gently reheat over low heat; do not let boil. Garnish with reserved broccoli.

Broccoli-Cheddar Soup

Southwestern Corn Chowder

MAKES 8 servings

PREP 10 minutes

COOK about 30 minutes

PER SERVING
207 calories, 7 g protein,
8 g fat, 31 g carbohydrate,
1,174 mg sodium,
13 mg cholesterol.

3 slices bacon, diced
½ cup chopped onion
1 cup finely chopped sweet red pepper
2 large baking potatoes, peeled and cubed
1 can (4½ ounces) chopped green chiles, drained
6 cups chicken broth
2 packages (10 ounces each) frozen whole-kernel corn
½ teaspoon salt
¼ teaspoon ground red pepper (cayenne)
¼ cup half-and-half
2 tablespoons chopped fresh cilantro (optional)

1. Sauté bacon and onion in a large saucepan over medium-high heat until onion is softened and lightly browned, about 5 minutes. Add sweet red pepper and sauté 1 minute. Add potatoes and chiles and cook, stirring, 5 minutes.

2. Add broth, corn, salt and ground red pepper. Reduce heat to medium; cover and simmer 15 minutes or until potatoes are fork-tender.

3. Transfer half of soup to a food processor or blender. Whirl to puree. Return to saucepan. Stir in half-and-half. Remove from heat. Add cilantro if desired.

Mexi-Chicken Soup

MAKES 8 servings

PREP 5 minutes

COOK 5 minutes

PER SERVING
243 calories, 18 g protein,
9 g fat, 25 g carbohydrate,
1,193 mg sodium,
38 mg cholesterol.

3 cans (13¾ ounces each) chicken broth
1 can (15¼ ounces) whole-kernel corn
1 can (14½ ounces) diced tomatoes
1 can (15 ounces) red kidney beans
1 pound boneless, skinless chicken breasts, cut into bite-size pieces

1. Combine broth, corn, tomatoes, beans and chicken in a large saucepan. Bring to boiling, stirring occasionally.

2. Cook soup 5 minutes. Remove from heat. Cover saucepan; let stand about 15 minutes.

Vegetable Soup with Pesto Swirl

onePOT

MAKES 10 servings

PREP 20 minutes

COOK 30 minutes

———————

PER SERVING
117 calories, 4 g protein,
7 g fat, 10 g carbohydrate,
901 mg sodium,
4 mg cholesterol.

1 tablespoon olive oil

½ cup diced carrot

½ cup diced celery

½ cup finely chopped leek

6 cups chicken broth

¾ pound red boiling potatoes, diced

½ pound green beans, cut in half

1 tomato, chopped

1 small yellow squash, diced

1 small zucchini, diced

¾ teaspoon salt

10 tablespoons prepared or homemade pesto (recipe, page 231)

1. Heat oil in a large nonstick saucepan. Add carrot, celery and leek; sauté over medium-high heat until very soft, 8 to 10 minutes. Add ¼ cup water if necessary to prevent sticking.

2. Add broth and potatoes; simmer until potatoes are almost tender, about 10 minutes.

3. Add green beans, tomato, squash, zucchini and salt; cook until tender, about 10 minutes.

4. Ladle soup into soup bowls. Swirl 1 tablespoon pesto into each serving.

Cream of Tomato Soup

onePOT

MAKES 4 servings

PREP 15 minutes

COOK about 35 minutes

———————

PER SERVING
150 calories, 5 g protein,
6 g fat, 23 g carbohydrate,
65 mg sodium,
9 mg cholesterol.

2 teaspoons canola oil

1 sweet onion, thinly sliced

1 small bay leaf

3 pounds tomatoes, peeled, seeded and chopped

2 teaspoons cornstarch

½ cup evaporated milk

¼ teaspoon black pepper

¼ teaspoon dried thyme

1. Heat oil in a large saucepan over medium heat. Add onion and bay leaf; cook 5 minutes, until softened. Add tomatoes; bring to simmering. Lower heat; cover; cook 20 minutes. Remove bay leaf.

2. Puree tomatoes in a food processor or blender. Pour back into saucepan.

3. Mix cornstarch and evaporated milk in a small bowl. Stir into soup. Cook, stirring, over medium heat until thickened, about 6 minutes. Stir in pepper and thyme.

Vichyssoise

quick PREP

MAKES 8 servings
PREP 10 minutes
COOK 20 minutes
REFRIGERATE 2 hours

PER SERVING
136 calories, 4 g protein,
5 g fat, 17 g carbohydrate,
781 mg sodium,
13 mg cholesterol.

2 leeks, trimmed and well washed
2 teaspoons vegetable oil
2 pounds all-purpose potatoes, peeled and cubed
7 cups lower-sodium chicken broth
½ teaspoon salt
¼ teaspoon black pepper
¼ cup half-and-half
Chopped fresh chives for garnish (optional)

1. Thinly slice white part of leeks; discard green portion.

2. Heat oil in a large saucepan; add leeks and cook over medium-high heat 5 minutes, until softened but not browned. Add up to ¼ cup water if necessary to prevent sticking.

3. Add potatoes, broth, salt and pepper. Simmer until potatoes are tender, about 15 minutes. Stir in half-and-half; heat through.

4. Working in batches, puree in a food processor or blender. Place in a large bowl and cover with plastic wrap. Refrigerate at least 2 hours. Ladle soup into soup bowls. Garnish each serving with chives if desired.

Cold Borscht

no COOK

MAKES 6 servings
PREP 10 minutes
REFRIGERATE 30 minutes

PER SERVING
101 calories, 4 g protein,
4 g fat, 0 g carbohydrate,
488 mg sodium,
0 mg cholesterol.

3 cans (14½ ounces each) beets
1 can (13¾ ounces) lower-sodium beef broth
⅔ cup reduced-fat sour cream
3 tablespoons cider vinegar
2 tablespoons chopped fresh dill
⅛ teaspoon salt
Fresh dill sprigs for garnish (optional)

1. Drain beets, reserving ½ cup liquid. Place beets, reserved liquid, broth, sour cream, vinegar, dill and salt in food processor or blender. Whirl until smooth. Transfer to a bowl and place in refrigerator to chill, about 30 minutes.

2. Ladle soup into soup bowls. Garnish each serving with a sprig of fresh dill if desired.

Tomato-Corn Soup

Tomato-Corn Soup

MAKES 6 servings

PREP 20 minutes

COOK 30 minutes

———

PER SERVING
243 calories, 10 g protein,
13 g fat, 25 g carbohydrate,
713 mg sodium,
41 mg cholesterol.

2 ears fresh corn, shucked

1 tablespoon vegetable oil

1 small onion, chopped

1 small all-purpose potato, peeled and diced

¼ teaspoon fennel seeds, crushed

6 large tomatoes, peeled, seeded and coarsely chopped

2 cans (13½ ounces each) chicken broth

½ teaspoon dried thyme

¼ teaspoon salt

¼ teaspoon black pepper

½ cup heavy cream

½ pound surimi (imitation crabmeat)

3 dashes liquid hot-pepper sauce, or to taste

1. Slice corn kernels from cobs; you should have about 1½ cups.

2. Heat oil in a large nonaluminum saucepan or Dutch oven over medium-high heat. Add onion; reduce heat to medium; sauté 5 minutes or until onion is slightly softened. Add potato and fennel seeds; cook, stirring, 2 minutes.

3. Add tomatoes, broth, half the corn and the thyme. Bring to boiling. Reduce heat to medium-low; simmer, stirring occasionally, 20 minutes. Season with salt and pepper.

4. Puree in a food processor or blender, working in batches if necessary.

5. Return soup to pot. Stir in cream, surimi and remaining corn. Gently reheat; do not let boil. Stir in hot-pepper sauce.

Avgolemono

MAKES 8 servings

PREP 5 minutes

STAND 10 minutes

COOK 5 minutes

PER SERVING
190 calories, 7 g protein,
4 g fat, 32 g carbohydrate,
661 mg sodium,
89 mg cholesterol.

2 cups water

2 cups instant rice

8 cups lower-sodium chicken broth

¼ cup lemon juice

1 box (10 ounces) frozen chopped spinach, thawed and
  squeezed dry

½ teaspoon salt

½ teaspoon black pepper

4 eggs

1. Bring water to boiling in a medium-size saucepan. Stir in rice; cover saucepan and set aside for 10 minutes or until water is completely absorbed by rice.

2. Bring broth to boiling in a large saucepan. Add lemon juice, spinach, salt and pepper.

3. Whisk eggs in a small bowl until frothy. Stir a little hot broth into eggs. Remove broth from heat. Gradually whisk egg mixture back into saucepan.

4. Place ½ cup rice in each soup bowl. Ladle soup over rice.

Avgolemono

Asian Grilled Chicken Salad

quick
COOK

MAKES 4 servings
PREP 10 minutes
COOK 30 seconds
GRILL OR BROIL 8 minutes

————

PER SERVING
279 calories, 28 g protein,
10 g fat, 20 g carbohydrate,
805 mg sodium,
72 mg cholesterol.

½ pound snow peas, trimmed and halved
1 sweet red pepper, cored, seeded and cut into thin
   strips
1 sweet yellow pepper, cored, seeded and cut into thin
   strips
1 medium-size carrot, peeled and cut into thin strips
6 ounces daikon (Asian white radish), peeled and cut
   into thin strips
3 tablespoons reduced-sodium soy sauce
3 tablespoons rice-wine vinegar
1 tablespoon grated fresh ginger or 1 teaspoon ground
   ginger
1 tablespoon honey
1 tablespoon dark Asian sesame oil
4 boneless, skinless chicken breast halves (about 1
   pound total)
½ teaspoon salt
¼ teaspoon black pepper

1. Bring a medium-size saucepan of water to boiling. Add snow peas; cook 30 seconds. Drain in a colander; rinse under cold running water to stop cooking.

2. Place snow peas, red and yellow peppers, carrot and daikon in a large bowl; toss to combine.

3. To prepare dressing, whisk together soy sauce, rice vinegar, ginger, honey and sesame oil in a small bowl.

4. Prepare a hot grill or heat broiler; position grill rack or broiler-pan rack 4 inches from heat.

5. Season chicken with salt and black pepper. Grill or broil 8 minutes or until internal temperature registers 170° on an instant-read thermometer, turning once halfway through cooking.

6. Slice chicken into ¼-inch-thick slices against grain at a 45° angle. Add to vegetables in bowl. Add dressing; toss to combine.

Warm Chicken Salad

2 tablespoons fresh lime juice

4 chicken cutlets (about 1 pound total), pounded thin

3 tablespoons garlic-flavored olive oil

1 package (1 pound) mixed salad greens

1 cup salsa

1. Combine 1 tablespoon lime juice and chicken in a shallow dish; turn chicken over to coat.

2. Heat 1 tablespoon oil in a large nonstick skillet over medium-high heat. Add chicken; cook, turning halfway through cooking, until browned and cooked through, about 6 minutes.

3. Combine greens, remaining 2 tablespoons oil and remaining 1 tablespoon lime juice in a large bowl; toss to coat.

4. Divide greens evenly among 4 dinner plates. Place a warm cutlet on top of each; top each cutlet with ¼ cup salsa.

Chicken, Mango & Bean Salad

4 boneless, skinless chicken breast halves
    (about 1 pound total)

1 lime

3 scallions, chopped, including some of the green

1 teaspoon chopped, seeded jalapeño chile or
    ¼ teaspoon liquid hot-pepper sauce

¼ cup sour cream

¾ teaspoon salt

1 large mango (1½ pounds), peeled, pitted and diced

1 can (15 ounces) red kidney beans, drained and rinsed

Assorted lettuce leaves for serving

1. Place chicken in a medium-size saucepan. Add enough water to cover. Bring to barely simmering. Cover; simmer 8 minutes or until internal temperature registers 170° on an instant-read thermometer. Cool chicken in liquid for 30 minutes. Remove chicken from liquid; cut into cubes.

2. Grate rind from lime; place in a medium-size bowl. Juice lime; add 2 tablespoons juice to rind. Stir in scallions, jalapeño, sour cream and salt.

3. Add chicken, mango and beans to mixture in bowl; toss gently to combine. Serve salad over assorted lettuce leaves on individual plates.

Turkey Waldorf Salad

quick COOK

MAKES 6 servings

PREP 10 minutes

COOK 3 minutes

———

PER SERVING
423 calories, 19 g protein,
31 g fat, 20 g carbohydrate,
303 mg sodium,
57 mg cholesterol.

¾ pound turkey cutlets, cubed

3 Red Delicious apples, cored and diced

3 ribs celery, diced

1 cup chopped walnuts

2 scallions, chopped, including some of the green

⅔ cup plain yogurt

⅔ cup mayonnaise

2 tablespoons frozen apple juice concentrate, thawed

¼ teaspoon salt

Salad greens (optional)

1. Bring a medium-size saucepan of water just to simmering over medium-high heat. Add turkey and cook 3 minutes. Drain and let cool briefly.

2. Combine apples, celery, walnuts and scallions in a large bowl. Mix in turkey.

3. In a small bowl, stir together yogurt, mayonnaise, apple juice concentrate and salt. Add to bowl with turkey; toss to combine. Serve over greens if desired.

Cran-Raspberry Vinaigrette

no COOK

MAKES 1½ cups

PREP 10 minutes

———

PER 2 TABLESPOONS
23 calories, 0 g protein,
1 g fat, 0 g carbohydrate,
133 mg sodium,
0 mg cholesterol.

¾ cup raspberries

½ cup cranberry juice

½ cup red- or white-wine vinegar

¼ cup hot water

1 tablespoon olive oil

¾ teaspoon salt

¼ teaspoon sugar

1. Place raspberries in a sieve over a small bowl. Press with back of a spoon to remove seeds; discard seeds.

2. Transfer puree to a food processor or blender; add cranberry juice, vinegar, water, oil, salt and sugar. Whirl to blend. Refrigerate, tightly covered, up to several days.

Cobb Salad

MAKES 8 servings

PREP 20 minutes

PER SERVING
WITHOUT DRESSING
176 calories, 14 g protein,
8 g fat, 14 g carbohydrate,
699 mg sodium,
71 mg cholesterol.

1 large head romaine lettuce, torn into bite-size pieces

1 large head chicory, torn into bite-size pieces

1 small avocado, halved, pitted, peeled and cut
   lengthwise into thin wedges

2 ounces blue cheese, crumbled (about ½ cup)

1 cup cherry tomatoes, halved

2 hard-cooked eggs, shelled and quartered

6 slices turkey bacon, cooked and crumbled

¼ pound cooked skinless, boneless turkey breast, cut into
   matchstick-size pieces

Cran-Raspberry Vinaigrette (recipe, opposite)

1. Combine romaine and chicory in a large shallow salad bowl.

2. Arrange avocado slices, blue cheese, cherry tomatoes, egg quarters, bacon and turkey in rows over lettuce mixture. Serve with Cran-Raspberry Vinaigrette drizzled over the top or on the side.

Cobb Salad

Endive Salad
with Tomato Vinaigrette

MAKES 8 servings

PREP 15 minutes

PER SERVING
78 calories, 1 g protein,
7 g fat, 3 g carbohydrate,
114 mg sodium,
0 mg cholesterol.

2 tablespoons cider vinegar

1½ tablespoons Dijon mustard

¼ teaspoon salt

⅛ teaspoon black pepper

¼ cup olive oil

¼ cup diced tomato

1 scallion, finely chopped, including part of the green

4 heads Belgian endive

2 bunches watercress, stemmed

1. Combine vinegar, mustard, salt and pepper in a small bowl. Whisk in oil until blended. Stir in tomato and scallion.

2. Halve endive lengthwise; remove core. Cut lengthwise into matchstick strips. Combine endive and watercress in a medium-size bowl.

3. Just before serving, toss endive and watercress with tomato vinaigrette.

Fast Fix

Super Salads. Simple!

SHREDDED VEGETABLES—cabbage, broccoli or carrots—are great starters for salad in a hurry. Each of these recipes makes 4 to 6 side servings.

Pesto Coleslaw

▶ Stir together ⅓ cup pesto, 2 teaspoons sugar, 1 teaspoon mustard, 1½ teaspoons white vinegar and ¼ teaspoon black pepper in a large bowl.

▶ Add 4 cups coleslaw mix; toss to combine.

Cool Crunchy Slaw

▶ Combine ½ can of water chestnuts, cut into slivers, with 1 package (12 ounces) coleslaw mix in a medium-size bowl.

▶ Mix ⅓ cup mayonnaise, 2 teaspoons soy sauce, 1 tablespoon cider vinegar, 2 tablespoons sour cream and 1 teaspoon sugar in a cup.

▶ Toss dressing with slaw.

Carrot Salad

▶ Combine 1 bag (8 ounces) shredded carrots; 1 can (8 ounces) crushed pineapple with juice; 2 tablespoons vegetable oil; 2 tablespoons soy sauce; ½ cup raisins and ¼ teaspoon salt in a medium-size bowl.

▶ Refrigerate, covered, 1 to 2 hours before serving.

Oriental Cabbage Slaw

▶ Combine 1 package (10 ounces) shredded cabbage with 2 chopped scallions (including part of the green) and 1 tablespoon toasted sesame seeds in a medium-size bowl.

▶ Mix 2 tablespoons vegetable oil, 2 tablespoons soy sauce, 1 tablespoon white vinegar and ⅓ cup sugar in a cup.

▶ Pour enough dressing over slaw to coat; refrigerate, covered, to blend flavors. Add more dressing if needed.

Broccoli-Carrot Slaw

MAKES 6 servings

PREP 10 minutes

———————

PER SERVING
65 calories, 3 g protein,
3 g fat, 8 g carbohydrate,
73 mg sodium,
3 mg cholesterol.

3 large carrots
3 broccoli stalks, peeled and tough ends trimmed
3 tablespoons bottled ranch dressing

1. Shred carrots and broccoli stalks using a food processor or the large holes on a grater.

2. Place carrots and broccoli in a medium-size bowl with dressing; toss to combine.

3. Serve immediately or refrigerate, covered, up to 24 hours.

Very Veggie Slaw

MAKES 8 servings

PREP 10 minutes

REFRIGERATE 30 minutes or

up to 24 hours

———————

PER SERVING
167 calories, 0 g protein,
17 g fat, 5 g carbohydrate,
256 mg sodium,
12 mg cholesterol.

¾ cup mayonnaise
2 tablespoons cider vinegar
1 tablespoon sugar
1 clove garlic, finely chopped
½ teaspoon salt
½ teaspoon black pepper
2 cups firmly packed finely shredded cabbage
1 small sweet red pepper, cored, seeded and thinly
   sliced
1 small sweet green pepper, cored, seeded and thinly
   sliced
8 radishes, trimmed and thinly sliced

1. Stir together mayonnaise, vinegar, sugar, garlic, salt and pepper in a large bowl. Add cabbage, red and green peppers and radishes; toss to coat evenly.

2. Cover and refrigerate at least 30 minutes or up to 24 hours.

Three-Bean Pasta Salad

MAKES 8 servings

PREP 10 minutes

COOK 12 minutes

———

PER SERVING
260 calories, 11 g protein,
3 g fat, 51 g carbohydrate,
539 mg sodium,
1 mg cholesterol.

1 pound penne
½ pound green beans, trimmed and halved crosswise
½ pound yellow wax beans, trimmed and halved crosswise
1 bottle (8 ounces) low-fat Italian salad dressing
1 tablespoon prepared or homemade pesto
   (recipe, page 231)
1 can (16 ounces) kidney beans, drained and rinsed
1 medium-size red onion, coarsely chopped
¼ cup chopped fresh basil

1. Cook penne in a large pot of lightly salted boiling water until al dente, firm but tender, about 12 minutes. During last 5 minutes, add green and wax beans. Drain in a colander; rinse under cold running water to stop cooking. Drain well. Transfer pasta and beans to a serving bowl.

2. Stir together dressing and pesto in a small bowl. Add to pasta mixture along with kidney beans, onion and basil; toss to mix.

Curried Chicken Salad

MAKES 8 servings

PREP 10 minutes

———

PER SERVING
289 calories, 16 g protein,
10 g fat, 35 g carbohydrate,
628 mg sodium,
32 mg cholesterol.

1 cup low-fat mayonnaise
½ cup chutney, chopped
1 teaspoon curry powder
½ teaspoon salt
½ teaspoon black pepper
2½ cups cubed cooked chicken (about 1 pound
   boneless, skinless chicken breasts)
1 cup seedless red grapes, halved
½ cup walnut pieces, toasted and coarsely chopped
Lettuce leaves for serving
8 dinner rolls for serving (optional)

1. Mix mayonnaise, chutney, curry powder, salt and pepper in a medium-size bowl. Add chicken, grapes and walnuts.

2. Line a serving platter with lettuce leaves. Mound chicken salad in center. Serve with rolls if desired.

Three-Bean Pasta Salad and
Curried Chicken Salad, *opposite*

Roasted Vegetable Caesar

MAKES 4 servings

PREP 10 minutes

BROIL OR GRILL 15 minutes

———

PER SERVING
WITHOUT DRESSING
92 calories, 4 g protein,
4 g fat, 13 g carbohydrate,
450 mg sodium,
0 mg cholesterol.

1 clove garlic, finely chopped

1 teaspoon dried oregano

1 teaspoon dried thyme

¾ teaspoon salt

½ teaspoon black pepper

1 tablespoon olive oil

1 sweet red pepper, halved, seeded and cut into
　2-inch-wide strips

1 sweet yellow pepper, halved, seeded and cut into
　2-inch-wide strips

1 sweet green pepper, halved, seeded and cut into
　2-inch-wide strips

1 zucchini, cut into ¼ -inch-thick slices

1 head romaine lettuce, torn into bite-size pieces

½ cup Basic or Low-Cal Caesar Dressing (recipes follow)

1. Prepare a hot grill or heat broiler, setting rack 6 inches from heat.

2. Mix garlic, oregano, thyme, salt, black pepper and oil in a medium-size bowl. Add peppers and zucchini to oil mixture; toss.

3. Broil or grill vegetables 15 minutes or until desired tenderness, turning once.

4. Place romaine in a large bowl. Add dressing; toss to coat. Arrange vegetables over greens.

Basic Caesar Dressing

MAKES about 1 cup

PREP 5 minutes

———

PER 2 TABLESPOONS
45 calories, 1 g protein,
4 g fat, 1 g carbohydrate,
123 mg sodium,
2 mg cholesterol.

6 tablespoons olive oil

Juice of 2 lemons (about ½ cup)

2 canned anchovy fillets

½ teaspoon Worcestershire sauce

3 cloves garlic, pressed

¼ cup grated Parmesan cheese

¼ teaspoon salt

⅛ teaspoon black pepper

Place oil, lemon juice, anchovy fillets and Worcestershire sauce in a blender. Whirl until smooth. Stir in garlic, Parmesan, salt and pepper. Refrigerate, tightly covered, up to several days.

Low-Cal Caesar Dressing

MAKES about 1 cup

PREP 5 minutes

———

PER 2 TABLESPOONS
112 calories, 2 g protein,
11 g fat, 2 g carbohydrate,
171 mg sodium,
3 mg cholesterol.

1 clove garlic, pressed
2 canned anchovy fillets
Juice of 1 lemon (about ¼ cup)
2 tablespoons olive oil
⅓ cup lower-sodium chicken broth
2 teaspoons Dijon mustard
½ teaspoon black pepper
1 teaspoon Worcestershire sauce
2 tablespoons grated Parmesan cheese

Place garlic, anchovy fillets, lemon juice, oil, broth, mustard, pepper and Worcestershire sauce in a blender. Whirl until smooth. Stir in Parmesan. Refrigerate, tightly covered, up to several days.

Spiced Steak Caesar

MAKES 4 servings

PREP 10 minutes

COOK 10 minutes

———

PER SERVING
WITHOUT DRESSING
191 calories, 21 g protein,
10 g fat, 5 g carbohydrate,
560 mg sodium,
46 mg cholesterol.

1 clove garlic, finely chopped
1 tablespoon fennel seeds, crushed
2 teaspoons dried thyme
¾ teaspoon salt
1½ teaspoons black pepper
1½ teaspoons olive oil
¾ pound flank steak
1 head romaine lettuce, torn into bite-size pieces
2 tablespoons grated Parmesan cheese
½ cup Basic or Low-Cal Caesar Dressing (recipes, opposite and above)

1. Mix garlic, fennel seeds, thyme, salt, ½ teaspoon pepper and ½ teaspoon oil in a small bowl. Rub over flank steak.

2. Heat remaining 1 teaspoon oil in a large skillet over medium-high heat. Add steak; cook 5 minutes on each side for medium-rare, until internal temperature registers 145°, or until desired doneness.

3. Place romaine in a large bowl. Add Parmesan, remaining 1 teaspoon pepper and dressing; toss to coat. Divide salad equally among 4 plates.

4. Slice steak into thin slices across grain at a 45° angle. Arrange over salad.

Mediterranean Rice Salad

1¼ cups water

½ teaspoon salt

2 cups instant brown rice

¾ cup bottled light Italian salad dressing

1 can (12 ounces) water-packed tuna, drained and flaked

1 package (9 ounces) frozen French-cut green beans,
    thawed and drained

1 cup small pitted ripe black olives

¼ to ½ teaspoon black pepper

Lettuce leaves for serving

3 small tomatoes, cored and cut into thin wedges

1. Combine water and salt in a medium-size saucepan. Bring to boiling. Stir in rice; cover saucepan and set aside for 10 minutes or until water is completely absorbed by rice. Transfer to a large bowl.

2. Gently stir dressing into rice, blending well. Fold in tuna, green beans, olives and pepper with a rubber spatula.

3. Serve salad immediately or refrigerate, covered, several hours or until well chilled. To serve, arrange lettuce leaves on 4 plates. Spoon salad over lettuce leaves on each plate. Surround with tomato wedges.

Grilled Tomato Salad

1 pound penne

1 bunch spinach (about 1 pound)

8 ounces fresh mozzarella cheese, cut into ½-inch
    cubes

½ cup Kalamata olives, pitted

¼ cup shredded fresh basil

¼ cup balsamic vinegar

1 tablespoon fresh lemon juice

1 teaspoon sugar

½ teaspoon salt

⅛ teaspoon black pepper

⅓ cup olive oil

3 large beefsteak tomatoes, cored

1. Prepare a medium-hot grill.

2. Cook penne in a large pot of lightly salted boiling water until al dente, firm but tender.

3. Meanwhile, stem, rinse and chop spinach. Transfer to a large bowl; add mozzarella, olives and basil.

4. Whisk together vinegar, lemon juice, sugar, salt, pepper and oil in a small bowl until blended.

5. Once grill is heated, cut tomatoes into ½- to ¾-inch-thick slices. Dip tomato slices into dressing. Grill 8 to 10 minutes, turning once. Reduce grilling time if tomatoes become too soft.

6. Drain pasta; add to spinach mixture in bowl. Toss with dressing and grilled tomatoes. Serve warm.

Note: Tomatoes can be cooked on the stovetop in a cast-iron skillet over medium heat. Cook for 2 minutes, turning once.

Grilled Tomato Salad

Potato Salad Rémoulade

quick
PREP

MAKES 8 servings

PREP 10 minutes

COOK 20 to 25 minutes

REFRIGERATE 1 hour or
overnight

PER SERVING
237 calories, 4 g protein,
17 g fat, 18 g carbohydrate,
408 mg sodium,
12 mg cholesterol.

2 pounds red new potatoes

¾ cup mayonnaise

3 tablespoons Dijon mustard

2 tablespoons fresh lemon juice

1 teaspoon liquid hot-pepper sauce

2 teaspoons sugar

½ teaspoon salt

¼ teaspoon black pepper

3 scallions, finely chopped, including part of the green

1 rib celery, finely diced

2 tablespoons chopped fresh parsley

1. Place potatoes in a medium-size saucepan; cover with water. Bring to boiling. Reduce heat; simmer 20 to 25 minutes or until knife-tender; do not overcook. Drain; cool completely. Leave skins on. Cut into ¾-inch cubes.

2. Combine mayonnaise, mustard, lemon juice, hot-pepper sauce, sugar, salt and pepper in a large bowl. Add potatoes, scallions, celery and parsley; toss gently to mix. Cover; refrigerate at least 1 hour or overnight.

Fast Fix

On the Side: Spectacular Spuds

HAVE A FAVORITE SEASONING? Chances are it works with potatoes. Here are three tasty salad ideas. To begin each, cook 2 pounds red potatoes in boiling salted water until tender, about 15 minutes, depending upon size. Drain and cool. Cut into 1-inch cubes. Each makes about 8 servings.

Parsleyed Potato Salad

▶ Combine 1 cup mayonnaise, ½ cup chopped scallion, ½ cup diced celery, ¼ cup chopped parsley, ½ teaspoon salt and ½ teaspoon black pepper in a large bowl.

▶ Add cubed potatoes and mix.

Classic Potato Salad

▶ Combine 1 cup mayonnaise; 2 hard-cooked eggs, shelled and chopped; 2 chopped sweet pickles; ½ teaspoon salt and ½ teaspoon black pepper in a large bowl.

▶ Add cubed potatoes and mix.

Italian Potato Salad

▶ Combine ½ cup mayonnaise, ½ cup sour cream, 2 tablespoons pesto, ¼ cup chopped red onion, 1 cup cooked green beans, ½ teaspoon salt and ½ teaspoon black pepper in a large bowl.

▶ Add cubed potatoes and mix.

Warm Creole Potato Salad

MAKES 4 servings
PREP 10 minutes
MICROWAVE 10½ minutes
STAND 8 minutes

———

PER SERVING
213 calories, 7 g protein,
7 g fat, 31 g carbohydrate,
458 mg sodium,
5 mg cholesterol.

4 slices bacon, diced
1 small onion, chopped
1½ pounds small new potatoes, scrubbed and
   cut into eighths
2 tablespoons cider vinegar
1½ tablespoons molasses
½ teaspoon salt
½ teaspoon liquid hot-pepper sauce
1½ tablespoons ketchup
1 tablespoon vegetable oil
1 rib celery, diced
2 tablespoons chopped fresh parsley

1. Scatter bacon across bottom of a microwave-safe 13 x 9 x 2-inch baking dish. Cover with paper toweling. Microwave at 100% power 1½ minutes. Uncover. Stir in onion. Microwave 1 minute.

2. Add potatoes to dish with bacon. Cover with lid. Microwave 4 minutes, stir, and microwave another 4 minutes or until tender.

3. Meanwhile, combine vinegar, molasses, salt, hot-pepper sauce, ketchup and oil in a medium-size bowl.

4. Add potato mixture to bowl with dressing, toss to combine. Let stand 8 minutes. Add celery and parsley; toss.

Mixed Greens with Blue Cheese

MAKES 8 servings
PREP 5 minutes

———

PER SERVING
152 calories, 6 g protein,
13 g fat, 4 g carbohydrate,
425 mg sodium,
16 mg cholesterol.

2 pounds mixed salad greens
6 ounces blue cheese, crumbled (about 1½ cups)
1 tablespoon Dijon mustard
1 teaspoon honey
¼ teaspoon salt
¼ cup balsamic vinegar
3 tablespoons olive oil
¼ cup coarsely chopped walnuts, toasted (recipe, page 231)

1. Place salad greens in a large serving bowl. Add blue cheese and toss.

2. Whisk mustard, honey and salt in a small bowl. Whisk in vinegar, then oil. Add to greens; toss. Sprinkle with nuts.

Sesame Shrimp Salad

MAKES 8 servings

PREP 10 minutes

REFRIGERATE 15 minutes
(while cooking noodles)

COOK noodles about 3
minutes, salad 5 minutes

PER SERVING
411 calories, 14 g protein,
21 g fat, 43 g carbohydrate,
1,348 mg sodium,
67 mg cholesterol.

1½ cups bottled Italian salad dressing

3 tablespoons reduced-sodium teriyaki sauce

2 teaspoons sugar

1 teaspoon dark Asian sesame oil

1 pound peeled, deveined medium shrimp

4 packages (3 ounces each) low-fat ramen noodles

½ pound snow peas, trimmed

12 leaves Napa cabbage or lettuce

4 scallions, chopped, including part of the green

2 tablespoons sesame seeds, toasted (recipe, page 231)

1. Combine Italian dressing, teriyaki sauce, sugar and oil in a small bowl. Place half the dressing in a resealable plastic bag. Add shrimp; refrigerate 15 minutes to marinate. Reserve remainder of dressing.

2. Meanwhile, cook ramen according to package directions, omitting seasoning packets. Drain in a colander; rinse under cold running water to stop cooking.

3. Cook snow peas in a saucepan of boiling water until crisp-tender, 2 minutes. Drain. Rinse under cold running water to stop cooking.

4. Remove shrimp from marinade; discard marinade. Sauté shrimp in a large nonstick skillet over medium-high heat 2 minutes or until cooked. Remove skillet from heat.

5. Line a serving bowl with cabbage leaves. Add ramen, snow peas, scallions and remaining dressing to shrimp in skillet; toss to combine. Spoon shrimp mixture into prepared bowl. Top with toasted sesame seeds.

Seafood Salad

Family Circle **Quick & Easy** Recipes

MAKES 4 servings

PREP 5 minutes

PER SERVING
149 calories, 10 g protein,
7 g fat, 11 g carbohydrate,
389 mg sodium,
17 mg cholesterol.

⅓ cup low-fat mayonnaise

2 tablespoons chili sauce

1 tablespoon sweet pickle relish

1 teaspoon lemon juice

½ pound surimi (imitation crabmeat), shredded

1 package (10 ounces) mixed salad greens

1. Mix mayonnaise, chili sauce, relish and lemon juice in a medium-size bowl. Remove and reserve ¼ cup.

2. Add surimi to remaining dressing in bowl.

3. Toss reserved dressing with greens in a large bowl. Arrange greens on 4 plates. Top with surimi mixture.

Lobster & Green Bean Salad

MAKES 6 servings

PREP 10 minutes

REFRIGERATE 2 hours or overnight

STAND 30 minutes

PER SERVING
229 calories, 9 g protein,
20 g fat, 6 g carbohydrate,
583 mg sodium,
28 mg cholesterol.

1 pound green beans, trimmed

3 tablespoons white-wine vinegar

1 teaspoon dried tarragon

1 teaspoon salt

1 clove garlic, finely chopped

½ cup vegetable oil

1½ cups cooked lobster meat (two 1¼-pound cooked lobsters)

1. Cook green beans in a large pot of boiling water until crisp-tender, about 8 minutes. Drain in a colander; rinse under cold running water to stop cooking. Blot beans dry with paper toweling.

2. Whisk together vinegar, tarragon, salt and garlic in a medium-size bowl until well blended. Gradually whisk in oil.

3. Add beans and lobster meat to dressing; toss to mix. Cover and refrigerate 2 hours or overnight.

4. To serve, let stand at room temperature for 30 minutes.

Seafood Salad, *opposite*

Lobster & Green Bean Salad

Green Garden Salad

no COOK

MAKES 8 servings

PREP 10 minutes

REFRIGERATE 1 hour

———

PER SERVING
53 calories, 2 g protein,
4 g fat, 4 g carbohydrate,
146 mg sodium,
0 mg cholesterol.

3 scallions, trimmed

1 sweet red pepper, cored, seeded and cut into chunks

1 cucumber, peeled, halved lengthwise, seeded and cut into chunks

2 tablespoons olive oil

1 tablespoon red-wine vinegar

½ teaspoon salt

¼ teaspoon liquid hot-pepper sauce (optional)

⅛ teaspoon black pepper

1 pint cherry tomatoes, halved

1 head romaine lettuce, separated into leaves

1. Separate white and green parts of scallions. Set green parts aside. Cut whites into chunks. Add whites to a food processor along with red pepper and cucumber. Pulse until finely chopped.

2. Whisk together oil, vinegar, salt, hot-pepper sauce if desired, and black pepper in a medium-size bowl. Add chopped vegetables and tomatoes; stir gently to combine. Refrigerate, covered, 1 hour, stirring occasionally.

3. Coarsely chop reserved green parts of scallions. To serve, arrange lettuce leaves on individual salad plates and spoon vegetable mixture over leaves. Or tear leaves into bite-size pieces and add to vegetable mixture; toss gently to combine. Garnish salad with chopped scallion greens.

Potato, Basil & Green Bean Salad

quick PREP

MAKES 8 servings

PREP 10 minutes

COOK 30 minutes

———

PER SERVING
137 calories, 3 g protein,
4 g fat, 24 g carbohydrate,
255 mg sodium,
0 mg cholesterol.

1½ pounds small red new potatoes with skins, halved

1 pound green beans, trimmed

⅛ cup extra-virgin olive oil

4½ teaspoons Dijon mustard

¾ teaspoon salt

⅜ teaspoon coarse black pepper

½ cup shredded fresh basil

2¼ teaspoons chopped fresh oregano

1. Cook potatoes in a large pot of boiling water until tender, 15 minutes. Transfer potatoes with a slotted spoon to a large bowl.

2. Add green beans to boiling water; cook until tender, 12 minutes. Drain in a colander; rinse under cold water to stop cooking. Add to bowl with potatoes.

3. Whisk together oil, mustard, salt, pepper, basil and oregano in a small bowl; mix into bowl with potatoes and beans. Serve or refrigerate until serving.

Winter Orange Salad

no COOK

MAKES 4 servings
PREP 10 minutes

———

PER SERVING
243 calories, 4 g protein,
19 g fat, 17 g carbohydrate,
393 mg sodium,
0 mg cholesterol.

1 small head romaine lettuce, separated into leaves
2 oranges, peeled and sliced crosswise into
   ¼-inch-thick rounds
1 small red onion, sliced into rings
12 pitted ripe black olives, sliced
⅓ cup sliced almonds, toasted (recipe, page 231)
¼ cup orange juice
2 teaspoons red-wine vinegar
1 tablespoon chopped fresh chives
2 teaspoons chopped fresh parsley
½ teaspoon salt
¼ teaspoon black pepper
¼ cup olive oil

1. Place a few romaine leaves in center of each of 4 salad plates. Top with orange rounds, then onion rings. Sprinkle with olives and almonds.

2. Puree orange juice, vinegar, chives, parsley, salt and pepper in a food processor or blender. With motor running, slowly pour in oil in a steady stream until dressing is thick. Drizzle over salad.

Fruit Salad with Strawberry Vinaigrette

no COOK

MAKES 8 servings
PREP 15 minutes

———

PER SERVING
WITHOUT DRESSING
97 calories, 1 g protein,
8 g fat, 8 g carbohydrate,
6 g sodium,
0 mg cholesterol.

1 cup olive oil
½ pint strawberries, hulled
2 tablespoons balsamic vinegar
½ teaspoon salt
¼ teaspoon black pepper
¼ teaspoon dried tarragon, crumbled
¼ teaspoon sugar
1 large head leaf lettuce, separated into leaves
1 red onion, halved lengthwise, then thinly sliced
   crosswise
2 avocados, peeled, pitted and sliced into wedges
2 oranges, peeled and sliced crosswise into rounds

1. Combine oil, strawberries, vinegar, salt, pepper, tarragon and sugar in a food processor. Whirl until strawberries are pureed.

2. Arrange lettuce leaves, onion slices, avocado wedges and orange rounds on a platter. Drizzle with dressing.

Pasta

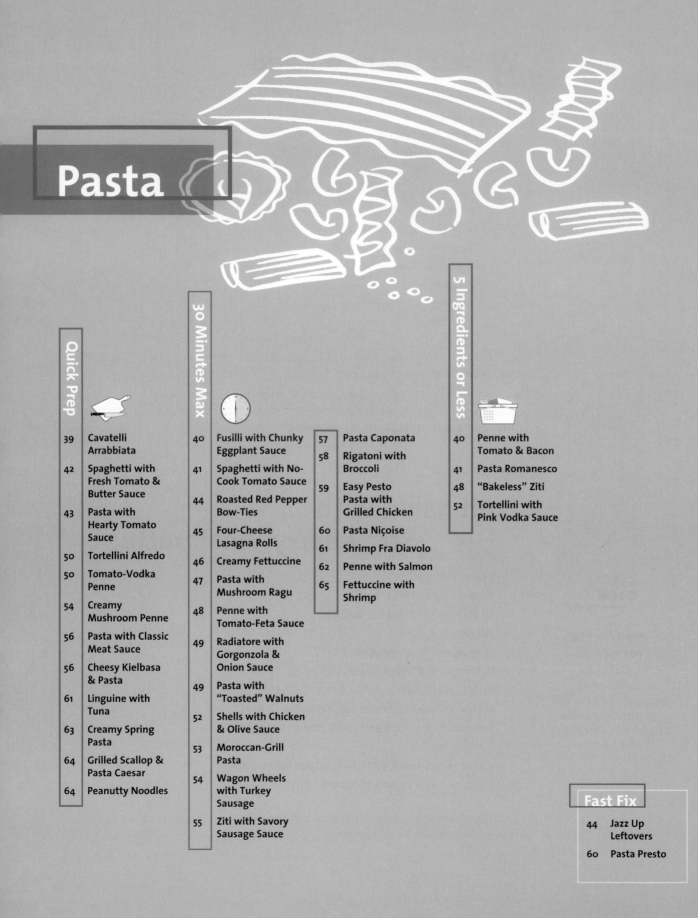

Cavatelli Arrabbiata

2 tablespoons olive oil

1 large onion, chopped

3 large cloves garlic, chopped

1 can (28 ounces) crushed tomatoes

1 tablespoon chopped fresh basil

¾ teaspoon red-pepper flakes

½ teaspoon salt

1 pound cavatelli

Slivered fresh basil for garnish (optional)

1. Heat oil in a saucepan over low heat. Add onion and garlic; cook, stirring occasionally, 12 minutes or until softened, making sure garlic does not burn. Add tomatoes, basil, red-pepper flakes and salt; cook 25 minutes.

2. Meanwhile, cook cavatelli in a large pot of lightly salted boiling water until al dente, firm but tender. Drain well. Toss cavatelli with sauce. Garnish with slivered basil if desired.

Cavatelli Arrabbiata

Penne with Tomato & Bacon

5 ingredients or LESS

MAKES 6 servings

PREP 5 minutes

COOK 15 minutes

———————

PER SERVING
351 calories, 13 g protein,
4 g fat, 67 g carbohydrate,
343 mg sodium,
4 g cholesterol.

1¼ cups chopped onion

4 slices bacon, diced

1 can (35 ounces) crushed tomatoes

½ teaspoon black pepper

1 pound penne or rigatoni

1. Sauté onion and bacon in a large nonstick skillet over medium-high heat, about 5 minutes or until onion is soft. Pour off excess fat.

2. Stir tomatoes into skillet; cook over medium-high heat, stirring occasionally, 8 to 10 minutes or until sauce is slightly thickened. Add pepper to sauce during last 5 minutes of cooking.

3. Meanwhile, cook penne in a large pot of lightly salted boiling water until al dente, firm but tender. Drain well.

4. Toss together penne and sauce in a large serving bowl.

Fusilli with Chunky Eggplant Sauce

30 minutes MAX

MAKES 6 servings

PREP 10 minutes

COOK 20 minutes

———————

PER SERVING
411 calories, 12 g protein,
9 g fat, 72 g carbohydrate,
220 mg sodium,
0 mg cholesterol.

1 pound fusilli

3 tablespoons olive oil

1 eggplant (1 pound), cut into 1-inch cubes

1 can (28 ounces) peeled Italian tomatoes

½ cup coarsely chopped fresh basil

Salt (optional)

Black pepper (optional)

1. Cook fusilli in a large pot of lightly salted boiling water until al dente, firm but tender. Drain well; keep warm.

2. Meanwhile, heat oil in a large nonstick skillet or Dutch oven over medium heat. Add eggplant. Drizzle a small amount of water over the eggplant. Cook, covered, stirring occasionally, until eggplant is tender, 8 to 10 minutes.

3. Add tomatoes with their liquid, breaking up tomatoes with a wooden spoon. Simmer, covered, about 10 minutes to blend flavors. Remove from heat. Stir in basil. Season with salt and pepper if desired.

4. Transfer fusilli to a serving platter; top with sauce.

Pasta Romanesco

MAKES 6 servings

PREP 10 minutes

COOK 10 minutes

———————

PER SERVING
395 calories, 21 g protein,
9 g fat, 57 g carbohydrate,
178 mg sodium,
23 mg cholesterol.

1 pound bow-tie pasta (farfalle) or penne
1 jar (7 ounces) roasted red peppers, drained
1 can (14½ ounces) chunky pasta-style tomatoes
1 package (8 ounces) low-sodium mozzarella cheese, cubed
3 tablespoons grated Parmesan cheese
Grated Parmesan cheese for serving (optional)

1. Cook pasta in a large pot of lightly salted boiling water until al dente, firm but tender. Drain well.

2. Meanwhile, prepare sauce. Place roasted red peppers in a food processor or blender. Whirl until a smooth puree. Scrape into a serving bowl.

3. Add tomatoes, mozzarella and Parmesan to serving bowl. Add drained pasta, tossing to coat. Serve with additional grated cheese if desired.

Spaghetti with No-Cook Tomato Sauce

MAKES 6 servings

PREP 15 minutes

COOK about 12 minutes

———————

PER SERVING
401 calories, 15 g protein,
9 g fat, 66 g carbohydrate,
369 mg sodium,
7 mg cholesterol.

1 pound spaghetti
2 pounds tomatoes, diced
½ cup shredded part-skim mozzarella cheese
2 cups chopped fresh basil
2 tablespoons olive oil
2 tablespoons grated Parmesan cheese
¾ teaspoon salt
1/2 teaspoon black pepper

1. Cook spaghetti in a large pot of lightly salted boiling water until al dente, firm but tender. Drain spaghetti, reserving ½ cup cooking water.

2. Meanwhile, combine tomatoes, mozzarella, basil, oil, Parmesan, salt and pepper in a large bowl.

3. Add spaghetti and reserved water to tomato mixture; toss to coat.

Spaghetti with Fresh Tomato & Butter Sauce

MAKES 4 servings

PREP 10 minutes

COOK 30 minutes

PER SERVING
560 calories, 16 g protein,
21 g fat, 79 g carbohydrate,
638 mg sodium,
50 mg cholesterol.

2 pounds tomatoes, peeled, seeded and coarsely chopped

6 tablespoons (¾ stick) butter

4 cloves garlic, lightly crushed

½ teaspoon salt

¾ pound spaghetti

3 tablespoons grated or shaved Parmesan cheese

2 tablespoons snipped fresh chives

1. Combine tomatoes, butter and garlic in a large saucepan. Simmer over medium heat, uncovered, until sauce has reduced, about 30 minutes. Add salt.

2. Meanwhile, cook spaghetti in a large pot of lightly salted boiling water until al dente, firm but tender. Drain well.

3. Toss spaghetti in a serving bowl with tomato sauce, Parmesan and chives.

Spaghetti with Fresh
Tomato & Butter Sauce

Pasta with Hearty Tomato Sauce

quick **PREP**

MAKES 6 servings

PREP 10 minutes

COOK about 30 minutes

―――――

PER SERVING
413 calories, 18 g protein,
8 g fat, 65 g carbohydrate,
914 mg sodium,
26 mg cholesterol.

½ pound ground chuck

1 large onion, chopped

2 small sweet green peppers, cored, seeded and chopped (about 1¼ cups)

3 cloves garlic, chopped

1 can (28 ounces) plum tomatoes, drained

2 cans (8 ounces each) tomato sauce

2 tablespoons tomato paste

¼ cup dry red wine

½ teaspoon red-pepper flakes

¼ teaspoon dried oregano

½ teaspoon salt

½ teaspoon black pepper

1 pound pasta, such as ziti

1. Heat a large nonaluminum saucepan over medium-high heat. Add ground chuck, onion, green peppers and garlic; sauté, breaking apart meat with a wooden spoon, 8 to 10 minutes or until vegetables are tender and meat is cooked.

2. Add tomatoes, tomato sauce, tomato paste, wine, red-pepper flakes, oregano, salt and black pepper to saucepan. Bring to boiling. Reduce heat to medium; simmer, stirring occasionally, 15 to 20 minutes.

3. Meanwhile, cook pasta in a large pot of lightly salted boiling water until al dente, firm but tender. Drain well; transfer to a large serving bowl. Taste sauce; adjust seasonings if desired. Spoon sauce over pasta.

Pasta with Hearty Tomato Sauce

Roasted Red Pepper Bow-Ties

MAKES 6 servings
PREP 10 minutes
COOK 20 minutes

───────────

PER SERVING
310 calories, 9 g protein,
5 g fat, 55 g carbohydrate,
358 mg sodium,
5 mg cholesterol.

1 tablespoon olive oil
½ cup finely chopped onion
2 cloves garlic, finely chopped
2 jars (12 ounces each) roasted red peppers, drained and
    coarsely chopped
1 tablespoon chopped fresh thyme or 1 teaspoon
    dried thyme
1 cup chicken broth
½ cup dry white wine
¼ cup half-and-half
¼ teaspoon salt
1 pound bow-tie pasta (farfalle)
¼ cup chopped fresh basil

1. Heat oil in a medium-size nonstick skillet over medium heat. Add onion and garlic. Cook until tender, about 5 minutes. If too dry, add water, 2 tablespoons at a time. Stir in peppers and thyme. Cook about 5 minutes. Add broth and wine. Simmer, uncovered, 10 minutes.

2. Add sauce in batches to a food processor or blender. Stir in half-and-half and salt; whirl to a puree.

3. Meanwhile, cook pasta in a large pot of lightly salted boiling water until al dente, firm but tender. Drain well. Place pasta in a large serving bowl. Toss with sauce. Stir in basil.

Fast Fix

Jazz Up Leftovers

DON'T NEGLECT THAT LEFTOVER PASTA. It takes just a little work to turn it into an easy-on-you main dish.

Creamy Italian-Style Pasta Pie

▶ Cook 3 slices chopped bacon and 1 chopped onion in a 9-inch cast-iron skillet over medium-high heat until tender, about 10 minutes.

▶ Stir in ½ cup grated Parmesan cheese, 1 cup cream, 4 beaten eggs, 1 cup frozen peas and 4 cups cooked pasta.

▶ Bake at 350°, covered, 30 minutes; uncover and bake 15 minutes more.

▶ Makes about 6 servings.

Mexican-Style Pasta Pie

▶ Heat 1 tablespoon olive oil in a 9-inch cast-iron skillet over medium-high heat.

▶ Add 2 cloves chopped garlic, ½ pound ground beef, 1½ teaspoons chili powder and ½ teaspoon salt; cook 5 minutes.

▶ Stir in 4 cups cooked spaghetti or other pasta, 1 cup salsa, 4 beaten eggs, and 1 cup shredded cheddar cheese.

▶ Bake at 350°, covered, 30 minutes; uncover and bake 15 minutes more.

▶ Makes about 6 servings.

Four-Cheese Lasagna Rolls

MAKES 6 servings

PREP 15 minutes

BAKE at 450° for 15 minutes

PER SERVING
461 calories, 28 g protein,
19 g fat, 44 g carbohydrate,
781 mg sodium,
53 mg cholesterol.

12 no-boil lasagna noodles

1 container (15 ounces) part-skim ricotta cheese

1½ cups shredded reduced-fat mozzarella cheese
   (6 ounces)

¾ cup shredded Monterey Jack cheese (3 ounces)

1 jar (7 ounces) roasted red peppers, drained and
   chopped

¼ cup grated Parmesan cheese

¼ cup finely chopped fresh basil

½ teaspoon red-pepper flakes

⅛ teaspoon black pepper

1 jar (14 ounces) pasta sauce

1. Heat oven to 450°. Soak lasagna noodles according to package directions. Drain; pat dry.

2. Meanwhile, combine ricotta, 1 cup mozzarella, ½ cup Monterey Jack, roasted red peppers, 2 tablespoons Parmesan, 2 tablespoons basil, red-pepper flakes and black pepper in a medium-size bowl.

3. Spread half the pasta sauce over bottom of a 13 x 9-inch baking dish. Spread 2 generous tablespoons cheese mixture along length of each noodle; roll up and place, seam side down, in dish.

4. Top rolls with remaining pasta sauce. Sprinkle remaining ½ cup mozzarella, ¼ cup Monterey Jack and 2 tablespoons Parmesan over rolls. Cover dish with aluminum foil.

5. Bake in heated 450° oven 10 minutes. Uncover; bake 5 minutes. Sprinkle with remaining 2 tablespoons basil.

Creamy Fettuccine

MAKES 6 servings

PREP 10 minutes

COOK 10 minutes

———

PER SERVING
402 calories, 19 g protein,
4 g fat, 72 g carbohydrate,
599 mg sodium,
9 mg cholesterol.

1 pound fettuccine

2 tablespoons all-purpose flour

¾ teaspoon salt

¼ teaspoon black pepper

¼ teaspoon ground nutmeg

2 cups skim milk

½ cup lower-sodium chicken broth

2 cups frozen peas, thawed

3 ounces Canadian bacon, diced (½ cup)

3 tablespoons grated Parmesan cheese

½ cup chopped fresh basil

1. Cook fettuccine in a large pot of lightly salted boiling water until al dente, firm but tender. Drain well.

2. Meanwhile, mix flour, salt, pepper and nutmeg in a large saucepan. Whisk in milk and chicken broth; cook over medium-high heat, stirring constantly, until mixture boils and thickens, about 6 minutes.

3. Stir in fettuccine, peas, bacon, Parmesan and basil. Heat through.

Creamy Fettuccine

Pasta with Mushroom Ragu

Pasta with Mushroom Ragu

MAKES 4 servings

PREP 15 minutes

COOK 17 minutes

PER SERVING
WITHOUT PASTA
142 calories, 5 g protein,
8 g fat, 16 g carbohydrate,
315 mg sodium,
8 mg cholesterol.

1 ounce dried wild mushrooms

1½ cups boiling water

¾ pound fettuccine or other flat pasta

1 tablespoon butter

1 tablespoon olive oil

1 leek, trimmed and well washed, white part sliced

¾ pound large white button mushrooms, sliced

2 teaspoons fresh thyme leaves

1 tablespoon chopped fresh parsley

1 large tomato, chopped

½ teaspoon salt

¼ teaspoon black pepper

Pasta

47

1. Soak wild mushrooms in boiling water in a small bowl for 15 minutes or until plumped. Remove mushrooms to paper toweling; gently squeeze out excess moisture. Coarsely chop; set aside. Strain soaking liquid through a coffee filter or sieve lined with dampened paper toweling into a small saucepan. Boil until reduced to ¼ cup, about 10 minutes.

2. Cook fettuccine in a large pot of lightly salted boiling water until al dente, firm but tender. Drain well.

3. Meanwhile, heat butter and oil in a large skillet over medium-high heat. Add leek; cook 1 minute. Add button mushrooms; cook 2 to 3 minutes or until slightly softened. Add reserved wild mushrooms; cook 1 minute. Add thyme, parsley, tomato, salt and pepper. Bring to simmering. Add mushroom liquid; simmer 2 minutes. Serve over fettuccine.

"Bakeless" Ziti

MAKES 4 servings

PREP 3 minutes

COOK 10 to 12 minutes

———————

PER SERVING
504 calories, 30 g protein,
11 g fat, 69 g carbohydrate,
698 mg sodium,
30 mg cholesterol.

¾ pound ziti

3 cups prepared fat-free spicy marinara sauce

1 cup reduced-fat ricotta cheese

1 cup shredded reduced-fat mozzarella cheese

¼ cup grated Parmesan cheese

1. Cook ziti in a large pot of lightly salted boiling water until al dente, firm but tender. Drain well.

2. Meanwhile, heat sauce in a medium-size saucepan over medium-high heat until warmed through.

3. Combine ziti, sauce, ricotta and mozzarella in a large serving bowl. Sprinkle with Parmesan.

Penne with Tomato-Feta Sauce

MAKES 6 servings

PREP 10 minutes

COOK 13 minutes

———————

PER SERVING
415 calories, 14 g protein,
13 g fat, 60 g carbohydrate,
569 mg sodium,
36 mg cholesterol.

1 pound penne

1 tablespoon olive oil

1 medium-size onion, diced

1 large zucchini, trimmed, halved lengthwise and sliced

½ teaspoon dried oregano

¼ teaspoon salt

¼ teaspoon black pepper

1 can (about 14 ounces) stewed tomatoes

⅛ teaspoon red-pepper flakes

6 ounces flavored crumbled feta cheese

¾ cup half-and-half

1. Cook penne in a large pot of lightly salted boiling water until al dente, firm but tender. Drain well.

2. Meanwhile, heat oil in a large skillet over medium-high heat. Add onion and cook 5 minutes or until slightly softened. Add zucchini, oregano, salt and pepper. Cook 3 to 4 minutes, stirring occasionally. Add tomatoes, red-pepper flakes, feta and half-and-half. Simmer 2 to 3 minutes or until slightly thickened. Serve over hot penne.

Radiatore with Gorgonzola & Onion Sauce

MAKES 4 servings

PREP 10 minutes

COOK about 12 minutes

———

PER SERVING
539 calories, 17 g protein,
24 g fat, 63 g carbohydrate,
783 mg sodium,
25 mg cholesterol.

¾ pound radiatore pasta

¼ cup olive oil

2 large Vidalia or other sweet onions, quartered and
thinly sliced

2 cloves garlic, finely chopped

2 tablespoons balsamic vinegar

½ teaspoon salt

¼ teaspoon black pepper

4 ounces Gorgonzola cheese, crumbled

1. Cook radiatore in a large pot of lightly salted boiling water until al dente, firm but tender. Drain well.

2. Meanwhile, heat oil in a large, deep, nonstick skillet over medium-high heat. Add onions; cook, stirring often, until very soft and golden brown, about 5 minutes. Add garlic; cook 1 minute. Remove from heat. Stir in vinegar, salt and pepper.

3. Toss radiatore with onions and Gorgonzola in a large serving bowl.

Pasta with "Toasted" Walnuts

MAKES 6 servings

PREP 10 minutes

MICROWAVE 3½ to
4½ minutes

COOK about 12 minutes

———

PER SERVING
484 calories, 15 g protein,
23 g fat, 56 g carbohydrate,
416 mg sodium,
2 mg cholesterol.

1 pound pasta, any shape

1 cup walnut pieces, chopped

¼ cup extra-virgin olive oil

2 cloves garlic, finely chopped

½ cup shredded fresh basil

1 tablespoon fresh lemon juice

1 teaspoon salt

¼ teaspoon black pepper

3 tablespoons grated Parmesan cheese

1. Cook pasta in a large pot of lightly salted boiling water until al dente, firm but tender. Drain well.

2. Meanwhile, mix walnuts and oil in a microwave-safe serving bowl large enough to hold the pasta. Microwave, uncovered, at 100% power 2 minutes. Stir and microwave an additional 1 to 2 minutes or until lightly toasted. Add garlic. Microwave 20 seconds. Stir in basil, lemon juice, salt and pepper.

3. Add hot pasta to walnut mixture. Sprinkle with Parmesan; toss.

Tortellini Alfredo

MAKES 4 servings

PREP 5 minutes

COOK about 12 minutes

———————

PER SERVING
752 calories, 25 g protein,
49 g fat, 52 g carbohydrate,
963 mg sodium,
183 mg cholesterol.

1 bag (15 ounces) cheese-filled tortellini
1 tablespoon butter
1½ cups heavy cream
⅛ teaspoon black pepper
Pinch ground nutmeg
⅔ cup grated Parmesan cheese
1 tablespoon chopped fresh parsley

1. Cook tortellini in a large pot of lightly salted boiling water until al dente, firm but tender. Drain well.

2. Meanwhile, heat butter in a medium-size skillet over medium-high heat. Add cream, pepper and nutmeg. Bring to boiling; reduce heat; simmer 7 minutes. Add Parmesan; cook 2 minutes or until sauce starts to thicken. Add tortellini; cook, stirring, 1 to 2 minutes to heat through. Sprinkle with parsley.

Tomato-Vodka Penne

MAKES 6 servings

PREP 10 minutes

COOK 30 minutes

———————

PER SERVING
491 calories, 16 g protein,
20 g fat, 61 g carbohydrate,
1,310 mg sodium,
57 mg cholesterol.

2 tablespoons olive oil
4 cloves garlic, chopped
6 ounces sliced prosciutto or Canadian bacon, chopped
3 scallions, finely chopped, including some of the green
½ teaspoon ground red pepper (cayenne)
¼ cup vodka
1 can (28 ounces) crushed tomatoes
1 pound penne
¾ cup heavy cream
1 teaspoon salt

1. Heat oil in a medium-size saucepan over low heat. Add garlic; cook, stirring occasionally, 8 minutes, making sure garlic doesn't burn. Add prosciutto, scallions, red pepper and vodka; cook 4 minutes over medium heat. Add tomatoes; cook, stirring occasionally, 15 minutes.

2. Meanwhile, cook penne in a large pot of lightly salted boiling water until al dente, firm but tender. Drain well and keep warm.

3. Add cream and salt to tomato mixture; cook 3 minutes. Toss penne with tomato-vodka sauce to coat evenly.

Tortellini Alfredo and Tomato-Vodka Penne, *opposite*

Tortellini with Pink Vodka Sauce

MAKES 6 servings

PREP 10 minutes

COOK about 12 minutes

———————

PER SERVING
367 calories, 14 g protein,
16 g fat, 41 g carbohydrate,
580 mg sodium,
66 mg cholesterol.

1 pound cheese-filled tortellini

3 tablespoons vodka

½ cup heavy cream

1 cup prepared marinara sauce

¼ cup grated Parmesan cheese

1. Cook tortellini in a large pot of lightly salted boiling water until al dente, firm but tender. Drain well.

2. Meanwhile, combine vodka and cream in a large skillet; bring to boiling. Reduce heat; simmer 5 minutes or until mixture is reduced to about half. Stir in marinara sauce; bring to a bare simmer.

3. Toss tortellini with sauce and half the cheese. Transfer to a serving dish. Top with remaining Parmesan.

Shells with Chicken & Olive Sauce

MAKES 4 servings

PREP 10 minutes

COOK about 12 minutes

———————

PER SERVING
532 calories, 24 g protein,
14 g fat, 78 g carbohydrate,
701 mg sodium,
26 mg cholesterol.

¾ pound medium-size pasta shells

2 tablespoons olive oil

1 large onion, chopped

½ pound boneless, skinless chicken breast halves, cut into 1-inch cubes

12 black olives, such as Kalamata, pitted and coarsely chopped

12 green olives, pitted and coarsely chopped

1 cup diced tomatoes, fresh or canned

3 tablespoons chopped fresh basil

¼ teaspoon salt

⅛ teaspoon black pepper

Grated Parmesan cheese (optional)

1. Cook shells in a large pot of lightly salted boiling water until al dente, firm but tender. Drain well, reserving 1 cup of cooking water.

2. Meanwhile, heat oil in a large heavy skillet over medium-high heat. Add onion; cook, stirring occasionally, until softened, about 2 minutes.

3. Add chicken to skillet; cook, stirring occasionally, until chicken loses its raw look, about 2 minutes. Add black and green olives, tomatoes and basil. Bring to boiling. Add reserved cooking water to skillet, stirring to mix. Return sauce to boiling over medium-high heat, stirring. Add salt and pepper to skillet, stirring to blend.

4. Toss shells with sauce in a large serving bowl until shells are well coated. If desired, sprinkle top with grated Parmesan or pass Parmesan separately in a bowl at the table.

Moroccan-Grill Pasta

MAKES 6 servings
PREP 10 minutes
BROIL 12 minutes
(while cooking pasta)
COOK 12 minutes

———

PER SERVING
323 calories, 17 g protein,
3 g fat, 57 g carbohydrate,
301 mg sodium,
21 mg cholesterol.

1 teaspoon curry powder
1 teaspoon ground cinnamon
½ teaspoon chili powder
½ teaspoon ground cumin
¼ teaspoon ground ginger
¾ teaspoon salt
¼ teaspoon black pepper
2 boneless, skinless chicken breast halves
    (about ½ pound total)
2 medium-size zucchini, halved lengthwise and
    scored lengthwise
¾ pound wagon wheel pasta
1 teaspoon olive oil
1½ pounds tomatoes, diced
1 tablespoon honey

1. Mix curry powder, cinnamon, chili powder, cumin, ginger, salt and pepper in a small bowl.

2. Heat broiler. Arrange chicken and zucchini on broiler-pan rack. Lightly coat with nonstick olive-oil cooking spray. Sprinkle with 1½ teaspoons spice mixture.

3. Broil 6 inches from heat 12 minutes, turning over once, or until internal temperature of chicken registers 170° on an instant-read thermometer and zucchini is fork-tender. Cool. Dice chicken and zucchini.

4. Meanwhile, cook wagon wheel pasta in a large pot of lightly salted boiling water until al dente, firm but tender. Drain well.

5. Heat oil in a medium-size nonstick skillet. Add remaining spice mixture; cook 30 seconds. Add tomatoes and honey; simmer 3 minutes or until softened. Mix pasta, zucchini, chicken and sauce in a serving bowl. Serve warm or at room temperature.

Creamy Mushroom Penne

quick PREP

MAKES 6 servings

PREP 5 minutes

COOK 20 minutes

PER SERVING
413 calories, 15 g protein,
13 g fat, 60 g carbohydrate,
438 mg sodium,
20 mg cholesterol.

1 envelope (0.9 ounce) garlic-mushroom recipe
   soup mix
2 cups water
1 pound penne
2 tablespoons olive oil
1 small sweet red pepper, cored, seeded and sliced
1½ pounds assorted presliced mushrooms
½ cup grated Parmesan cheese
½ cup chopped fresh flat-leaf parsley
¼ cup heavy cream

1. Whisk together soup mix and water in a small bowl; set aside.

2. Cook penne in a large pot of lightly salted boiling water until al dente, firm but tender. Drain well.

3. Meanwhile, heat oil in a large skillet over medium heat. Add sweet pepper and mushrooms; sauté until partially tender, about 10 minutes. Stir in soup mixture. Increase heat to medium-high; cook, uncovered, until slightly thickened, about 8 minutes. Stir in ¼ cup Parmesan, parsley and cream. Cook another minute or until heated through.

4. Transfer penne to a serving bowl. Add mushroom sauce and remaining ¼ cup Parmesan; toss well.

Wagon Wheels with Turkey Sausage

Family Circle **Quick & Easy** Recipes

30 minutes MAX

MAKES 6 servings

PREP 5 minutes

COOK 15 minutes

PER SERVING
388 calories, 18 g protein,
6 g fat, 77 g carbohydrate,
439 mg sodium,
32 mg cholesterol.

1 pound wagon wheel pasta
4 links hot Italian-style turkey sausage (½ pound total),
   casings removed
½ pound mushrooms, thinly sliced
1 cup chicken broth
1 package (10 ounces) frozen chopped spinach, thawed
¼ cup raisins, coarsely chopped

1. Cook wagon wheel pasta in a large pot of lightly salted boiling water until al dente, firm but tender. Drain well.

2. Meanwhile, sauté sausage in a large skillet over medium heat, breaking up with a wooden spoon, 3 minutes. Add mushrooms; cover and simmer 5 minutes or until mushrooms are soft and sausage is cooked through. Add broth, spinach and raisins; gently heat through.

3. Toss together hot pasta and sausage sauce in a large serving bowl.

Ziti with Savory Sausage Sauce

MAKES 6 servings

PREP 5 minutes

COOK 25 minutes

———

PER SERVING
403 calories, 20 g protein,
9 g fat, 80 g carbohydrate,
830 mg sodium,
47 mg cholesterol.

1 teaspoon olive oil

¼ cup chopped onion

1 clove garlic, finely chopped

4 links sweet Italian-style turkey sausage (½ pound total), casings removed

1 can (14½ ounces) diced tomatoes

1 cup fat-free half-and-half

¼ teaspoon salt

⅛ teaspoon black pepper

1 pound ziti

1 teaspoon cornstarch

1 tablespoon cold water

1 cup frozen peas, thawed

1. Heat oil in a large skillet over medium heat. Add onion and garlic; sauté until fragrant, about 1 minute. Add sausage to skillet; sauté, breaking up with a wooden spoon, 7 minutes or until lightly browned.

2. Stir in tomatoes, half-and-half, salt and pepper; simmer, uncovered, stirring occasionally, 15 minutes or until slightly thickened.

3. Meanwhile, cook ziti in a large pot of lightly salted boiling water until al dente, firm but tender. Drain well.

4. Dissolve cornstarch in water in a small bowl. Gently stir into sausage mixture. Add peas; cook until heated through.

5. Transfer ziti to a large serving bowl; toss with sausage sauce.

Ziti with Savory Sausage Sauce

Pasta with Classic Meat Sauce

quick PREP

MAKES 8 servings

PREP 10 minutes

COOK 30 minutes

———

PER SERVING
333 calories, 18 g protein,
9 g fat, 47 g carbohydrate,
404 mg sodium,
29 mg cholesterol.

1 tablespoon olive oil

½ cup chopped onion

2 cups sliced mushrooms

¾ pound lean ground beef

½ cup dry white wine

1 can (28 ounces) Italian peeled tomatoes

½ cup water

¾ teaspoon salt

½ teaspoon black pepper

1 pound pappardelle or other wide noodles

1. Heat oil in a large nonstick skillet over medium heat. Add onion; cook until softened, 4 minutes. Add mushrooms; cook until liquid evaporates, 5 minutes.

2. Add beef; cook, breaking up clumps with a wooden spoon, until browned. Add wine; cook until wine evaporates. Add tomatoes with their liquid, water, salt and pepper; simmer, uncovered, stirring occasionally until sauce thickens, about 15 minutes.

3. Meanwhile, cook pappardelle in a large pot of lightly salted boiling water until al dente, firm but tender. Drain well. Add to skillet; toss.

Cheesy Kielbasa & Pasta

quick PREP

MAKES 8 servings

PREP 10 minutes

COOK about 12 minutes

BAKE at 350° for 30 minutes

———

PER SERVING
530 calories, 21 g protein,
24 g fat, 56 g carbohydrate,
1,367 mg sodium,
62 mg cholesterol.

1 pound bow-tie pasta (farfalle)

1 package (10 ounces) frozen peas, thawed

1 pound kielbasa, cut into ½-inch-thick slices

2 cans (10¾ ounces each) condensed cheddar cheese soup

2⅔ cups whole milk

1 teaspoon liquid hot-pepper sauce

¼ teaspoon black pepper

1. Heat oven to 350°.

2. Cook pasta in a large pot of lightly salted boiling water until al dente, firm but tender. Drain well. Place in a 13 x 9 x 2-inch baking dish. Add peas, sprinkling evenly over pasta.

3. Meanwhile, brown kielbasa in a medium-size nonstick skillet over medium-high heat 5 to 7 minutes. Add to pasta in baking dish.

4. Whisk together soup, milk, hot-pepper sauce and black pepper in a medium-size bowl. Add to baking dish and toss to coat pasta.

5. Bake in heated 350° oven about 30 minutes or until heated through.

Pasta Caponata

30 minutes MAX

MAKES 6 servings

PREP 20 minutes

COOK 12 minutes

BROIL 8 minutes

(while cooking pasta)

———

PER SERVING
393 calories, 11 g protein,
14 g fat, 58 g carbohydrate,
492 mg sodium,
52 mg cholesterol.

1 pound penne

1 pound eggplant, cut into 3 x ¼-inch strips

¾ teaspoon salt

½ teaspoon black pepper

10 oil-cured black olives, pitted and chopped

2 tablespoons capers

½ cup chopped fresh basil

15 cherry tomatoes, quartered

2 tablespoons pine nuts, toasted

1 clove garlic, mashed

2 tablespoons olive oil

2 tablespoons grated Parmesan cheese

Shaved Parmesan cheese (optional)

1. Heat broiler. Coat broiler-pan rack with nonstick olive-oil cooking spray.

2. Cook penne in a large pot of lightly salted boiling water until al dente, firm but tender. Drain well; spray lightly with nonstick olive-oil cooking spray and toss. Keep warm.

3. Meanwhile, coat eggplant strips with nonstick olive-oil cooking spray. Sprinkle with ½ teaspoon salt and pepper. Place eggplant on prepared rack. Broil 8 minutes or until golden on both sides, turning once.

4. Combine penne, eggplant, olives, capers, basil, tomatoes, nuts, garlic, oil, grated Parmesan and remaining ¼ teaspoon salt in a large bowl; toss gently to mix. Serve with shaved Parmesan if desired.

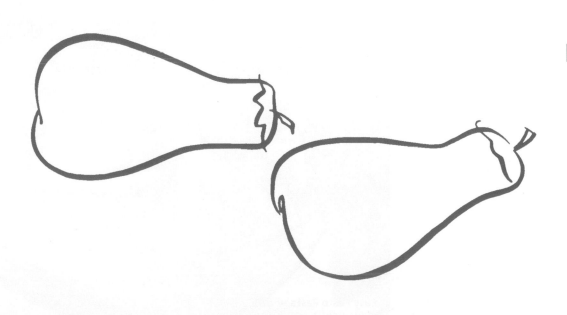

Rigatoni with Broccoli

30 minutes MAX

MAKES 6 servings

PREP 10 minutes

COOK 17 minutes

———————

PER SERVING
488 calories, 19 g protein,
21 g fat, 55 g carbohydrate,
544 mg sodium,
51 mg cholesterol.

2 tablespoons olive oil

1 onion, diced

1 sweet red pepper, thinly sliced

2 cups broccoli flowerets

¼ teaspoon dried basil

½ teaspoon salt

¼ teaspoon black pepper

1 clove garlic, finely chopped

6 links hot Italian sausage (¾ pound total), casings
    removed and filling crumbled

⅓ cup white wine

1 pound rigatoni

¼ cup heavy cream

1 cup shredded mozzarella cheese

1. Heat oil in a large skillet over medium-high heat. Add onion, red pepper, broccoli, basil, salt, black pepper and garlic. Cook 6 minutes. Add sausage and cook 4 more minutes. Add wine and cook another 3 minutes.

2. Meanwhile, cook rigatoni in a large pot of lightly salted boiling water until al dente, firm but tender. Drain well, reserving ½ cup cooking water.

3. Add reserved water, cream and mozzarella to skillet and cook 2 minutes. Remove from heat; add rigatoni and toss to coat.

**Easy Pesto Pasta with
Grilled Chicken,** *opposite*

Easy Pesto Pasta with Grilled Chicken

MAX

MAKES 6 servings

PREP 15 minutes

COOK 10 minutes

GRILL OR BROIL 8 minutes

(while cooking pasta)

———————

PER SERVING
306 calories, 12 g protein,
7 g fat, 48 g carbohydrate,
336 mg sodium,
14 mg cholesterol.

2 boneless, skinless chicken breast halves
  (5 ounces each)
½ pound cherry tomatoes, halved
¾ pound penne
½ pound green beans, trimmed and cut into 1-inch pieces
½ cup reduced-fat mayonnaise
1 tablespoon prepared or homemade pesto
  (recipe, page 231)
3 tablespoons distilled white vinegar
¼ teaspoon salt
¼ teaspoon black pepper

1. Prepare a hot grill or heat broiler. Lightly brush grill rack or broiler-pan rack with vegetable oil; set rack 6 inches from source of heat.

2. Place chicken breast halves between sheets of plastic wrap. Lightly pound until ¼ inch thick.

3. Place tomato halves upside down on paper toweling; let drain about 10 minutes.

4. Meanwhile, grill or broil chicken breasts, about 4 minutes per side or until internal temperature registers 170° on an instant-read thermometer. Remove chicken from grill and cut into 1-inch pieces.

5. Meanwhile, cook penne in a large pot of lightly salted boiling water. After cooking 5 minutes, add green beans; continue cooking until penne is al dente, firm but tender, and beans are crisp-tender. Drain penne and beans in a colander; rinse under cool running water. Drain well.

6. Transfer penne and beans to a large bowl. Add grilled chicken. Stir together mayonnaise, pesto and vinegar in a small bowl. Add to pasta mixture along with salt and pepper. Gently toss to combine.

Pasta

Pasta Niçoise

MAKES 4 servings
PREP 10 minutes
COOK 12 minutes

———

PER SERVING
356 calories, 22 g protein,
4 g fat, 60 g carbohydrate,
1163 mg sodium,
13 mg cholesterol.

¾ pound spinach spaghetti
1 can (14½ ounces) diced tomatoes, drained
1 can (8 ounces) tomato sauce
2 cloves garlic, finely chopped
2 tablespoons tomato paste
¼ teaspoon red-pepper flakes
4 scallions, chopped, including part of the green
1 can (6 ounces) water-packed tuna, drained
2 tablespoons chopped pitted oil-cured black olives
3 tablespoons capers, drained and rinsed
⅓ cup chopped fresh parsley

1. Cook spaghetti in a large pot of lightly salted boiling water until al dente, firm but tender. Drain well.

2. Meanwhile, in a large skillet, combine tomatoes, tomato sauce, garlic, tomato paste and red-pepper flakes. Bring to simmering; simmer 4 minutes or until slightly thickened.

3. Add scallions, tuna, olives and capers. Bring to simmering, breaking up tuna with a wooden spoon; simmer 1 minute. Stir in parsley. Spoon over spaghetti.

Fast Fix

Pasta Presto

BOIL UP that pasta and whip up these extra-fast dishes in no time.

Penne with Instant Artichoke Sauce

▸ Drain 1 jar (6½ ounces) marinated artichoke hearts, reserving marinade.

▸ Chop artichoke hearts. Chop 2 tomatoes.

▸ Combine artichoke hearts, tomatoes and reserved marinade in a serving bowl; set aside to meld flavors.

▸ Cook ½ pound penne or rigatoni in a large pot of lightly salted boiling water until al dente, firm but tender; drain well.

▸ Add hot pasta to artichoke-tomato mixture. Toss to mix and "cook" sauce.

▸ Makes about 4 servings.

Pasta with Mushroom-Cognac Sauce

▸ Cook 1 pound pasta in a large pot of lightly salted boiling water until al dente, firm but tender; drain well.

▸ Meanwhile, place ½ cup dried mushrooms, 3 tablespoons cognac and 5 tablespoons hot water in a glass measure; soak 10 minutes.

▸ Strain liquid into a serving bowl. Chop mushrooms.

▸ Mix mushrooms, ½ cup grated Parmesan cheese and 1 jar (16 ounces) prepared Alfredo sauce with mushroom liquid in serving bowl.

▸ Add hot pasta to sauce. Toss to mix and "cook" sauce.

▸ Makes about 6 servings.

Shrimp Fra Diavolo

MAKES 6 servings

PREP 15 minutes

COOK about 15 minutes

————

PER SERVING
406 calories, 19 g protein,
7 g fat, 67 g carbohydrate,
474 mg sodium,
67 mg cholesterol.

2 tablespoons olive oil

¾ pound peeled, deveined large shrimp, cut in half lengthwise

3 tablespoons finely chopped garlic

1 teaspoon red-pepper flakes

³/₈ teaspoon salt

1 pound linguine

1 can (28 ounces) Italian-style peeled tomatoes, drained and coarsely chopped

2 tablespoons tomato paste

1 teaspoon dried basil

1. Heat oil in a large skillet over medium-high heat. Add shrimp; cook 30 seconds. Add garlic, red-pepper flakes and ¼ teaspoon salt; cook, stirring occasionally, 2 minutes or until shrimp are curled and pink. Be careful not to overcook. With a slotted spoon, remove shrimp to a bowl.

2. Cook linguine in a large pot of lightly salted boiling water until al dente, firm but tender. Drain well.

3. Meanwhile, add tomatoes, tomato paste, basil and remaining ⅛ teaspoon salt to skillet; stir to combine. Bring to boiling over medium-high heat; cook 10 minutes or until sauce is thickened.

4. To serve, add cooked shrimp to sauce; gently heat through very briefly. Toss with linguine or serve on top of it.

Linguine with Tuna

MAKES 6 servings

PREP 5 minutes

COOK 10 minutes

————

PER SERVING
360 calories, 19 g protein,
5 g fat, 57 g carbohydrate,
415 mg sodium,
16 mg cholesterol.

1 pound linguine

1 tablespoon olive oil

2 cloves garlic, finely chopped

1 can (6 ounces) water-packed tuna, drained

1 can (3 ounces) water-packed tuna, drained

1 can (13¾ ounces) chicken broth

¼ cup finely chopped parsley

¼ to ½ teaspoon red-pepper flakes

1. Cook linguine in a large pot of lightly salted boiling water until al dente, firm but tender. Drain well.

2. Meanwhile, heat oil in a large skillet over medium-low heat. Add garlic; sauté 2 minutes. Add tuna, broth, parsley and red-pepper flakes. Increase heat to medium; cook just until heated through.

3. Add linguine to skillet. Toss.

Penne with Salmon

MAKES 4 servings

PREP 15 minutes

COOK 15 minutes

PER SERVING
204 calories, 20 g protein,
9 g fat, 8 g carbohydrate,
755 mg sodium,
48 mg cholesterol.

½ pound penne

¼ cup lower-sodium chicken broth

3 tablespoons oyster sauce (see Note below)

3 tablespoons rice-wine vinegar

1 tablespoon reduced-sodium soy sauce

½ teaspoon liquid hot-pepper sauce

2 teaspoons cornstarch

1 tablespoon canola oil

3 cloves garlic, finely chopped

3 scallions, separated into white and green parts, each finely chopped

1 tablespoon finely chopped peeled fresh ginger

1 boneless, skinless salmon fillet (about 1 pound), cut into 1 x ¼-inch strips

6 ounces fresh shiitake mushrooms, stemmed and quartered

5 cups spinach leaves (4 ounces), stemmed

1. Cook penne in a large pot of lightly salted boiling water until al dente, firm but tender. Drain well and keep warm.

2. Meanwhile, combine broth, oyster sauce, vinegar, soy sauce, hot-pepper sauce and cornstarch in a small bowl.

3. Heat oil in a large nonstick wok or skillet over high heat. Add garlic, white part of scallions and ginger; sauté 15 seconds. Add salmon and mushrooms; cook, stirring often, 4 to 5 minutes or until salmon is cooked.

4. Stir cornstarch mixture and add to wok along with spinach. Heat to boiling. Stir in penne. Heat 1 minute. Transfer to a serving bowl. Garnish with green part of scallions.

Note: Oyster sauce is a tangy brown sauce that is flavored with oysters and often used in Cantonese cooking. If unavailable, substitute soy sauce.

Creamy Spring Pasta

quick
PREP

MAKES 6 servings

PREP 5 minutes

COOK 10 minutes

PER SERVING
507 calories, 20 g protein,
19 g fat, 64 g carbohydrate,
471 mg sodium,
97 mg cholesterol.

1 pound bow-tie pasta (farfalle)

1 box (10 ounces) frozen peas

1 tablespoon butter

1 can (15 ounces) stewed tomatoes, drained

1 cup heavy cream

½ teaspoon salt

¼ teaspoon black pepper

½ pound crabmeat or surimi (imitation crabmeat),
   coarsely chopped

1. Cook pasta in a large pot of lightly salted boiling water. After cooking 6 minutes, add frozen peas; continue cooking 4 minutes.

2. Meanwhile, melt butter in a medium-size skillet over high heat. Add tomatoes, breaking up with a wooden spoon. Add cream, salt and pepper; lower heat to medium-high and simmer 5 minutes. Add crabmeat.

3. Drain pasta and peas; toss with sauce.

Penne with Salmon,
opposite

Grilled Scallop & Pasta Caesar

½ pound bow-tie pasta (farfalle)

1¼ pounds sea scallops

½ teaspoon salt

¼ teaspoon black pepper

1 teaspoon olive oil

1 head romaine lettuce, torn into bite-size pieces

1 sweet red pepper, cored, seeded and thinly sliced

½ cup Basic or Low-Cal Caesar Dressing
   (recipes, pages 28 and 29)

1. Cook pasta in a large pot of lightly salted boiling water until al dente, firm but tender. Drain well.

2. Meanwhile, season scallops with salt and black pepper. Heat oil in a large nonstick skillet over medium-high heat. Working in 2 batches, sauté scallops just until opaque in center, 3 minutes per batch.

3. Place romaine in a large bowl. Add red pepper, pasta and scallops. Drizzle with dressing; toss to coat.

Peanutty Noodles

1 pound fettuccine

1 box (10 ounces) frozen green beans

1 cup peanut butter

¾ cup water

¼ cup rice-wine vinegar

3 tablespoons soy sauce

2 teaspoons lime juice

½ teaspoon salt

½ teaspoon liquid hot-pepper sauce

1 tablespoon vegetable oil

2 cups shredded cooked chicken or beef (about ½ pound)

2 scallions, chopped, including part of the green

1. Cook fettuccine in a large pot of lightly salted boiling water. After cooking 6 minutes, add frozen green beans; continue cooking 4 minutes.

2. Meanwhile, whisk together peanut butter, water, vinegar, soy sauce, lime juice, salt and hot-pepper sauce in a serving bowl.

3. Drain fettuccine and green beans. Return to pot and toss with oil and chicken. Then add to sauce in serving bowl. Toss to combine. Sprinkle scallions on top.

Fettuccine with Shrimp

MAX

MAKES 6 servings

PREP 8 minutes

COOK 17 minutes

PER SERVING
612 calories, 37 g protein,
21 g fat, 67 g carbohydrate,
477 mg sodium,
217 mg cholesterol.

1 pound fettuccine
2 tablespoons olive oil
3 cloves garlic, finely chopped
3 shallots, finely chopped
1 tablespoon flour
1 cup chicken broth
1 cup heavy cream
⅛ teaspoon saffron
1½ pounds peeled, deveined medium shrimp
1 tomato, seeded and chopped
2 teaspoons lemon juice
¼ teaspoon salt
⅛ teaspoon black pepper
Pinch red-pepper flakes

1. Cook fettuccine in a large pot of lightly salted boiling water until al dente, firm but tender. Drain well.

2. Meanwhile, heat oil in a large nonstick skillet over medium-high heat. Add garlic and shallots; sauté 7 minutes or until softened; be careful not to let them burn. Stir in flour and cook, stirring, 2 minutes.

3. Add broth, cream, saffron and shrimp to skillet. Simmer, stirring occasionally, 5 to 7 minutes. Add tomato, lemon juice, salt, black pepper and red-pepper flakes. Simmer 3 minutes. Serve sauce over fettuccine.

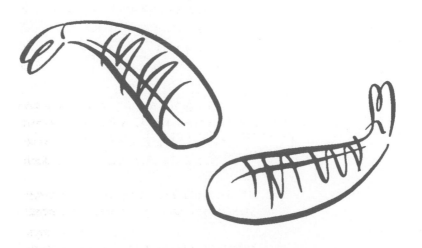

Fish & Shellfish

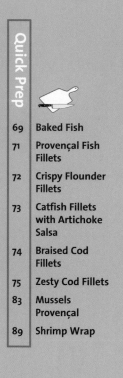

Creole-Style Flounder

MAKES 6 servings

PREP 15 minutes

COOK 10 to 12 minutes

PER SERVING
175 calories, 25 g protein,
5 g fat, 7 g carbohydrate,
596 mg sodium,
70 mg cholesterol.

2 tablespoons butter
¼ cup chopped celery
¼ cup chopped onion
2 cloves garlic, finely chopped
1 large sweet green pepper, cored, seeded and thinly
    sliced lengthwise
6 flounder fillets (1½ pounds total)
½ teaspoon salt
¼ teaspoon black pepper
⅛ teaspoon ground red pepper (cayenne)
1 can (8 ounces) tomato sauce
1 tablespoon fresh lemon juice

1. Heat butter in a large nonstick skillet over medium-high heat. Add celery, onion, garlic and green pepper; cook until tender, about 5 minutes.

2. Season fillets with salt, black pepper and red pepper. Place on top of vegetables in skillet. Pour tomato sauce evenly over top of fish. Drizzle with lemon juice. Cover and cook over medium-high heat 7 minutes or until fish is cooked through.

Creole-Style Flounder

Aegean Sole

MAKES 6 servings

PREP 8 minutes

COOK 30 minutes

———

PER SERVING
235 calories, 27 g protein,
11 g fat, 6 g carbohydrate,
465 mg sodium
95 mg cholesterol.

1 bag (10 ounces) fresh spinach

¼ cup dry seasoned bread crumbs

4 ounces feta cheese, crumbled

6 small sole fillets (1¾ pounds total)

3 tablespoons butter

1. Remove 2 spinach leaves and cut into strips for garnish; reserve. Rinse remaining spinach leaves in water; shake to dry. Steam in a medium-size skillet, covered, over medium-high heat about 4 minutes. Let cool, then squeeze dry. Chop and mix with bread crumbs and feta cheese.

2. Heat oven to 350°.

3. Arrange fillets on a work surface. Place spinach mixture in center of each fillet; roll up. Cut butter into small pieces. Scatter half the butter in bottom of a 12 x 8 x 2-inch casserole. Place rolled fillets, seam side down, in casserole. Sprinkle remaining butter on top. Cover with aluminum foil.

4. Bake in heated 350° oven 25 minutes or until cooked through. Garnish with reserved spinach strips.

Fish 'n' Chips in a Bun

30 minutes MAX

MAKES 4 servings

PREP 15 minutes

COOK 6 minutes

———

PER SERVING
662 calories, 38 g protein,
37 g fat, 45 g carbohydrate,
1005 mg sodium,
145 mg cholesterol.

SAUCE

½ cup mayonnaise

2 tablespoons capers, drained and rinsed

1 tablespoon chopped fresh parsley

1 teaspoon fresh lemon juice

1 teaspoon dry mustard

½ teaspoon dried tarragon

¼ teaspoon salt

⅛ teaspoon ground red pepper (cayenne)

⅔ cup cornflake crumbs

1 egg

2 tablespoons milk

4 flounder or sole fillets (about 1¼ pounds total)

2 tablespoons vegetable oil

4 seeded hamburger buns

4 green lettuce leaves

1 cup potato chips

1. Prepare sauce: Whisk together mayonnaise, capers, parsley, lemon juice, mustard, tarragon, salt and red pepper in a small bowl.

2. Place crumbs on waxed paper. Whisk together egg and milk in a small bowl. Dip fish into egg mixture, then into crumbs, pressing crumbs onto fish to coat.

3. Heat oil in a nonstick skillet over medium-high heat. Add fish; cook, turning once, until golden brown and fish just begins to flake easily when tested with a fork, 6 minutes. Drain on paper toweling.

4. Layer bun bottoms with lettuce, fish, sauce and chips. Add bun tops.

Baked Fish

MAKES 4 servings

PREP 10 minutes

BAKE at 450° for 25 to 30 minutes

———

PER SERVING
522 calories, 33 g protein, 15 g fat, 61 g carbohydrate, 773 mg sodium, 91 mg cholesterol.

¼ cup (½ stick) butter

¼ cup water

¼ cup dry white wine

3 tablespoons fresh lemon juice

½ teaspoon salt

¼ teaspoon black pepper

8 large basil leaves, shredded

1⅓ cups instant white rice

1 medium-size red onion, thinly sliced

1 small sweet red pepper, cored, seeded and thinly sliced

1 cup frozen peas

4 sole, flounder or haddock fillets (about 1 pound total)

¼ teaspoon lemon-pepper seasoning

1 plum tomato, thinly sliced

Loaf semolina bread or other favorite bread

Lemon wedges for garnish (optional)

1. Heat oven to 450°.

2. Combine butter, water, wine, lemon juice, ¼ teaspoon salt, black pepper and basil in a small saucepan. Heat over medium heat until butter melts.

3. Lay out 4 squares of heavy-duty aluminum foil. Spread ⅓ cup rice in center of each piece. Top with equal amounts of onion, red pepper and peas. Sprinkle vegetables with remaining ¼ teaspoon salt. Top with fillets, tucking any rice under. Sprinkle each fillet with lemon-pepper seasoning and top with tomato.

4. Curl edges of foil up slightly. Evenly divide butter mixture among packets. Fold together 2 opposite edges of foil, then fold ends up and over to seal each packet completely. Place on a baking sheet.

5. Bake in heated 450° oven 20 to 25 minutes. Warm bread in oven during last few minutes of baking. Open packets carefully, as steam may escape. Serve with bread and lemon wedges if desired.

Baked Stuffed Flounder

MAKES 6 servings

PREP 15 minutes

BAKE at 400° for 42 minutes

COOK 4 minutes

───────

PER SERVING
306 calories, 32 g protein,
14 g fat, 11 g carbohydrate,
552 mg sodium,
103 mg cholesterol.

3 ribs celery, cut into 2½-inch-long thin strips

2 carrots, cut into 2½-inch-long thin strips

1 leek, trimmed and well washed, white part and 1 inch
   of green cut lengthwise into 2½-inch-long thin strips

2 tablespoons olive oil

1 medium-size tomato, seeded and diced

½ pound surimi (imitation crabmeat), cut into
   2½-inch-long thin strips

1 teaspoon salt

½ teaspoon garlic powder

½ teaspoon onion powder

¼ teaspoon black pepper

6 large flounder fillets (about 2 pounds total)

½ cup fresh basil leaves, coarsely chopped

6 sprigs fresh thyme or ½ teaspoon dried thyme

⅓ cup dry white wine

¼ cup (½ stick) unsalted butter

2 tablespoons fresh lemon juice

1. Heat oven to 400°.

2. Toss together celery, carrots, leek and oil in a flameproof 13 x 9 x 2-inch baking pan. Roast in heated 400° oven 20 minutes, stirring once or twice.

3. Add tomato and surimi to pan with vegetables. Roast 10 minutes. Remove mixture from pan and reserve. Leave oven on.

4. Mix salt, garlic and onion powders and pepper in a small cup. Season skinned side of each fish fillet with half of salt mixture. Divide vegetable mixture among fillets; top with basil. Fold fish in half over filling. Season with remaining salt mixture. Place fillets in a single layer in same baking pan. Top each with a sprig of thyme. Drizzle with wine. Cover pan with aluminum foil.

5. Return pan to oven and bake 12 minutes or until fish is cooked through. Remove fish to a platter using a slotted spoon; cover to keep warm.

6. Place baking pan on stovetop burner. Bring juices to boiling over high heat; boil about 3 minutes or until reduced by half. Whisk in butter and lemon juice until creamy. Serve with fish.

Provençal Fish Fillets

quick PREP

MAKES 4 servings

PREP 5 minutes

COOK 20 minutes

BAKE at 350° for 10 minutes

BROIL 5 minutes

———

PER SERVING
357 calories, 57 g protein,
10 g fat, 7 g carbohydrate,
334 mg sodium,
101 mg cholesterol.

1 tablespoon olive oil

1 medium-size onion, sliced

2 cloves garlic, finely chopped

4 large canned tomatoes, chopped, or 1 cup drained
   canned diced tomatoes

½ teaspoon dried thyme

2 bay leaves

10 oil-cured black olives, pitted and sliced

1 teaspoon capers, drained, rinsed and mashed

4 firm white fish fillets such as snapper
   (about 1½ pounds total)

1. Heat oil in a medium-size saucepan. Add onion and garlic; sauté 5 minutes or until softened. Add tomatoes, thyme, bay leaves, olives and capers; simmer, uncovered, over medium heat 15 minutes. Remove and discard bay leaves.

2. Heat oven to 350°. Coat a broilerproof baking dish large enough to hold fish in a single layer with nonstick cooking spray.

3. Place fish in baking dish. Bake in heated 350° oven 10 minutes.

4. Remove dish from oven. Increase oven temperature to broil. Spoon sauce over fish. Broil fish 3 to 4 inches from source of heat 5 minutes.

Baked Stuffed Flounder, *opposite*

Crispy Flounder Fillets

MAKES 4 servings

PREP 5 minutes

BAKE at 450° for 8 minutes

———

PER SERVING
188 calories, 23 g protein,
2 g fat, 19 g carbohydrate,
710 mg sodium,
53 mg cholesterol.

¾ cup cornflake crumbs

1 teaspoon dried oregano

½ teaspoon salt, plus additional pinch

¼ teaspoon black pepper, plus additional pinch

⅛ teaspoon ground red pepper (cayenne)

2 tablespoons all-purpose flour

2 egg whites

1 tablespoon Dijon mustard

4 flounder fillets (1 pound total)

1. Heat oven to 450°. Coat a baking sheet with nonstick cooking spray.

2. Combine crumbs, oregano, ½ teaspoon salt, ½ teaspoon black pepper and red pepper in a shallow dish. Place flour in another shallow dish. Beat egg whites in a medium-size bowl until stiff, glossy peaks form. Fold in mustard.

3. Season fish fillets with a pinch each salt and black pepper. Dip fillets into flour to coat both sides, shaking off any excess flour. Spread egg mixture on both sides of floured fish; dip into crumbs, coating well. Place fish on prepared baking sheet.

4. Bake in heated 450° oven 8 minutes or until fish is crisp and cooked through.

Fast Fix

Fish Flair

TRY THESE SIMPLE TRICKS for delicious baked fish in a flash. Begin each of these recipes with 4 fish fillets (about 1½ pounds total).

Caponata Catfish

▶ Place catfish fillets on a cutting board; spread 1 can (7½ ounces) caponata over them, dividing evenly.

▶ Top each fillet with a little lemon juice, chopped parsley and grated Parmesan cheese.

▶ Roll up each fillet; place seam side down in a lightly buttered baking dish. Add a little white wine.

▶ Cover and bake at 350° about 20 minutes or until fish is cooked through.

▶ Makes 4 servings.

Italian Tomato-Olive-Garlic Flounder

▶ Combine 1½ tablespoons capers; 3 cloves garlic, finely chopped; ⅓ cup chopped black olives; ⅓ cup white wine; ¼ teaspoon dried rosemary, ¼ teaspoon dried thyme and ¼ cup marinara sauce in a bowl.

▶ Season flounder fillets with salt and pepper to taste; roll and place in a lightly buttered baking dish. Pour sauce on and around fish.

▶ Cover and bake at 375° about 25 minutes or until cooked.

▶ Makes 4 servings.

Mustard-Herb Snapper

▶ Blend 1 tablespoon Dijon mustard, 3 tablespoons chopped fresh parsley, 2 tablespoons bread crumbs and 1 teaspoon dried tarragon or rosemary in a small bowl.

▶ Spread on red snapper fillets; place fish in a lightly buttered baking dish.

▶ Bake at 375° until fish is crisped and cooked through, about 15 minutes.

▶ Makes 4 servings.

Catfish Fillets with Artichoke Salsa

MAKES 4 servings

PREP 5 minutes

COOK 10 minutes

PER SERVING
478 calories, 34 g protein,
30 g fat, 18 g carbohydrate,
743 mg sodium,
148 mg cholesterol.

1 egg
¼ cup milk
⅓ cup cornmeal
½ teaspoon salt
¼ teaspoon black pepper
¼ teaspoon dried thyme
Pinch ground red pepper (cayenne)
4 catfish fillets (1½ pounds total)
⅓ cup vegetable oil

ARTICHOKE SALSA
1 jar (6½ ounces) marinated artichoke hearts
1 tomato, chopped
1 red onion, diced
¼ teaspoon salt
1 teaspoon lime juice

1. Mix egg and milk in a shallow bowl. Mix cornmeal, salt, black pepper, thyme and red pepper in a second shallow bowl. Dip fillets in egg mixture, then cornmeal mixture.

2. Heat oil in a large skillet over medium-high heat. Add fish; cook 10 minutes or until golden, turning once.

3. Meanwhile, prepare salsa: Drain liquid from artichoke hearts into a small bowl. Chop artichoke hearts and add to liquid along with tomato, onion, salt and lime juice; stir to combine.

4. Transfer fish to a platter and serve topped with artichoke salsa.

Fish & Shellfish

73

Braised Cod Fillets

MAKES 6 servings

PREP 10 minutes

BAKE 20 minutes

COOK 7 minutes

PER SERVING
119 calories, 18 g protein,
5 g fat, 4 g carbohydrate,
667 mg sodium,
40 mg cholesterol.

2 tablespoons Dijon mustard
1 teaspoon grated fresh ginger
1 small clove garlic, finely chopped
6 cod fillets (1½ pounds total)
¾ teaspoon salt
½ teaspoon black pepper
1 cup vegetable broth
½ cup dry white wine
2 tablespoons butter
1 medium-size onion, diced
1½ bags (10 ounces each) fresh spinach

1. Heat oven to 425°.

2. Mix mustard, ginger and garlic in a small bowl. Season fillets with ¼ teaspoon salt and ¼ teaspoon pepper. Spread each with 1 teaspoon mustard mixture. Arrange in a baking dish large enough to hold them in a single layer. Add broth and wine.

3. Bake fish, uncovered, in heated 425° oven 20 minutes.

4. Meanwhile, heat butter in a medium-size skillet. Add onion and cook over medium heat 4 minutes or until tender. Add spinach; cover and cook 3 minutes, until wilted. Season with remaining ½ teaspoon salt and ¼ teaspoon pepper. Serve fish over spinach.

Cod Fillets Adobo

MAKES 4 servings

PREP 5 minutes

REFRIGERATE 20 minutes

BROIL 5 to 7 minutes

PER SERVING
155 calories, 20 g protein,
8 g fat, 0 g carbohydrate,
195 mg sodium,
49 mg cholesterol.

2 tablespoons vegetable oil
2 tablespoons lemon juice
¾ teaspoon paprika
¾ teaspoon dried oregano
¼ teaspoon ground cumin
¼ teaspoon salt
⅛ teaspoon black pepper
4 cod fillets (1¼ pounds total)

1. Combine oil, lemon juice, paprika, oregano, cumin, salt and pepper in a small bowl. Using a basting brush, spread mixture on both sides of fish. Place fillets in a pie plate. Cover and refrigerate 20 minutes.

2. Heat broiler. Arrange fillets in a broilerproof baking dish large enough to hold them in a single layer; position in broiler so top of fish is 3 inches from heat.

3. Broil 5 to 7 minutes or until fish just begins to flake when tested with a fork.

Zesty Cod Fillets

Zesty Cod Fillets

MAKES 4 servings

PREP 10 minutes

COOK 10 minutes

BAKE at 350° for 20 minutes

———

PER SERVING
166 calories, 21 g protein,
5 g fat, 10 g carbohydrate,
1,047 mg sodium,
46 mg cholesterol.

2 teaspoons olive oil

1 medium-size onion, thinly sliced

1 clove garlic, finely chopped

1 can (14½ ounces) whole tomatoes, drained and
    coarsely chopped

1 cup chicken broth

¼ cup dry white wine

½ teaspoon dried thyme

1 teaspoon salt

½ teaspoon black pepper

4 cod fillets (about 1 ½ pounds)

½ pound fresh spinach, tough stems removed

1. Heat oven to 350°.

2. Heat oil in a nonstick skillet. Add onion and garlic; cook until onion is very soft, 5 minutes. Add tomatoes, broth, wine, thyme, ½ teaspoon salt and ¼ teaspoon pepper; simmer, uncovered, until sauce is reduced and thickened slightly, 5 minutes.

3. Season fish with remaining ½ teaspoon salt and ¼ teaspoon pepper. Place in a 13 x 9 x 2-inch baking dish. Add sauce; cover.

4. Bake in heated 350° oven 15 minutes. Add spinach to sauce around fish. Bake 5 minutes or until fish flakes when tested with a fork.

Terrific Tuna

HAVING A CAN OF TUNA in the cupboard is a guarantee that lunch or dinner can be on the table in minutes.

Hurry-up Paella

▶ Cook 1 package (5 ounces) yellow rice mix following package directions.

▶ Meanwhile, coarsely chop one ⅛-inch-thick slice deli ham.

▶ Just before rice is done, add ham and 1 can (6 ounces) drained and flaked water-packed tuna to saucepan along with 1 box (10 ounces) frozen peas, thawed. Stir to combine; heat through.

▶ Makes about 4 servings.

Toasty Tuna Melt

▶ Toast 4 English muffin bottoms and place on a baking sheet.

▶ Combine 1 can (6 ounces) drained and flaked water-packed tuna, 2 chopped ribs celery, 3 tablespoons chopped red onion, ¼ cup mayonnaise, 1 teaspoon Dijon mustard, 5 drops liquid hot-pepper sauce and ⅛ teaspoon black pepper in a small bowl.

▶ Divide tuna mixture among muffin bottoms. Top each with a tomato slice and 1 ounce shredded cheddar cheese.

▶ Broil to melt cheese; toast muffin tops.

▶ Top each tuna melt with a muffin top.

▶ Makes 4 servings.

Speedy Sandwich Filling

▶ Mix 1 cup seeded, chopped cucumber, 1 cup drained canned chick-peas, 1 can (6 ounces) drained and flaked water-packed tuna, 3 tablespoons bottled Italian salad dressing, 1 tablespoon fresh lemon juice and ¼ teaspoon salt.

▶ Use to fill pitas or another favorite sandwich bread.

▶ Makes about 6 servings.

Grilled Tuna on Sourdough

quick COOK

MAKES 4 sandwiches
PREP 10 minutes
REFRIGERATE 15 minutes
GRILL OR COOK 6 minutes

———
PER SERVING
668 calories, 43 g protein, 24 g fat, 69 g carbohydrate, 1,060 mg sodium, 54 mg cholesterol.

4 tuna steaks (about 1 pound total)
2 tablespoons plus 1 teaspoon soy sauce
1 tablespoon dark Asian sesame oil
1 tablespoon fresh lemon juice
4 teaspoons chopped peeled fresh ginger
2 tablespoons mayonnaise
8 slices sourdough bread
4 leaves red-leaf lettuce
1 avocado, peeled, pitted and lightly mashed

1. Arrange tuna steaks in a baking dish large enough to hold them in a single layer. Whisk 2 tablespoons soy sauce, oil, lemon juice and 1 tablespoon ginger in a small bowl. Pour over tuna in baking dish. Refrigerate 15 minutes, turning after 8 minutes.

2. Mix mayonnaise, remaining 1 teaspoon ginger and remaining 1 teaspoon soy sauce in a bowl. Refrigerate.

3. Prepare a medium-hot grill; coat rack with cooking spray and position 6 inches from heat. Alternatively, coat a stovetop grill pan; heat over high heat until pan starts to smoke slightly, about 3 minutes.

4. Remove tuna from marinade; pat dry with paper toweling. Cook on grill or pan 3 minutes per side for medium. Transfer to a platter; tent with foil.

5. Spread bread with mayonnaise mixture; make 4 sandwiches with lettuce, avocado and tuna.

Orange-Ginger Tuna Steak

MAKES 4 servings
PREP 15 minutes
REFRIGERATE 30 minutes
GRILL 6 minutes
COOK 5 minutes

———

PER SERVING
53 calories, 41 g protein,
13 g fat, 18 g carbohydrate,
1,267 mg sodium,
63 mg cholesterol

2 teaspoons grated orange rind

1 cup orange juice

½ cup reduced-sodium soy sauce

2 tablespoons dark-brown sugar

4 teaspoons dark Asian sesame oil

4 teaspoons finely chopped peeled fresh ginger

2 tablespoons finely chopped fresh cilantro

4 tuna steaks, about 1 inch thick (1½ pounds total)

2 tablespoons sweetened dried cranberries

1. Combine rind, orange juice, soy sauce, brown sugar, oil, ginger and cilantro in a baking dish large enough to hold tuna steaks in a single layer. Add tuna to dish; turn to coat. Cover; refrigerate 30 minutes, turning once.

2. Prepare a medium-hot grill and position rack about 2 inches from heat. Alternatively, heat broiler; coat broiler-pan rack with nonstick cooking spray and position rack about 2 inches from heat. Remove tuna from marinade. Reserve marinade.

3. Grill or broil tuna until cooked through, about 3 minutes per side for medium. Transfer to a platter.

4. Meanwhile, place marinade in a medium-size saucepan; cook over medium-high heat until thick and syrupy, about 5 minutes. Stir in cranberries during last 2 minutes of cooking.

5. To serve, spoon cranberry sauce over tuna steaks.

Lemon-Pepper Tuna

MAKES 4 servings

PREP 5 minutes

COOK 10 minutes

───────

PER SERVING
217 calories, 41 g protein,
5 g fat, 1 g carbohydrate,
388 mg sodium,
79 mg cholesterol.

4 tuna steaks, ¾ inch thick (about 2 pounds total)
½ teaspoon salt
½ teaspoon coarsely ground black pepper
1 tablespoon vegetable oil
½ cup chicken broth
1 tablespoon lemon juice
1 tablespoon grainy Dijon mustard
1 tablespoon finely chopped fresh chives

1. Sprinkle both sides of tuna steaks with salt and pepper.

2. Heat oil in a large nonstick skillet over medium-high heat. Add tuna; cook until browned on both sides and just slightly pink in center, about 8 minutes. Transfer tuna to a platter.

3. To same skillet, add broth and lemon juice. Heat to boiling. Remove from heat. Swirl in mustard and chives. Spoon sauce over tuna.

Dill-Baked Salmon

MAKES 4 servings

PREP 10 minutes

COOK 18 minutes

BAKE at 350° for 15 minutes

(while cooking greens)

───────

PER SERVING
429 calories, 38 g protein,
25 g fat, 15 g carbohydrate,
601 mg sodium,
138 mg cholesterol.

4 salmon fillets (1½ pounds total)
¾ teaspoon salt
¼ teaspoon black pepper
2 tablespoons lemon juice
1 tablespoon chopped fresh dill
4 lemon slices
3 shallots, chopped
1 clove garlic, finely chopped
2 tablespoons butter
2 bags (10 ounces each) fresh spinach
2 cups lightly packed fresh basil leaves
¼ cup heavy cream

1. Heat oven to 350°.

2. Arrange fillets in a baking dish large enough to hold them in a single layer. Mix salt and pepper and sprinkle half over fish along with lemon juice and dill. Top each fillet with a lemon slice.

3. Heat butter in a medium-size nonstick skillet over medium heat. Add shallots and garlic; sauté 6 minutes. Add spinach and basil and cook 8 minutes. Add remaining salt mixture and cream. Boil 4 minutes.

4. Meanwhile, bake fish in heated 350° oven 15 minutes. Serve over greens.

Salmon with Pesto

Salmon with Pesto

quick **COOK**

MAKES 4 servings

PREP 10 minutes

COOK 5 to 8 minutes

———

PER SERVING
289 calories, 43 g protein
11 g fat, 3 g carbohydrate,
542 mg sodium,
111 mg cholesterol.

4 salmon steaks (2 pounds total)

½ teaspoon salt

¾ teaspoon black pepper

2 tablespoons prepared or homemade pesto
  (recipe, page 231)

2 tablespoons fresh lemon juice

2 teaspoons Dijon mustard

1 teaspoon olive oil

½ teaspoon sugar

1 small tomato, seeded and diced

Fresh basil leaves for garnish (optional)

1. Heat broiler. Coat broiler-pan rack with nonstick cooking spray.

2. Sprinkle salmon steaks with salt and ½ teaspoon pepper. Place on broiler-pan rack. Broil 5 inches from heat 5 to 8 minutes or until cooked through.

3. Meanwhile, combine pesto, lemon juice, mustard, oil, sugar and remaining ¼ teaspoon pepper in a small bowl.

4. Arrange salmon on a platter. Drizzle with sauce. Top with tomato and basil if desired.

Fish & Shellfish

79

Scallops & Vegetables

MAKES 4 servings

PREP 10 minutes

COOK 10 minutes

———————

PER SERVING
125 calories, 14 g protein,
2 g fat, 12 g carbohydrate,
414 mg sodium,
21 mg cholesterol.

2 strips bacon, chopped

1 small onion, chopped

½ pound bay scallops

½ pound mushrooms, sliced

½ pound snow peas, trimmed

1 tablespoon dry sherry

2 teaspoons cornstarch

1 tablespoon water

1 tablespoon lemon juice

½ teaspoon salt

1. Brown bacon in a nonstick skillet. Remove to paper toweling to drain. Drain all but 1 tablespoon fat from skillet.

2. Add onion and scallops to skillet; cook, stirring, until scallops are white, 3 to 5 minutes. Remove.

3. Add mushrooms, snow peas and sherry to skillet; cover and cook 3 minutes. Combine cornstarch and water. Add to skillet; cook, stirring, until thickened. Stir in bacon and scallops. Stir in lemon juice and salt; warm through.

Scallop Sauté

MAKES 4 servings

PREP 15 minutes

COOK 10 minutes

———————

PER SERVING
462 calories, 17 g protein,
19 g fat, 57 g carbohydrate,
1,584 mg sodium,
23 mg cholesterol.

2 medium-size carrots

1 package (8 ounces) flat rice noodles or capellini

3 tablespoons dark Asian sesame oil

2 cloves garlic, sliced

1¼ pounds sea scallops, halved or quartered if large

2 tablespoons soy sauce

1 tablespoon honey

½ teaspoon ground ginger

½ teaspoon salt

¼ teaspoon black pepper

1 tablespoon fresh lime juice

½ cup chopped scallions, including part of the green

¼ cup fresh cilantro leaves, chopped

1 teaspoon sesame seeds, toasted (recipe, page 231), for garnish (optional)

1. Using a vegetable peeler, slice carrots into long ribbons.

2. Cook rice noodles and carrots in a large pot of boiling water 4 to 5 minutes. Drain well; rinse with warm water and transfer to a large serving bowl.

3. Meanwhile, heat 1 tablespoon oil in a medium-size skillet over medium-high heat. Add garlic and scallops; cook until scallops are white, about 5 minutes.

4. Whisk together remaining 2 tablespoons oil, soy sauce, honey, ginger, salt, pepper and lime juice in a small bowl. Add to skillet along with scallions; cook 1 minute.

5. Add scallop mixture and cilantro to noodle-carrot mixture; toss to combine. Top with sesame seeds if desired.

Parsleyed Scallops

MAKES 4 servings

PREP 15 minutes

BROIL scallops 4 minutes, tomatoes 3 minutes

———

PER SERVING
160 calories, 14 g protein,
8 g fat, 9 g carbohydrate,
771 mg sodium,
33 mg cholesterol.

1¼ pounds sea scallops

3 tablespoons dry seasoned bread crumbs

1 tablespoon chopped fresh parsley

1 teaspoon grated lemon rind

1 teaspoon vegetable oil

2 tomatoes, cut into ½-inch-thick slices

½ teaspoon salt

2 tablespoons grated Parmesan cheese

½ teaspoon coarse black pepper

1 tablespoon butter or margarine

1 teaspoon lemon juice

Fresh parsley sprigs for garnish (optional)

1. Heat broiler. Coat a large baking sheet with nonstick cooking spray.

2. Toss scallops, bread crumbs, parsley, rind and oil in a medium-size bowl until scallops are well coated.

3. Place scallops on prepared baking sheet. Broil 4 inches from heat until golden brown, about 4 minutes. Do not turn.

4. Remove scallops from broiler; keep broiler on. Transfer scallops to serving plates; tent with aluminum foil and keep warm.

5. Place tomatoes on same baking sheet. Sprinkle with salt, Parmesan and pepper. Broil 4 inches from heat until golden and bubbly, about 3 minutes.

6. Meanwhile, heat butter and lemon juice in a small saucepan over low heat. Drizzle over scallops. Serve scallops with tomato slices; garnish with parsley sprigs if desired.

Clam Pie

5 ingredients or **LESS**

MAKES 4 servings

PREP 5 minutes

COOK about 3 minutes

BAKE at 400° for 20 minutes

———

PER SERVING
556 calories, 33 g protein,
22 g fat, 53 g carbohydrate,
767 mg sodium,
71 mg cholesterol.

2 tablespoons garlic-flavored olive oil
2 cans (6½ ounces each) chopped clams, drained
1 prepared pizza shell
⅓ cup ricotta cheese
1 cup shredded mozzarella cheese

1. Heat oven to 400°.

2. Heat oil in a medium-size skillet over low heat. Add clams, cook 2 minutes.

3. Spread clam mixture over pizza shell. Arrange ricotta and mozzarella cheeses evenly over top.

4. Place on a baking sheet and bake in heated 400° oven 20 minutes.

Clam Pie

Mussels Provençal

MAKES 6 servings

PREP 10 minutes

COOK 30 minutes

PER SERVING
242 calories, 10 g protein,
4 g fat, 41 g carbohydrate,
475 mg sodium,
8 mg cholesterol.

1 tablespoon vegetable oil
1 large onion, quartered and
   separated
2 cloves garlic, crushed
1 can (14 ounces) crushed
   tomatoes
¾ cup dry white wine
   or chicken broth
1 bay leaf
1 teaspoon dried thyme
¼ teaspoon salt
⅛ teaspoon black pepper
1 sweet yellow pepper, cored,
   seeded and cut into thin strips
1½ teaspoons capers, drained and
   rinsed
2 teaspoons sugar
½ pound spaghetti
1 pound mussels in shells, cleaned
Chopped parsley for garnish (optional)

1. Heat 1½ teaspoons oil in a large nonstick skillet over medium heat. Add onion; sauté 3 minutes or until slightly softened. Add garlic; sauté 1 to 2 minutes. Add tomatoes, ½ cup wine, bay leaf, thyme, salt and pepper. Bring to boiling; cook, uncovered, 10 minutes. Remove skillet from heat. Remove and discard bay leaf.

2. Heat remaining 1½ teaspoons oil in a separate large skillet with a tight-fitting lid over medium-high heat. Add yellow pepper; cook 2 minutes. Add tomato sauce, remaining ¼ cup wine, capers and sugar; cook 2 minutes.

3. Meanwhile, cook spaghetti in a large pot of lightly salted boiling water until al dente, firm but tender. At the same time, add mussels to skillet with sauce. Cover; simmer, stirring occasionally, 9 minutes or until mussels open. Discard any mussels that do not open.

4. Drain spaghetti; transfer to a large bowl. Top with sauce and mussels. Garnish with parsley if desired.

Shrimp Melts

MAKES 4 servings

PREP 5 minutes

COOK 7 minutes

―――――――

PER SERVING
551 calories, 30 g protein,
31 g fat, 39 g carbohydrate,
1,188 mg sodium,
159 mg cholesterol.

¾ pound peeled, deveined medium shrimp, diced
¾ cup salsa
2 avocados, peeled and pitted
1 loaf Italian bread (14 inches long), halved lengthwise
6 ounces Monterey Jack cheese, shredded

1. Cook shrimp and salsa in a medium-size skillet over medium-high heat about 4 minutes or until shrimp are cooked through.

2. Heat broiler.

3. Slice avocados and layer on bread halves, dividing evenly. Spoon shrimp mixture on avocado. Top with cheese.

4. Broil about 6 inches from heat 2 to 3 minutes or until cheese melts. Cut into 4 pieces.

Fast Fix

Shrimp Savvy

FOR A SPEEDY main dish with shrimp, try these accents.

Salsa-Pepper Shrimp Sauté

► Core, seed and slice 1 sweet green pepper and 1 sweet red pepper. Finely chop 3 cloves garlic.

► Heat 2 tablespoons olive oil in a large skillet over high heat.

► Add peppers and garlic; cook until slightly soft, about 3 minutes.

► Add 1 pound peeled, deveined shrimp and cook 4 minutes.

► Stir in 1½ cups salsa.

► Makes about 6 servings.

Roasted Pepper & Shrimp Bake

► Whirl ½ cup roasted red pepper strips, 2 cloves garlic, ½ cup chopped parsley and 1 tablespoon lemon juice in a food processor or blender.

► Place 1 pound peeled, deveined shrimp in a lightly oiled baking pan; brush with roasted pepper mixture.

► Bake at 350° until cooked through, about 10 minutes.

► Makes about 6 servings.

Lime-Cumin-Garlic Shrimp

► Combine 1 clove finely chopped garlic, 2 tablespoons olive oil, 2 tablespoons lime juice, ¼ teaspoon cumin and salt and pepper to taste in a small bowl.

► Skewer 1 pound peeled, deveined shrimp; brush with marinade.

► Grill or broil 4 to 5 minutes or until cooked.

► Makes about 6 servings.

Festive Paella

MAKES 8 servings

PREP 15 minutes

COOK about 40 minutes

PER SERVING
336 calories, 24 g protein,
7 g fat, 41 g carbohydrate,
1,126 mg sodium,
85 mg cholesterol.

1 tablespoon olive oil

½ pound hot Italian-style chicken or turkey sausage,
   cut into coins

2 onions, chopped

6 cloves garlic, coarsely chopped

1 can (13¾ ounces) reduced-sodium chicken broth

1 bottle (8 ounces) clam juice

1 can (16 ounces) stewed tomatoes

1 cup water

½ cup dry white wine or water

½ teaspoon ground turmeric

1 small bay leaf

½ teaspoon liquid hot-pepper sauce

¾ teaspoon salt

1½ cups long-grain white rice

1 sweet green pepper, cored, seeded and diced

1 piece baked ham (6 ounces), cut into ¾-inch cubes

¾ pound boneless, skinless chicken breast halves, cut
   into ¾-inch cubes

½ pound peeled, deveined medium shrimp

1 box (10 ounces) frozen peas

1. Heat oil in a Dutch oven over medium heat. Add sausage; cook, turning, until browned, 10 minutes. Transfer sausage to a large bowl.

2. Add onions and garlic to pot; sauté 4 minutes or until softened. Add broth, clam juice, tomatoes, water, wine, turmeric, bay leaf, hot-pepper sauce and salt. Bring to boiling. Stir in rice, pepper and ham. Reduce heat; cover and simmer 12 minutes.

3. Stir in chicken and sausage; simmer 8 minutes. Stir in shrimp and peas; simmer 6 minutes or until shrimp are pink and curled and rice is tender.

Shrimp & Vegetable Stir-Fry

MAKES 4 servings

PREP 5 minutes

COOK 10 minutes

———————

PER SERVING
211 calories, 20 g protein,
7 g fat, 19 g carbohydrate,
1,361 mg sodium,
166 mg cholesterol.

½ cup bottled stir-fry sauce
¾ pound peeled, deveined medium shrimp
1 tablespoon vegetable oil
2 packages (10 ounces each) coleslaw mix
3 scallions, chopped, including part of the green

1. Combine 2 tablespoons stir-fry sauce and shrimp in a small bowl.

2. Heat oil in a large nonstick skillet over medium-high heat. Add shrimp with sauce; stir-fry 5 minutes. Remove shrimp; set aside.

3. Add 1 tablespoon stir-fry sauce and coleslaw mix to skillet; cook 5 minutes while slowly adding remaining 1 tablespoon sauce. Add reserved shrimp and scallions; heat through.

Middle Eastern Shrimp

MAX

MAKES 6 servings

PREP 10 minutes

COOK 15 minutes

———————

PER SERVING
346 calories, 21 g protein,
14 g fat, 36 g carbohydrate,
871 mg sodium,
132 mg cholesterol.

2 cans (14½ ounces each) stewed tomatoes
½ cup frozen chopped onions, thawed
3 tablespoons pine nuts
2 tablespoons olive oil
2 tablespoons balsamic vinegar
2 teaspoons bottled chopped garlic
¾ teaspoon ground cumin
½ teaspoon ground allspice
¼ teaspoon black pepper
¼ teaspoon salt
⅛ teaspoon ground red pepper (cayenne)
1⅓ cups water
1 cup couscous
¾ teaspoon dried mint
⅔ cup crumbled feta cheese
1 pound peeled, deveined medium shrimp
Fresh mint leaves for garnish (optional)

1. Stir together tomatoes with their liquid, onions, pine nuts, oil, vinegar, garlic, cumin, allspice, black pepper, salt and red pepper in a medium-size saucepan; break up tomatoes slightly with a wooden spoon.

2. Cook, covered, over medium heat 10 to 12 minutes or until mixture is slightly thickened.

3. Meanwhile, bring water to boiling in a small saucepan. Combine couscous and dried mint in a small bowl. Add to boiling water; stir. Cover saucepan; remove from heat. Let stand, covered, 5 minutes. Uncover; fluff with fork. Stir in ⅓ cup feta cheese. Cover saucepan again.

4. Add shrimp to tomato mixture; cover and cook, stirring occasionally, 2 to 3 minutes or until shrimp are cooked through.

5. To serve, spoon couscous onto a large platter; top with shrimp mixture and sprinkle with remaining ⅓ cup feta. Garnish with mint leaves if desired.

Middle Eastern Shrimp

Pineapple Shrimp

MAKES 6 servings

PREP 5 minutes

COOK 17 minutes

PER SERVING
153 calories, 11 g protein,
3 g fat, 20 g carbohydrate,
404 mg sodium,
90 mg cholesterol.

1 can (20 ounces) juice-packed pineapple chunks

2 carrots, thinly sliced

1 tablespoon vegetable oil

2 sweet red peppers, cored, seeded and diced

¾ cup orange juice

2 tablespoons white-wine vinegar

¾ teaspoon salt

1 tablespoon cornstarch

1 tablespoon water

1 pound peeled, deveined medium shrimp, sliced
   lengthwise

Cooked white rice for serving (optional)

1. Drain pineapple, reserving liquid. Mix 2 tablespoons reserved pineapple juice with carrots in a large skillet. Cover and cook over medium heat 5 minutes. Add oil and peppers and cook another 5 minutes.

2. In a small bowl, mix remaining pineapple juice, orange juice, vinegar and salt; add to skillet along with pineapple chunks. Simmer 5 minutes. Mix cornstarch with water. Add to skillet along with shrimp. Cook 2 minutes or until shrimp are cooked through. Serve over rice if desired.

Balsamic Shrimp

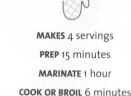

MAKES 4 servings

PREP 15 minutes

MARINATE 1 hour

COOK OR BROIL 6 minutes

PER SERVING
316 calories, 23 g protein,
22 g fat, 5 g carbohydrate,
302 mg sodium,
173 mg cholesterol.

BALSAMIC VINAIGRETTE

¾ cup olive oil

3 tablespoons balsamic vinegar

3 tablespoons red-wine vinegar

1 tablespoon packed light-brown sugar

1 teaspoon crumbled dried oregano

1 teaspoon crumbled dried rosemary

½ teaspoon salt

¼ teaspoon crumbled dried thyme

⅛ teaspoon black pepper

1 pound peeled, deveined medium shrimp

2 sweet green or red peppers, cored, seeded, halved
   crosswise and sliced into thin strips

Cooked white rice for serving (optional)

1. Prepare balsamic vinaigrette: Stir together oil, vinegars, brown sugar, oregano, rosemary, salt, thyme and black pepper in a small bowl.

2. Mix shrimp and peppers with 3 tablespoons of balsamic vinaigrette in a medium-size bowl. Refrigerate shrimp mixture, covered, 1 hour.

3. If planning to broil, heat broiler and brush broiler-pan rack with olive oil and position it 4 inches from heat. Alternatively, heat a large stovetop grill or cast-iron skillet over medium heat; coat with nonstick cooking spray.

4. Working in batches if necessary, place shrimp and peppers in a single layer in broiler-pan rack or stovetop grill. Cook 6 minutes or until shrimp are pink, curled and firm-tender and peppers are firm-tender. If broiling, turn once; if grilling, toss or turn occasionally. Transfer to a clean bowl; keep warm.

5. Meanwhile, heat 4 tablespoons balsamic vinaigrette to boiling in a small saucepan; reserve remainder of vinaigrette for another use. Pour hot vinaigrette over shrimp-and-pepper mixture in bowl, tossing until well coated. Serve over rice if desired.

Shrimp Wrap

MAKES 8 servings

PREP 10 minutes

COOK 27 minutes

PER SERVING
287 calories, 13 g protein,
6 g fat, 45 g carbohydrate,
745 mg sodium,
61 mg cholesterol.

1 package (5 ounces) yellow rice mix
1 tablespoon olive oil
1 cup chopped onion
1 cup diced sweet red pepper
2 cloves garlic, finely chopped
1 tablespoon tomato paste
3 tablespoons lemon juice
¾ cup water
½ teaspoon dried thyme
⅛ teaspoon ground red pepper (cayenne)
1 medium-size zucchini, sliced into coins
1 large tomato, peeled, seeded and diced
¾ pound peeled, deveined medium shrimp
8 red pepper–flavored flour tortillas (8-inch)
Chopped tomato for garnish (optional)

1. Prepare rice according to package directions, but do not add any oil or butter.

2. Meanwhile, heat oil in a large nonstick skillet. Add onion and sweet red pepper; sauté until tender, about 8 minutes. Add garlic; sauté 1 minute. Stir in tomato paste. Add lemon juice, water, thyme and ground red pepper; cook 3 minutes.

3. Add zucchini; cook, covered, 5 minutes, adding a little water if mixture becomes too dry. Stir in tomato and shrimp; cover and simmer 10 minutes or until shrimp are cooked through. Remove from heat.

4. Warm tortillas according to package directions. Spoon about ⅓ cup rice and ½ cup shrimp mixture down center of each tortilla. Roll tortillas up; place, seam side down, on serving dish. Garnish tortillas with chopped tomato if desired.

Imperial Crab Bake

MAKES 6 servings

PREP 10 minutes

BAKE at 350° for 30 minutes

———

PER SERVING
61 calories, 1 g protein,
6 g fat , 2 g carbohydrate,
71 mg sodium,
9 mg cholesterol.

1 can (14 ounces) sliced white potatoes, drained

1 teaspoon chopped fresh thyme

1 package (8 ounces) light cream cheese,
   at room temperature

¼ cup finely chopped celery

¼ cup finely chopped sweet red or green pepper

¼ cup finely chopped onion

¼ cup heavy cream

1 tablespoon all-purpose flour

2 teaspoons Worcestershire sauce

½ teaspoon salt

¼ teaspoon black pepper

Few drops liquid hot-pepper sauce

1 pound crabmeat or surimi (imitation crabmeat),
   broken apart

1 bag (6 ounces) fresh baby spinach, trimmed

¼ cup crushed oyster (soup) crackers

1 tablespoon chopped fresh parsley

1. Heat oven to 350°.

2. Combine potatoes and thyme in a small bowl. Combine cream cheese, celery, red pepper, onion, heavy cream, flour, Worcestershire sauce, salt, black pepper and hot-pepper sauce in a medium-size bowl. Stir in crabmeat.

3. Layer potatoes and spinach in an 8 x 8 x 2-inch glass baking dish. Top with crabmeat mixture. Sprinkle with crackers and parsley.

4. Bake in heated 350° oven 30 minutes or until heated and lightly browned.

Imperial Crab Bake

Seafood Stuffed
Tomatoes

Seafood Stuffed Tomatoes

MAKES 8 servings

PREP 25 minutes

REFRIGERATE about 15

minutes (optional)

PER SERVING
195 calories, 11 g protein,
9 g fat, 19 g carbohydrate,
381 mg sodium,
23 mg cholesterol.

8 large red or yellow tomatoes (8 to 10 ounces each)
½ teaspoon salt
1 pound surimi (imitation crabmeat), shredded
1 small red onion, finely chopped
1 medium-size sweet yellow pepper, cored,
    seeded and diced
1 large carrot, finely chopped
⅓ cup mayonnaise
⅓ cup low-fat mayonnaise
2 tablespoons fresh lemon juice
⅛ teaspoon ground celery seeds
Pinch ground nutmeg
2 tablespoons milk
1½ tablespoons chopped fresh cilantro

1. Slice ½ inch from top of each tomato. With a spoon, hollow out insides, leaving a ¼-inch shell. Salt inside of tomato shells lightly; invert onto paper toweling to drain.

2. Combine surimi, onion, pepper and carrot in a medium-size bowl. Mix together regular mayonnaise, low-fat mayonnaise, lemon juice, celery seeds and nutmeg in a small bowl. Whisk in milk until smooth. Stir in cilantro. Add to surimi mixture and gently mix to combine.

3. Stuff each tomato with seafood salad, dividing equally. Chill slightly if desired.

Shrimp & Mango Pitas

no COOK

MAKES 4 servings

PREP 15 minutes

PER SERVING
343 calories, 30 g protein,
5 g fat, 43 g carbohydrate,
698 mg sodium,
221 mg cholesterol.

1 mango, peeled, pitted and chopped
¼ cup apricot nectar
1 tablespoon olive oil
½ teaspoon grated fresh ginger
1 pound medium shrimp, cooked, peeled, deveined and chopped
¼ cup chopped scallions, including part of the green
¼ teaspoon fresh lemon juice
¼ teaspoon salt
⅛ teaspoon black pepper
1 package (8 ounces) small pita bread (8 pitas)
1 small bunch watercress

1. Puree 2 tablespoons chopped mango, apricot nectar, oil and ginger in a food processor until smooth.

2. Combine shrimp, scallions, lemon juice, salt, pepper, remaining chopped mango and pureed mango mixture in a large bowl.

3. Split open each pita. Spoon shrimp mixture into each pocket. Top with sprigs of watercress.

Warm Shrimp & Feta Salad

quick COOK

MAKES 4 servings

PREP 10 minutes

COOK 6 minutes

PER SERVING
343 calories, 21 g protein,
26 g fat , 8 g carbohydrate,
847 mg sodium,
162 mg cholesterol.

¼ cup plus 2 teaspoons olive oil
3 tablespoons bottled clam juice
1 tablespoon lemon juice
½ teaspoon dried Italian seasoning
¼ teaspoon salt
⅛ teaspoon black pepper
1 sweet red pepper, cored, seeded and chopped
1 small onion, chopped
2 cloves garlic, chopped
1 sprig fresh rosemary
1 pound peeled, deveined medium shrimp
1 bunch baby spinach leaves, trimmed
10 Kalamata olives, pitted and chopped
½ cup crumbled flavored feta cheese

1. Combine ¼ cup oil, clam juice, lemon juice, Italian seasoning, salt and black pepper in a small bowl; set dressing aside.

2. Heat remaining 2 teaspoons oil in a large nonstick skillet over medium heat. Add red pepper, onion, garlic and rosemary. Sauté 1 to 2 minutes or until vegetables have softened.

3. Add shrimp and dressing to skillet, cook 3 minutes. Discard rosemary sprig.

4. Place spinach in a large serving bowl. Pour shrimp mixture from skillet over spinach; toss well.

5. Top with olives and feta cheese. Serve warm.

Summer Shrimp & Artichoke Salad

MAKES 6 servings

PREP 20 minutes

COOK 5 minutes

REFRIGERATE 3 hours or overnight

PER SERVING
215 calories, 12 g protein, 16 g fat, 8 g carbohydrate, 729 mg sodium, 91 mg cholesterol.

1 pound peeled, deveined medium shrimp
1 cup chicken broth
½ cup dry white wine
1 can (14 ounces) artichoke hearts, drained and quartered
2 tomatoes, cut into eighths
½ cup black olives, cut in half
¼ cup olive oil
2 tablespoons fresh lemon juice
¼ cup chopped fresh parsley
¼ teaspoon salt
⅛ teaspoon black pepper
Lettuce leaves for serving
4 scallions, chopped, including part of the green, for garnish (optional)

1. Place shrimp, broth and wine in a medium-size saucepan. Bring to boiling over low heat; shrimp should be cooked by the time liquid reaches boiling. Remove pan from heat. Let shrimp cool in cooking liquid.

2. Remove shrimp from liquid; discard liquid. Combine shrimp, artichoke hearts, tomatoes and olives in a medium-size bowl.

3. Whisk together oil, lemon juice, parsley, salt and pepper in a small bowl. Pour over shrimp mixture; toss to mix. Refrigerate, covered, at least 3 hours or overnight.

4. To serve, line a large bowl with lettuce. Spoon in shrimp mixture. Garnish with scallions if desired.

Poultry

Lemon-Pepper Chicken Breasts

MAKES 6 servings

PREP 10 minutes

GRILL OR BROIL about
12 minutes

PER SERVING
179 calories, 29 g protein,
4 g fat, 7 g carbohydrate,
716 mg sodium,
79 mg cholesterol.

2 lemons, ends removed

6 boneless, skinless chicken breast halves
(about 1¼ pounds total)

2 tablespoons lemon-pepper seasoning

½ teaspoon salt

2 tablespoons sugar

2 teaspoons chili powder

1. Prepare a hot grill or heat broiler; lightly brush grill rack with vegetable oil or broiler-pan rack with nonstick cooking spray and position 6 inches from heat.

2. Slice each lemon into 6 thin rounds. Remove seeds and discard. Arrange slices in a single layer on a microwave-safe plate. Cover plate and microwave at 100% power 1 minute. Set slices aside to cool.

3. Place chicken between sheets of plastic wrap. Lightly pound to an even thickness. Sprinkle with lemon-pepper seasoning and salt.

4. Grill or broil chicken breasts until firm and browned, about 5 minutes per side or until internal temperature registers 170° on an instant-read thermometer. Transfer to a platter; keep warm.

5. Sprinkle lemon slices with sugar and chili powder. Grill or broil on same rack as chicken until browned on both sides, about 40 seconds per side. Place 2 lemon slices on each chicken breast and drizzle with any juice remaining from microwave plate.

Lemon-Pepper Chicken Breasts

Five-Spice Chicken

MAKES 4 servings

PREP 10 minutes

COOK 20 minutes

BROIL about 6 minutes

(while cooking vegetables)

———

PER SERVING
292 calories, 28 g protein,
9 g fat, 25 g carbohydrate,
730 mg sodium,
63 mg cholesterol.

1¼ pounds red new potatoes, quartered

½ pound green beans, trimmed

1 medium-size tomato, chopped

1 tablespoon plus 2 teaspoons olive oil

1 teaspoon dried oregano

1¼ teaspoons salt

½ teaspoon black pepper

1 tablespoon Chinese five-spice powder

4 boneless, skinless chicken breast halves (about 1
   pound total)

1. Heat broiler; coat broiler-pan rack with nonstick cooking spray and position 4 inches from heat.

2. Cook potatoes in a large pot of boiling water 15 minutes or until almost tender. Add green beans to pot; cook 5 minutes or until tender. Drain; transfer to a large bowl. Add tomato, 1 tablespoon oil, oregano, ¾ teaspoon salt and pepper; mix well.

3. Meanwhile, mix five-spice powder, remaining 2 teaspoons oil and remaining ½ teaspoon salt in a small bowl. Rub mixture over chicken.

4. Place chicken on prepared rack. Broil 6 minutes or until internal temperature registers 170° on an instant-read thermometer, turning once.

5. Serve chicken with potato-bean salad.

Chicken Cheese Steaks

MAKES 4 servings

PREP 10 minutes

GRILL OR BROIL 12 minutes

———

PER SERVING
743 calories, 50 g protein,
24 g fat, 80 g carbohydrate,
346 mg sodium,
123 mg cholesterol.

1 large sweet red pepper, cored, seeded and cut
   lengthwise into 8 strips

1 medium-size onion, cut into ¼-inch-thick slices

½ cup bottled or homemade Caesar dressing
   (recipes, pages 28 and 29)

4 boneless, skinless chicken breast halves
   (1¼ pounds total)

1 cup shredded mozzarella cheese (4 ounces)

4 torpedo rolls, split in half

1. Prepare a hot grill; brush rack and hinged grill basket with vegetable oil and position 3 to 4 inches from heat. Alternatively, heat broiler; coat broiler-pan rack with nonstick cooking spray and position 3 to 4 inches from heat.

2. Toss pepper and onion with 2 tablespoons dressing in a small bowl.

3. Coat chicken breast halves with 2 tablespoons dressing. Place chicken between sheets of plastic wrap. Lightly pound until ¼ inch thick. Leave plastic wrap on chicken and refrigerate.

4. Grill or broil pepper strips and onion in basket until tender and browned, 2 to 3 minutes per side. Coarsely chop. Toss with remaining ¼ cup dressing in bowl.

5. Remove plastic wrap from chicken. Grill or broil 3 minutes per side or until internal temperature registers 170° on an instant-read thermometer.

6. Place ¼ cup mozzarella on each breast; grill or broil until cheese melts (if grilling, cover grill). Place chicken in rolls and top with vegetables.

Fast Fix

Broiled Chicken Fix-Ups

START WITH ONE 3-pound chicken, cut into 8 serving pieces. Heat broiler, placing oiled rack 6 inches from heat. Broil chicken, turning several times, 20 minutes or until internal temperature of breast registers 170° on an instant-read thermometer; thigh, 180°. Serve with one of these tasty sauces. Makes 4 servings.

Mushroom Sauce

- Melt 1 tablespoon butter in a medium-size skillet over medium heat.
- Add ¼ cup chopped onion; cook 4 minutes.
- Add ¾ cup sliced mushrooms; cook 3 minutes.
- Add 2 tablespoons chopped black olives, 1 tablespoon ketchup, ¼ teaspoon salt, ¼ teaspoon black pepper, 1 cup chicken broth and ¼ cup red wine.
- Transfer 2 tablespoons liquid from skillet to a small cup and mix with 1 tablespoon cornstarch.
- Return mixture to skillet, stir, and cook until thickened, about 3 minutes.
- Makes about 1½ cups.

Cranberry Sauce

- Place 2 cups cranberry juice, ¼ cup dried cranberries, ¼ teaspoon salt and ¼ teaspoon black pepper in a medium-size saucepan.
- Bring to boiling and boil to reduce, about 8 minutes.
- Transfer 2 tablespoons cranberry liquid to a small cup and mix with 1 tablespoon cornstarch.
- Return mixture to saucepan, stir, and cook until thickened, about 3 minutes.
- Makes about 1½ cups.

Cheddar Sauce

- Melt 2 tablespoons butter in a medium-size saucepan over medium heat.
- Stir in 2 tablespoons flour; cook to brown slightly.
- Whisk in 1¾ cups milk; cook until thickened, about 5 minutes. Remove saucepan from heat.
- Stir in 1 cup shredded cheddar cheese, ¼ cup salsa, dash liquid hot-pepper sauce and ¼ teaspoon salt.
- Makes about 3 cups.

Teriyaki Chicken

MAKES 4 servings

PREP 5 minutes

REFRIGERATE 3 hours or
overnight

BROIL 8 to 10 minutes

COOK 8 minutes

———————

PER SERVING
549 calories, 40 g protein,
12 g fat, 73 g carbohydrate,
1,179 mg sodium,
68 mg cholesterol.

¾ cup roasted-garlic teriyaki sauce

3 tablespoons honey

4 boneless, skinless chicken breast halves (about 1½
pounds total), partially halved horizontally, then
opened like a book

1 package (about 8 ounces) soba noodles or vermicelli

2 scallions, chopped, including part of the green

1. Mix teriyaki sauce and honey in a medium-size bowl. Add chicken, making sure marinade covers it. Refrigerate, covered, 3 hours or overnight.

2. Heat broiler; coat broiler-pan rack with nonstick cooking spray and position 6 inches from heat. Broil chicken 4 to 5 minutes on one side, brushing with marinade. Turn chicken over and brush again; broil an additional 4 to 5 minutes or until internal temperature registers 170° on an instant-read thermometer.

3. Boil remaining marinade in a small saucepan until reduced by a third.

4. Meanwhile, cook noodles in a large pot of lightly salted boiling water until al dente, firm but tender, about 8 minutes. Drain well. Toss with 3 tablespoons reduced marinade.

5. Slice chicken; serve over noodles. Sprinkle with scallions.

Chicken Niçoise

MAKES 6 servings

PREP 20 minutes

MICROWAVE 20 minutes

STAND 3 minutes

———————

PER SERVING
401 calories, 33 g protein,
14 g fat, 35 g carbohydrate,
946 mg sodium,
68 mg cholesterol.

1½ pounds boneless, skinless chicken breast halves

2 tablespoons olive oil

½ medium-size onion, thinly sliced

2 cloves garlic, finely chopped

¾ teaspoon dried thyme

½ teaspoon salt

¼ teaspoon black pepper

2 jars (6½ ounces each) marinated artichoke hearts,
drained

2 cans (14½ ounces each) diced tomatoes, drained

3 tablespoons tomato paste

1 can (6 ounces) sliced ripe black olives, drained

2 tablespoons balsamic vinegar

¼ cup plus 2 tablespoons grated Parmesan cheese

Cooked orzo for serving (optional)

1. Cut chicken breasts into 1-inch chunks.

2. Stir together oil, onion and garlic in a large microwave-safe glass bowl or a 13 x 9 x 2-inch microwave-safe glass baking dish. Microwave, uncovered, at 100% power 4 minutes or until onion is slightly softened.

3. Stir in thyme, salt, pepper, artichokes, tomatoes, tomato paste, olives and vinegar until well blended. Microwave, uncovered, at 100% power 3 minutes; stir mixture and microwave an additional 3 minutes.

4. Add chicken to sauce; stir to combine. Microwave, uncovered, at 100% power 5 minutes; stir mixture and microwave an additional 5 minutes. Let stand about 3 minutes.

5. Toss chicken with ¼ cup Parmesan. Serve over cooked orzo if desired; sprinkle with remaining 2 tablespoons Parmesan.

Chicken Niçoise, *opposite*

Teriyaki Chicken, *opposite*

Great Last-Minute Glazes

PLAIN CHICKEN ON THE GRILL? Again? Gussy it up with these easy glazes. Begin with a hot grill and chicken cutlets or whole chicken cut into serving pieces. Grill cutlets about 5 minutes per side or until internal temperature registers 170° on an instant-read thermometer. Grill serving pieces 25 to 35 minutes or until internal temperature of breast registers 170°; thigh or leg, 180°.

Mexican-Style Sauce

▶ Mix 1 cup ketchup, 2 tablespoons red-wine vinegar, 2 tablespoons light-brown sugar, ½ teaspoon cumin, pinch ground red pepper (cayenne) and 1 can (4½ ounces) chopped green chiles in a small saucepan.

▶ Bring to simmering and simmer 5 minutes.

▶ Brush over chicken during last few minutes of grilling.

▶ Makes about 1¼ cups.

Tangy Barbecue Sauce

▶ Combine 2 tablespoons Worcestershire sauce, 2 tablespoons light-brown sugar and 2 tablespoons mustard with 1 cup chili sauce in a small bowl.

▶ Brush over chicken during last few minutes of grilling.

▶ Makes about 1¼ cups.

Sweet-Tangy-Hot Glaze

▶ Combine ½ cup pureed raspberries, 2 tablespoons honey, 1 teaspoon raspberry vinegar and a dash of liquid hot-pepper sauce in a cup.

▶ Brush over chicken during last few minutes of grilling

▶ Makes about ½ cup.

Scallion Chicken

30 minutes MAX

MAKES 4 servings

PREP 15 minutes

BROIL 14 minutes

COOK sauce 2 minutes

(while broiling chicken)

———

PER SERVING
263 calories, 28 g protein,
13 g fat, 9 g carbohydrate,
536 mg sodium,
97 mg cholesterol.

¼ cup finely chopped shallots

1 tablespoon grated fresh ginger or 1 teaspoon ground ginger

1 clove garlic, finely chopped

3 tablespoons reduced-sodium soy sauce

1 tablespoon red-wine vinegar

1 tablespoon honey

2 teaspoons dark Asian sesame oil

8 boneless, skinless chicken thighs, trimmed of all fat (1½ pounds total)

1 bunch scallions, sliced into 3-inch pieces, including part of the green

1. Combine shallots, ginger, garlic, soy sauce, vinegar, honey and oil in a medium-size bowl. Add chicken and scallions; toss.

2. Heat broiler. Line broiler-pan rack with aluminum foil and coat with nonstick cooking spray; position 5 inches from heat.

3. Thread chicken and green onions alternately on four 8-inch metal skewers. Transfer honey mixture to a small saucepan and set aside. Place skewers on prepared rack.

4. Broil chicken 7 minutes. Turn; broil 6 minutes or until internal temperature registers 180° on an instant-read thermometer.

5. Meanwhile, boil honey mixture in saucepan 2 minutes.

6. Transfer chicken to a platter. Pour sauce over.

Grilled Paillard of Chicken with Artichoke Mole

MAKES 6 servings

PREP 15 minutes

GRILL 2 minutes

OR BROIL 4 minutes

PER SERVING
238 calories, 30 g protein,
11 g fat, 5 g carbohydrate,
274 mg sodium,
78 mg cholesterol.

2 tablespoons shelled pumpkin seeds, toasted (recipe, page 231)
1 jar (6½ ounces) marinated artichoke hearts, drained
½ to 1 jalapeño chile, seeded and chopped
1 clove garlic, finely chopped
2 tablespoons fresh lemon juice
2 tablespoons chopped fresh cilantro
3 tablespoons extra-virgin olive oil
½ teaspoon salt
6 boneless, skinless chicken breast halves (about 2 pounds total)
⅛ teaspoon black pepper
1 medium-size tomato, cut into 6 wedges

1. Prepare a hot grill or heat broiler. Lightly brush grill rack with vegetable oil or coat broiler-pan rack with nonstick cooking spray; position rack as close as possible to heat.

2. To make mole, combine pumpkin seeds, artichoke hearts, jalapeño, garlic, lemon juice, cilantro and 1 tablespoon oil in a food processor or blender. Process until uniformly and finely chopped. Season with ¼ teaspoon salt.

3. Coat chicken breast halves with remaining 2 tablespoons oil. Season with remaining ¼ teaspoon salt and pepper. Place chicken between sheets of plastic wrap. Lightly pound until ⅛ inch thick.

4. Grill breasts 1 minute per side or broil 2 minutes per side, until browned and internal temperature registers 170° on an instant-read thermometer.

5. To serve, top each breast with several tablespoons of artichoke mole.

Skillet Chicken & Yellow Rice

MAKES 4 servings
PREP 5 minutes
COOK 24 minutes

SHOWN ON FRONT COVER.

———

PER SERVING
341 calories, 25 g protein,
7 g fat, 49 g carbohydrate,
1,180 mg sodium,
47 mg cholesterol.

1 tablespoon olive oil
1 sweet green pepper, cored, seeded and diced
1 cup frozen chopped onion
1 package (5 ounces) yellow rice mix
1 can (14½ ounces) diced or stewed Mexican-style
   tomatoes
1¼ cups water
¾ pound chicken tenders
¼ teaspoon salt
1 cup drained canned pinto beans, rinsed
¼ cup sliced pimiento-stuffed green olives
¼ teaspoon liquid hot-pepper sauce
¼ cup chopped fresh cilantro (optional)

1. Heat oil in a large nonstick skillet over medium heat. Add green pepper and onion; cook, stirring, 4 minutes or until softened. Add rice mix, tomatoes and water. Simmer, covered, 10 minutes.

2. Sprinkle chicken with salt. Stir into rice along with beans, olives and hot-pepper sauce; cook, covered, 8 to 10 minutes or until rice is tender and chicken cooked through. Sprinkle with cilantro if desired.

Sweet & Sour Chicken, *opposite*

Sweet & Sour Chicken

MAKES 4 servings

PREP 20 minutes

COOK 12 minutes

———

PER SERVING
402 calories, 21 g protein,
5 g fat, 66 g carbohydrate,
704 mg sodium,
47 mg cholesterol.

2 teaspoons olive oil

1 onion, cut into slivers

1 sweet green pepper, cored, seeded and cut into
½-inch squares

¾ pound boneless, skinless chicken breasts, cut
into ¾-inch-wide strips

1 tomato, cut into 1-inch cubes

1 cup Chinese duck sauce or apricot basting sauce

1 tablespoon ketchup

1 tablespoon cider vinegar

2 teaspoons soy sauce

2 teaspoons cornstarch, dissolved in 1 tablespoon water

1. Heat oil in a large nonstick skillet over medium heat. Add onion; sauté 2 minutes. Add pepper; sauté 3 minutes.

2. Increase heat to medium-high. Stir in chicken; sauté 5 minutes or until cooked through. Stir in tomato, duck sauce, ketchup, vinegar, soy sauce and cornstarch mixture. Bring to boiling; cook, stirring, until thickened, about 1 minute.

Thai Sandwiches

MAKES 6 servings

PREP 5 minutes

BROIL 6 minutes

———

PER SERVING
336 calories, 29 g protein,
12 g fat, 44 g carbohydrate,
338 mg sodium,
65 mg cholesterol.

2 drops liquid hot-pepper sauce

½ cup plus 1 tablespoon bottled peanut sauce

1 pound chicken tenders

1 package (8 ounces) shredded coleslaw mix

1 cucumber, peeled and thinly sliced

6 large flour tortillas (10-inch)

½ cup plain yogurt

1. Heat broiler; position broiler-pan rack 6 inches from heat.

2. Add hot-pepper sauce to ½ cup peanut sauce in a large bowl. Add chicken tenders; stir to coat.

3. Stir together coleslaw mix, cucumber and remaining 1 tablespoon peanut sauce in a second large bowl.

4. Place chicken on broiler-pan rack. Broil 3 minutes. Turn over; broil another 3 minutes or until cooked through.

5. Meanwhile, warm tortillas according to package directions.

6. Fill warmed tortillas with chicken and coleslaw-cucumber mixture. Top each with yogurt.

Curried Chicken

MAKES 4 servings

PREP 5 minutes

COOK 11 minutes

———————

PER SERVING
183 calories, 15 g protein,
9 g fat, 12 g carbohydrate,
343 mg sodium,
37 mg cholesterol.

4 boneless, skinless chicken breast halves (about 1
    pound total)
2 tablespoons chopped garlic
2 tablespoons curry powder
2 tablespoons vegetable oil
½ teaspoon salt
¼ teaspoon black pepper
¼ cup chutney
1 bunch scallions, sliced into 1-inch pieces,
    including part of the green

1. Place chicken breast halves between sheets of plastic wrap. Lightly pound until thin.

2. Combine garlic, curry powder, 1 tablespoon oil, salt and pepper and rub over chicken breasts.

3. Heat remaining 1 tablespoon oil in a large nonstick skillet over medium-high heat. Add chicken; sauté 4 minutes per side or until internal temperature registers 170° on an instant-read thermometer.

4. Transfer chicken to a plate. Spread chutney evenly over each piece.

5. Add scallions to remaining pan juices; cook over medium heat 3 minutes. Spoon over chicken.

Chicken Cutlets with Corn Bread Stuffing

MAKES 4 servings

PREP 10 minutes

COOK 5 minutes

BAKE at 400° for 25 minutes

———————

PER SERVING
401 calories, 27 g protein,
20 g fat, 27 g carbohydrate,
657 mg sodium,
96 mg cholesterol.

Family Circle **Quick & Easy** Recipes

4 boneless, skinless chicken breast halves (about 1
    pound total)
1¾ cups seasoned corn bread stuffing mix
3 tablespoons butter
4 scallions, chopped, including part of the green
1 Granny Smith apple, peeled, cored and diced

1. Place chicken breast halves between sheets of plastic wrap. Lightly pound until thin.

2. Place ¼ cup stuffing mix in a food processor or blender. Whirl to break into fine crumbs. (Alternatively, place stuffing mix in a paper bag and crush with a rolling pin.) Sprinkle crumbs on a sheet of waxed paper. Dip chicken breasts in crumbs to coat.

3. Heat 2 tablespoons butter in a small skillet over medium heat. Add scallions and apple; sauté 4 minutes or until softened. Stir in remaining 1½ cups stuffing mix until mixture is well combined.

4. Heat oven to 400°.

5. Spoon stuffing mixture into an 11 x 7 x 2-inch baking dish, shaping into an oval the size of chicken breasts. Arrange chicken breasts in a single layer over stuffing to cover. Melt remaining 1 tablespoon butter; drizzle over chicken.

6. Bake in heated 400° oven 25 minutes or until internal temperature registers 170° on an instant-read thermometer.

Deviled Chicken Cutlets

MAKES 4 servings

PREP 10 minutes

BAKE at 450° for 15 minutes

———————

PER SERVING
297 calories, 36 g protein,
14 g fat, 6 g carbohydrate,
616 mg sodium,
100 mg cholesterol.

4 boneless, skinless chicken breast halves (about
   1½ pounds total)
3 tablespoons mayonnaise
3 tablespoons Dijon mustard
1 teaspoon chopped garlic
½ teaspoon ground sage
½ teaspoon liquid hot-pepper sauce
¼ cup dry plain bread crumbs
¼ teaspoon salt

1. Place oven rack in upper third of oven. Heat oven to 450°. Line a baking sheet with aluminum foil. Lightly coat foil with nonstick cooking spray. Place chicken pieces on foil.

2. Stir together mayonnaise, mustard, garlic, sage and hot-pepper sauce in a small bowl until well blended. Mix bread crumbs and salt in another small bowl. Brush mayonnaise mixture evenly over top of chicken breast halves. Sprinkle half of crumbs evenly on top of chicken. Turn chicken over; repeat brushing with mayonnaise mixture and sprinkling with remaining crumbs.

3. Bake in heated 450° oven 15 minutes or until internal temperature registers 170° on an instant-read thermometer and crumbs are golden.

Basil Stuffed Chicken

MAKES 6 servings

PREP 15 minutes

BROIL 8 to 10 minutes

___

PER SERVING
238 calories, 31 g protein,
8 g fat, 10 g carbohydrate,
683 mg sodium,
76 mg cholesterol.

6 boneless, skinless chicken breast halves (about
   2 pounds total)
½ teaspoon salt
½ teaspoon black pepper
6 slices part-skim mozzarella cheese (about
   4 ounces total)
1 tomato, cut into 6 slices
6 fresh basil leaves
½ cup dry seasoned bread crumbs
2 tablespoons grated Parmesan cheese
2 tablespoons reduced-fat mayonnaise

1. Heat broiler. Brush broiler-pan rack with olive oil; place 8 inches from heat.

2. Place chicken breast halves between sheets of plastic wrap. Lightly pound. Season chicken with salt and pepper. Slice each breast horizontally almost in half, but leaving one side attached. Arrange a mozzarella slice, tomato slice and basil leaf on bottom half of each breast, keeping filling in center. Fold top of chicken over filling, pressing around edges to seal.

3. Combine bread crumbs and Parmesan on a sheet of waxed paper. Brush chicken with mayonnaise. Dip chicken into crumbs; press to adhere.

4. Lightly coat both sides of chicken with nonstick cooking spray. Place chicken on prepared broiler-pan rack. Broil 8 to 10 minutes, turning once, or until internal temperature registers 170° on an instant-read thermometer.

Mustard Chicken

MAKES 6 servings

PREP 5 minutes

COOK 20 minutes

___

PER SERVING
362 calories, 32 g protein,
22 g fat, 6 g carbohydrate,
534 mg sodium,
143 mg cholesterol.

2 tablespoons butter
6 boneless, skinless chicken breast halves (about
   2 pounds total)
¼ cup dry white wine
¼ cup coarse-grained mustard
1 cup heavy cream
½ teaspoon salt
¼ teaspoon black pepper
2 boxes (10 ounces each) frozen broccoli spears, thawed

1. Heat butter in a large nonstick skillet over medium-high heat. Add chicken; sauté about 12 minutes, turning once, or until internal temperature registers 170° on an instant-read thermometer. Transfer to a platter; keep warm.

2. Add wine, mustard, cream, salt, pepper and broccoli to skillet. Simmer over medium heat 6 to 8 minutes or until broccoli is tender. Pour over chicken.

Basil Stuffed Chicken,
opposite

Tex-Mex Chicken Casserole

one**POT**

MAKES 8 servings

PREP 20 minutes

BAKE at 350° for 25 minutes

___

PER SERVING
293 calories, 20 g protein,
10 g fat, 35 g carbohydrate,
930 mg sodium,
43 mg cholesterol.

1 package (10 ounces) frozen corn kernels,
   thawed slightly
12 corn tortillas (6-inch)
1 cup hot salsa
1 can (14 to 16 ounces) stewed tomatoes
1 container (8 ounces) plain low-fat yogurt
½ cup low-fat (1%) milk
¾ teaspoon salt
24 pitted ripe black olives, sliced
1 can (16 ounces) black beans, rinsed and drained
1½ cups shredded cooked chicken
2 large scallions, chopped, including part of the green
¼ cup chopped fresh cilantro
¼ teaspoon black pepper
1 teaspoon ground cumin
1 teaspoon dried oregano
1 cup shredded sharp cheddar cheese (4 ounces)
Sour cream for serving (optional)
Radishes for serving (optional)

1. Heat oven to 350°. Lightly oil a 13 x 9 x 2-inch baking dish.

2. Sprinkle ½ cup corn kernels in prepared dish. Tear 6 corn tortillas into 4 or 5 pieces each. Overlap in bottom of dish to cover.

3. Mix salsa and tomatoes in a small bowl. In another small bowl, stir together yogurt, milk and ¼ teaspoon salt.

4. Spoon 1 cup salsa mixture over tortillas in dish. Drizzle with ½ cup yogurt mixture; sprinkle with olives. Reserve ¼ cup each corn and beans; sprinkle remaining corn and beans over casserole. Top with chicken, scallions and cilantro. Sprinkle with remaining ½ teaspoon salt, pepper, cumin and oregano. Sprinkle with half of cheddar; spoon ½ cup salsa mixture over top.

5. Tear remaining tortillas into pieces. Overlap on top of casserole to cover. Sprinkle with reserved corn and beans. Spoon on remaining salsa mixture. Drizzle remaining yogurt mixture on top; sprinkle with remaining cheddar.

6. Bake, covered, in heated 350° oven 15 minutes. Uncover; bake 10 minutes or until hot and lightly browned. Serve with sour cream and radish slices if desired.

Triple-Play Chicken

ADD PIZZAZZ to basic sautéed chicken the fast and easy way—just whip up a sauce right in the skillet. Here are three tasty ideas. To make 4 servings, start with 4 boneless, skinless chicken breast halves (1½ pounds total).

Place chicken between sheets of plastic wrap. Lightly pound until ¼ inch thick. Sprinkle with ⅛ teaspoon salt and ⅛ teaspoon black pepper. Place 2 tablespoons flour on a sheet of waxed paper. Dip chicken in flour to coat lightly, shaking off excess. Heat 2 tablespoons butter in a large skillet over medium-high heat. When butter starts to brown, add chicken; sauté 3 minutes per side or until internal temperature registers 170° on an instant-read thermometer. Transfer chicken to a platter; keep warm while you prepare a sauce.

Raisin & Pine Nut Sauce

▶ Add 1 cup dry white wine or chicken broth, ½ cup raisins, ½ cup pine nuts, ½ teaspoon dried rosemary, ¼ teaspoon salt and pinch black pepper to hot skillet in which you cooked chicken.

▶ Cook over medium-high heat, scraping browned bits from pan, 6 minutes or until syrupy.

▶ Makes about 1½ cups.

Olive, Caper & Tomato Sauce

▶ Add ½ cup dry white vermouth or chicken broth to hot skillet in which you cooked chicken; cook over medium-high heat, scraping browned bits from pan, 4 minutes.

▶ Add 2 tablespoons halved ripe black olives, 1 tablespoon drained capers, 1 diced tomato, pinch salt and pinch red-pepper flakes. Cook 5 minutes or until slightly thickened.

▶ Makes about 1 cup.

Tarragon-Mustard Cream Sauce

▶ Add ⅔ cup dry white wine or chicken broth to hot skillet in which you cooked chicken.

▶ Cook over medium-high heat, scraping browned bits from pan, 4 minutes.

▶ Add 1 teaspoon dried tarragon, 1 cup broth and ½ cup cream; cook, stirring, 8 minutes or until thickened.

▶ Remove from heat. Stir in 2 teaspoons coarse-grained mustard.

▶ Makes about 2 cups.

Chicken Enchiladas

Chicken Enchiladas

30 minutes MAX

MAKES 5 servings
PREP 10 minutes
MICROWAVE 1 minute
BAKE at 375° for 10 minutes
BROIL 5 minutes

———
PER SERVING
578 calories, 40 g protein,
30 g fat, 38 g carbohydrate,
586 mg sodium,
128 mg cholesterol.

1 tablespoon vegetable oil

1 medium-size onion, chopped

1 clove garlic, finely chopped

1 can (4 ounces) chopped green chiles

3 cups shredded cooked chicken

1 can (10 ounces) mild enchilada sauce

2 cups shredded pepper-Jack cheese (8 ounces)

10 corn tortillas (6-inch)

1 cup half-and-half

1. Heat oven to 375°.

2. Heat oil in a large nonstick skillet over medium heat. Add onion and garlic; sauté about 5 minutes. Add chiles, chicken and enchilada sauce; cook 2 minutes. Stir in ½ cup cheese. Remove from heat.

3. Coat a 13 x 9 x 2-inch baking dish with nonstick cooking spray. Wrap tortillas in damp paper toweling and warm in microwave 1 minute; dip each tortilla in warm water, shaking off excess. Fill each with ⅓ cup chicken mixture; roll up and place, seam side down, in pan. Top with half-and-half. Sprinkle with remaining cheese.

4. Bake in heated 375° oven 10 minutes. Adjust oven temperature to broil; broil 5 minutes or until enchiladas are golden.

Tortilla Pie

5 ingredients or **LESS**

MAKES 4 servings

PREP 5 minutes

MICROWAVE 8 minutes

OR BAKE at 400° for 25 minutes

BROIL 30 seconds

_____

PER SERVING
522 calories, 38 g protein,
19 g fat, 50 g carbohydrate,
1,066 mg sodium,
96 mg cholesterol.

4 flour tortillas (8-inch)
1 can (16 ounces) refried beans (1½ cups)
1 cup shredded Monterey Jack cheese (4 ounces)
1 cup salsa
2 cups shredded cooked chicken

1. Heat broiler (see note below). Coat a 10-inch microwave-safe pie plate with nonstick cooking spray.

2. Place a tortilla in prepared pie plate. Spread with one-third each of refried beans, cheese, salsa and chicken. Top with a tortilla. Repeat layers, top with third tortilla. Repeat layers and finish with fourth tortilla.

3. Cover with plastic wrap; microwave at 100% power 8 minutes.

4. Uncover pie and broil 30 seconds. To serve, cut into wedges.

Note: If you prefer, cover pie with aluminum foil and bake in heated 400° oven 25 minutes instead of cooking in a microwave. Adjust oven to broil when pie is baked, and proceed with step 4 above.

Spanish-Style Chicken

one**POT**

MAKES 4 servings

PREP 10 minutes

COOK 20 to 25 minutes

_____

PER SERVING
333 calories, 31 g protein,
19 g fat, 8 g carbohydrate,
1,039 mg sodium,
105 mg cholesterol.

4 whole chicken legs (about 1¾ pounds total)
1 teaspoon salt
½ teaspoon black pepper
1 tablespoon vegetable oil
1 large onion, coarsely chopped
1 clove garlic, pressed
1 can (8 ounces) tomato sauce
¼ cup chicken broth
1 teaspoon dried thyme

1. Sprinkle chicken legs with ½ teaspoon salt and ¼ teaspoon black pepper.

2. Heat oil in a large skillet over medium-high heat. Add chicken; brown about 4 minutes per side. Transfer to paper toweling to drain.

3. Reduce heat to medium. Add onion and garlic to skillet; sauté until almost tender, 1 to 2 minutes.

4. Return chicken to skillet along with tomato sauce, broth, thyme and remaining ½ teaspoon salt and ¼ teaspoon pepper. Cover; cook 10 to 15 minutes or until internal temperature registers 180° on instant-read thermometer.

Spicy Chicken Sausage Jambalaya

MAKES 6 servings

PREP 10 minutes

COOK 23 to 28 minutes

PER SERVING
355 calories, 15 g protein,
10 g fat, 51 g carbohydrate,
1,069 mg sodium,
44 mg cholesterol.

4 links smoked chicken andouille sausage or chicken
   kielbasa (¾ pound total), cut into coins
1 large onion, chopped
1 sweet green pepper, cored, seeded and chopped
1 rib celery, chopped
1½ tablespoons Cajun spice mix
½ bay leaf
1 can (14½ ounces) reduced-sodium stewed tomatoes
3 cups lower-sodium chicken broth
1½ cups long-grain white rice

1. Cook sausage, onion, pepper and celery in a large nonstick saucepan over medium-high heat 3 minutes. Add spice mix and bay leaf; cook 5 minutes. Add tomatoes and broth. Stir in rice.

2. Simmer, covered, over medium heat 15 to 20 minutes or until rice is tender. Remove bay leaf before serving.

Chile Chicken Potpies

MAKES 8 servings

PREP 10 minutes

COOK 15 minutes

BAKE at 350° for 15 minutes

PER SERVING
431 calories, 26 g protein,
13 g fat, 60 g carbohydrate,
569 mg sodium,
36 mg cholesterol.

1 tablespoon vegetable oil
1 medium-size onion, diced
1½ pounds ground chicken
1 tablespoon chili powder
¾ teaspoon salt
½ teaspoon black pepper
1 can (13¾ ounces) chicken broth
3 tablespoons flour
1 can (10 ounces) Mexicali corn
1 can (4½ ounces) chopped green chiles
1 large tomato, diced
1 tube (1 pound, 1.3 ounces) refrigerated corn biscuits

1. Heat oven to 350°.

2. Heat oil in a large skillet over medium-high heat. Add onion and cook 4 minutes or until softened. Add chicken, chili powder, salt and pepper; cook 5 minutes, breaking up chicken with a wooden spoon.

3. In a small bowl, whisk together broth and flour. Stir into skillet along with corn and chiles. Cook 5 minutes. Remove from heat. Stir in tomato.

4. Transfer chicken mixture to 8 individual disposable foil tart pans or to 1½-cup ramekins, dividing equally. Divide contents of tube into individual corn biscuits and roll out slightly. Place each on top of a tart pan and crimp to seal edge. Cut an X to vent in center.

5. Bake in heated 350° oven 15 minutes or until top is browned and filling bubbly.

Apple Chicken Legs

MAKES 6 servings

PREP 5 minutes

REFRIGERATE 1 hour

GRILL OR BAKE 30 to 40

minutes

———

PER SERVING
291 calories, 30 g protein,
16 g fat, 6 g carbohydrate,
636 mg sodium,
105 mg cholesterol.

1 can (6 ounces) frozen apple juice concentrate, thawed
¼ cup cider vinegar
1½ teaspoons ground red pepper (cayenne)
1 tablespoon coarse (kosher) salt
6 whole chicken legs, with or without skin (about 3
    pounds total)

1. Combine apple juice concentrate, vinegar, red pepper and salt in a large nonmetallic bowl or plastic food-storage bag. Add chicken legs and toss to coat. Cover bowl or seal bag and refrigerate 1 hour to marinate.

2. Prepare a grill to low heat; lightly brush grill rack with vegetable oil and position 6 inches from heat. Alternatively, heat oven to 375°; coat broiler-pan rack with nonstick cooking spray.

3. Remove chicken from marinade; grill or bake as follows.

To grill: Grill chicken, uncovered, 10 minutes, turning once and coating with more marinade. Then cover grill and grill chicken 10 minutes, turning once and coating with more marinade. Uncover and, turning every 5 minutes, continue grilling 10 to 15 minutes more or until internal temperature registers 180° on an instant-read thermometer.

To bake: Place chicken on prepared broiler-pan rack. Bake in heated 375° oven 15 minutes; turn, baste with marinade. Bake 15 minutes more. Turn chicken; baste; bake 10 minutes or until internal temperature registers 180° on an instant-read thermometer.

Note: Do not continue basting during last period of cooking unless you boil marinade at least 3 minutes first.

Grilled Chicken with Peach Barbecue Sauce

MAKES 4 servings

PREP 5 minutes

MICROWAVE sauce 4 minutes; chicken 10 minutes

STAND 5 minutes

GRILL OR BROIL 8 minutes

———————

PER SERVING
348 calories, 27 g protein,
8 g fat, 43 g carbohydrate,
888 mg sodium,
90 mg cholesterol.

PEACH BARBECUE SAUCE

1 medium-size peach, pitted and cut into chunks

½ cup peach preserves

¼ cup cider vinegar

¼ cup packed dark-brown sugar

2 tablespoons soy sauce

¼ teaspoon ground ginger

2 tablespoons cornstarch, dissolved in 2 tablespoons
   water

4 whole chicken legs (about 2½ pounds total)

½ teaspoon salt

¼ teaspoon black pepper

1. Prepare a hot grill, positioning rack 6 inches from heat, or heat broiler, positioning broiler-pan rack 2 inches from heat.

2. Meanwhile, prepare peach barbecue sauce: Place peach in a food processor and pulse until chunky. Combine peach, preserves, vinegar, brown sugar, soy sauce and ginger in a medium-size microwave-safe glass bowl. Microwave, uncovered, at 100% power 1 minute; stir once and microwave 1 minute more or until peach is slightly softened.

3. Stir cornstarch mixture into peach sauce. Microwave, uncovered, at 100% power 1 minute; stir once and microwave 1 minute more or until slightly thickened. Reserve half the sauce to serve with chicken.

4. Remove skin from chicken legs. Salt and pepper both sides of legs. Arrange legs in a single layer in a 13 x 9 x 2-inch microwave-safe baking dish, with thickest part of each chicken leg facing outside of dish. Loosely cover dish with plastic wrap.

5. Microwave at 100% power 5 minutes. Turn chicken legs over. Loosely cover again with plastic wrap. Microwave an additional 5 minutes. Let chicken stand, covered, about 5 minutes. Brush remaining half of sauce over legs.

6. Grill or broil legs about 4 minutes on each side or until chicken becomes dark in color and internal temperature registers 180° on an instant-read thermometer. Serve with reserved sauce on the side.

Thai Cilantro Chicken Legs

MAKES 4 servings

PREP 10 minutes

REFRIGERATE overnight

BROIL OR GRILL 45 to 50

minutes

———

PER SERVING
279 calories, 32 g protein,
14 g fat, 4 g carbohydrate,
413 mg sodium,
103 mg cholesterol.

½ cup buttermilk

¼ cup flake coconut

1 cup chopped fresh cilantro

2 cloves garlic, crushed

½ teaspoon salt

⅛ teaspoon black pepper

4 whole chicken legs (2 pounds total)

Chopped fresh cilantro for garnish (optional)

1. Combine buttermilk, coconut, cilantro, garlic, salt and pepper in a blender. Whirl at high speed until pureed. Pour into a plastic food-storage bag.

2. Loosen skin on chicken legs. Pull back from meat, leaving skin attached.

3. Add chicken legs to bag, squishing to coat with marinade. Push out all air; seal and marinate in refrigerator overnight.

4. Prepare a hot grill or heat broiler; position rack 6 inches from heat.

5. Remove chicken from bag. Pull skin back over meat. Grill or broil 45 to 50 minutes or until internal temperature registers 180° on an instant-read thermometer, turning legs over halfway through cooking. Garnish with cilantro if desired.

Grilled Chicken with
Peach Barbecue
Sauce, *opposite*

Poultry

Baked Chicken Bonanza

THERE'S SCARCELY ANYTHING EASIER than baking chicken. Here's how to make it special. Begin with one 3-pound chicken cut into 8 pieces (or 8 of any piece). Heat oven to 350°. Place chicken in a baking pan, adding embellishents as explained below, and bake 40 to 50 minutes or until internal temperature of breast registers 170° on an instant-read thermometer; thigh or drumstick, 180°. Makes 4 servings.

Dried-Fruit Sauce

▶ Combine 1 sliced onion, 2 sliced carrots, 4 chopped dried apricots and 4 chopped dates (or dried fruit of your choice) in a small bowl.

▶ Season chicken with 1 teaspoon ground cinnamon and ½ teaspoon ground cumin; place in baking dish. Add fruit-vegetable mixture and ½ cup chicken broth.

Chinese Maple Glaze

▶ Combine ⅓ cup soy sauce, ⅓ cup maple syrup, 3 tablespoons vinegar and 1 teaspoon Chinese five-spice powder in a small bowl.

▶ Remove skin from chicken; brush mixture on top.

▶ During baking, brush chicken occasionally with mixture.

Artichoke Companion

▶ Drain 1 jar (6½ ounces) marinated artichoke hearts; cut into quarters.

▶ Add artichokes to baking dish with chicken during last 15 minutes of cooking.

Caribbean Jerk Chicken

MAKES 4 servings

PREP 10 minutes

REFRIGERATE overnight

BAKE at 500° for 30 minutes

PER SERVING
532 calories, 53 g protein,
31 g fat , 10 g carbohydrate,
706 mg sodium,
166 mg cholesterol.

MARINADE

2 tablespoons fresh lime juice

1 tablespoon soy sauce

1 tablespoon peanut oil

1 tablespoon liquid hot-pepper sauce

1 tablespoon chopped fresh ginger

3 cloves garlic, coarsely chopped

½ teaspoon dried thyme

¼ teaspoon black pepper

¼ teaspoon ground allspice

¼ teaspoon salt

2½ pounds chicken parts

1. Prepare marinade: Place lime juice, soy sauce, oil, hot-pepper sauce, ginger, garlic, thyme, pepper, allspice and salt in a food processor or blender; whirl to puree. Combine marinade with chicken in a large plastic food-storage bag. Seal. Marinate in refrigerator overnight.

2. Heat oven to 500°. Place oven rack in top position.

3. Drain chicken; discard marinade. Pat chicken dry. Arrange in a roasting pan.

4. Roast in heated 500° oven 25 minutes for breasts, 30 minutes for thighs and drumsticks, or until internal temperature of breasts registers 170° on an instant-read thermometer; thighs and drumsticks, 180°.

Chicken with Diablo Sauce

MAKES 6 servings

PREP 10 minutes

REFRIGERATE 2 hours or overnight

BAKE 30 to 35 minutes

PER SERVING
277 calories, 26 g protein,
15 g fat, 9 g carbohydrate,
661 mg sodium,
71 mg cholesterol.

2 tablespoons honey
1 tablespoon Worcestershire sauce
2 teaspoons paprika
1 teaspoon curry powder
1 teaspoon chili powder
1 teaspoon salt
1 teaspoon black pepper
½ teaspoon ground red pepper (cayenne)
1 whole chicken (3½ to 4 pounds), cut into 10 serving pieces, skin removed from breasts, drumsticks and thighs

DIABLO SAUCE
½ jar (about 7 ounces) roasted red peppers, drained
2 tablespoons olive oil
1 tablespoon balsamic vinegar
½ teaspoon salt
¼ teaspoon liquid hot-pepper sauce

1. Stir together honey and Worcestershire sauce in a small bowl. In another small bowl, mix paprika, curry powder, chili powder, salt, black pepper and red pepper.

2. Place chicken on a 15 x 10-inch baking sheet. Brush honey mixture over chicken; sprinkle evenly with spice mixture. Turn chicken over and repeat brushing and sprinkling on other side. Cover; refrigerate at least 2 hours or overnight.

3. Heat oven to 450°. Arrange chicken in a large roasting pan, placing wings skin side up.

4. Bake in heated 450° oven 30 to 35 minutes or until well browned and internal temperature of breasts registers 170° on an instant-read thermometer; thighs and drumsticks, 180°.

5. Meanwhile, prepare sauce: Puree peppers, oil, vinegar, salt and hot-pepper sauce in a food processor or blender.

6. Arrange chicken on a serving platter. Serve sauce on the side.

Chicken Thighs with Sweet Spice Rub

MAKES 4 servings

PREP 5 minutes

REFRIGERATE 1 hour

GRILL OR BAKE 30 to 35 minutes

PER SERVING
WITHOUT SKIN
236 calories, 33 g protein,
7 g fat, 10 g carbohydrate,
1,065 mg sodium,
134 mg cholesterol.

⅓ cup coarse (kosher) salt

⅓ cup granulated sugar

4 cups water

8 chicken thighs (about 2½ pounds), with or without skin

SWEET SPICE RUB

1 tablespoon brown sugar

¼ cup paprika

1 teaspoon ground cumin

⅛ teaspoon ground red pepper (cayenne)

½ teaspoon black pepper

½ teaspoon garlic powder

¼ teaspoon onion powder

1. Add salt and granulated sugar to water in a large nonmetallic bowl; stir to dissolve completely. Add thighs, making sure all pieces are submerged. Cover bowl with plastic wrap and refrigerate 1 hour.

2. Meanwhile, make spice rub: Mix together brown sugar, paprika, cumin, red pepper, black pepper, garlic powder and onion powder in a small bowl.

3. Prepare a grill to low heat; lightly brush grill rack with vegetable oil and position 6 inches from heat. Alternatively, heat oven to 375°; coat broiler-pan rack with nonstick cooking spray.

4. Remove thighs from soaking liquid and pat dry. Dust thighs on both sides with spice rub, pressing gently to make sure rub adheres; if keeping skin on, spread rub evenly under skin with your fingers.

5. Grill or bake thighs as follows.

To grill: Grill, uncovered, 5 minutes per side or until surfaces begin to brown. Turn thighs. Cover grill and cook 5 minutes more per side. Uncover and, turning thighs every 5 minutes, continue grilling until internal temperature registers 180° on an instant-read thermometer, about 10 to 15 minutes more.

To bake: Place thighs on prepared broiler-pan rack. Bake in heated 375° oven 5 minutes per side. Turn thighs; bake 10 minutes. Repeat. Turn again and bake 5 minutes more or until internal temperature registers 180° on an instant-read thermometer. If cooking thighs with skin on, turn oven to broil and broil thighs 3 minutes so skin is crisp if desired.

Chicken with Portabellas

one**POT**

MAKES 4 servings

PREP 10 minutes

COOK about 35 minutes

———

PER SERVING
238 calories, 18 g protein,
16 g fat, 4 g carbohydrate,
425 mg sodium,
58 mg cholesterol.

4 boneless chicken thighs (about 1 pound total)

½ teaspoon salt

¼ teaspoon black pepper

1 tablespoon olive oil

1 package (6 ounces) sliced fresh portabella mushrooms

¼ cup plus 2 tablespoons chicken broth

¼ cup dry white wine

1 teaspoon dried rosemary

2 teaspoons all-purpose flour

¼ cup sour cream

1. Season thighs with salt and pepper. Heat oil in a large skillet over medium-high heat. Sauté thighs 3 minutes per side or until golden. Transfer to a plate. Drain all but 1 tablespoon drippings.

2. Add mushrooms to skillet and sauté 5 minutes. Add chicken, ¼ cup broth, wine and rosemary. Cover; simmer 15 minutes.

3. Whisk flour and remaining 2 tablespoons broth in a small bowl. Whisk into skillet; cook, stirring, 4 minutes or until thickened and bubbly. Lower heat. Stir in sour cream and gently heat through (do not let boil).

Chicken Thighs with Sweet Spice Rub, *opposite*

Herb-Glazed Turkey on Skewers

quick COOK

MAKES 8 servings

PREP 15 minutes

BROIL 6 minutes

———

PER SERVING
94 calories, 14 g protein,
1 g fat, 8 g carbohydrate,
148 mg sodium,
39 mg cholesterol.

6 ounces (½ jar) apple jelly

4½ teaspoons Dijon mustard

1½ teaspoons fresh lemon juice

1 tablespoon chopped fresh sage or
    ¼ teaspoon dried sage

1 teaspoon ground ginger

2 pounds turkey cutlets

½ teaspoon salt

¼ teaspoon black pepper

1. Prepare a hot grill or heat broiler; position grill rack or broiler-pan rack 6 inches from heat.

2. Whisk together jelly, mustard, lemon juice, sage and ginger in a small bowl. Pour ½ cup jelly mixture into a small saucepan; set aside.

3. Cut each turkey cutlet lengthwise in half or into enough pieces to make total of 32. Folding accordion-style, thread 2 slices per skewer onto sixteen 12-inch metal skewers. Season with salt and pepper.

4. Broil or grill skewers 3 minutes per side, brushing with glaze from bowl. Discard any remaining glaze. Transfer skewers to a platter.

5. Bring remaining jelly mixture in saucepan to boiling. Spoon sauce over turkey skewers on platter.

Turkey Paprikash

Family Circle **Quick & Easy** Recipes

quick PREP

MAKES 4 servings

PREP 5 minutes

COOK 12 minutes

———

PER SERVING
318 calories, 20 g protein,
17 g fat, 23 g carbohydrate,
628 mg sodium,
47 mg cholesterol.

¾ pound wide egg noodles

⅓ cup all-purpose flour

¾ pound turkey cutlets, cut crosswise into 1-inch strips

1 tablespoon olive oil

1½ cups frozen chopped onion

1 cup frozen chopped sweet green pepper

2 tablespoons paprika

⅛ teaspoon ground red pepper (cayenne)

1 can (14¾ ounces) chicken broth

¾ cup reduced-fat sour cream

1 tablespoon fresh lemon juice

¼ teaspoon salt

Paprika for garnish (optional)

1. Cook egg noodles in a large pot of lightly salted boiling water until al dente, firm but tender. Drain well.

2. Meanwhile, combine flour and turkey in a plastic food-storage bag; seal and shake to coat.

3. Heat oil in a nonstick skillet over medium heat. Add onion and green pepper; cook, stirring, 8 minutes. Stir in paprika, red pepper and turkey. Stir in broth. Bring to simmering, stirring; simmer 2 minutes or until turkey is cooked through.

4. Remove skillet from heat. Stir in sour cream, lemon juice and salt.

5. Transfer noodles to plates. Spoon turkey mixture on top. Sprinkle with paprika if desired.

Skillet Turkey Sauerbraten

MAKES 4 servings
PREP 10 minutes
COOK 10 minutes

PER SERVING
459 calories, 28 g protein,
16 g fat, 50 g carbohydrate,
542 mg sodium,
101 mg cholesterol.

1 tablespoon vegetable oil
4 turkey cutlets (1 pound total)
¾ cup frozen chopped onion, thawed and drained
½ cup frozen sliced carrots, thawed
1 cup beef broth
¼ cup dry red wine
¼ cup crumbled ginger cookies
2 tablespoons red-wine vinegar
½ teaspoon ground ginger
¼ teaspoon salt
¼ teaspoon black pepper
¼ cup reduced-fat sour cream
2 teaspoons all-purpose flour
½ pound thin egg noodles
2 tablespoons dried parsley

1. Heat oil in a large nonstick skillet over medium heat. Working in batches if necessary to avoid crowding skillet, cook turkey cutlets 30 seconds per side. Transfer to a platter.

2. Add onion and carrots to skillet; sauté 2 to 3 minutes or until tender. Add broth, wine, cookies, vinegar, ginger, salt and pepper. Bring to boiling.

3. Return turkey to skillet. Reduce heat; cover and simmer 2 to 3 minutes or until turkey is cooked through.

4. Meanwhile, combine sour cream and flour in a small bowl.

5. Transfer turkey to a platter. Add sour cream mixture to skillet; cook, stirring, 1 to 2 minutes or until thickened.

6. Meanwhile, cook noodles in a large pot of lightly salted boiling water until al dente, firm but tender. Drain well. Toss with dried parsley.

7. Spoon sauce over turkey. Serve over noodles.

Schnitzel & Salad

quick **COOK**

MAKES 4 servings

PREP 15 minutes

BROIL 6 to 8 minutes

———————

PER SERVING
325 calories, 27 g protein,
17 g fat, 19 g carbohydrate,
828 mg sodium,
58 mg cholesterol.

2 tablespoons cider vinegar

3 tablespoons plus 1 teaspoon Dijon mustard

⅛ teaspoon salt

⅛ teaspoon black pepper

¼ cup olive oil

2 bunches arugula, trimmed and torn into bite-size
    pieces

½ head radicchio, trimmed and torn into bite-size pieces

1 head Belgian endive, cored and cut lengthwise into
    strips

½ cup dry seasoned bread crumbs

4 turkey cutlets (about ¾ pound total)

1. Whisk vinegar, 1 teaspoon mustard, salt, pepper and oil in a large bowl. Add arugula, radicchio and endive; toss to coat.

2. Heat broiler; coat broiler-pan rack with nonstick cooking spray and position 4 inches from heat.

3. Place bread crumbs on a sheet of waxed paper. Brush cutlets with remaining 3 tablespoons mustard. Dip into crumbs, pressing to adhere. Lightly coat cutlets with nonstick cooking spray. Place on broiler-pan rack.

4. Broil 3 to 4 minutes per side or until turkey is cooked through and golden.

5. Divide greens evenly among 4 dinner plates. Arrange turkey on greens.

Turkey Pizzaiola

Family Circle **Quick & Easy** Recipes

quick **PREP**

MAKES 6 servings

PREP 10 minutes

COOK turkey about 16
minutes; spaghetti 10
minutes

BAKE at 450° for 10 minutes
(while cooking spaghetti)

———————

PER SERVING
414 calories, 38 g protein,
23 g fat, 15 g carbohydrate,
878 mg sodium,
94 mg cholesterol.

2 tablespoons olive oil

6 turkey cutlets (1½ pounds total)

1 sweet green pepper, cored, seeded and cut into
    ½-inch-wide strips

1 sweet red pepper, cored, seeded and cut into
    ½-inch-wide strips

1 large onion, thinly sliced

1 jar (28 ounces) marinara sauce

1 cup shredded mozzarella cheese (4 ounces)

1 pound spaghetti

1. Heat oven to 450°.

2 Heat oil in a large nonstick skillet over medium-high heat. Reduce heat to medium. Add turkey and sauté 3 to 4 minutes per side or until lightly browned. Remove turkey and reserve.

3. Add green and red peppers and onion to skillet; sauté, stirring occasionally, about 8 minutes or until vegetables are softened.

4. Spread ½ cup marinara sauce evenly over bottom of a 13 x 9 x 2-inch glass baking dish. Arrange turkey cutlets over sauce, slightly overlapping if necessary. Spoon 1 cup sauce evenly over turkey. Top with pepper-and-onion mixture. Sprinkle with mozzarella.

5. Cook spaghetti in a large pot of lightly salted boiling water until al dente, firm but tender. Drain well.

6. Meanwhile, bake turkey mixture in heated 450° oven 10 minutes or until mozzarella is melted.

7. Toss hot spaghetti with remaining marinara sauce. Serve turkey mixture over spaghetti.

Turkey Pizzaiola, *opposite*

Schnitzel & Salad, *opposite*

Turkey Meat Loaf

MAKES 6 servings
PREP 10 minutes
COOK 12 minutes
BAKE at 350° for 30 minutes

PER SERVING
227 calories, 19 g protein,
10 g fat, 14 g carbohydrate,
549 mg sodium,
91 mg cholesterol.

3 slices white bread
¼ cup low-fat (1%) milk
2 teaspoons vegetable oil
½ pound mushrooms, chopped
1 medium-size onion, chopped
1 rib celery, chopped
2 carrots, chopped
1 teaspoon salt
⅓ cup water
1 pound ground turkey
¼ cup dry unseasoned bread crumbs
1 egg, lightly beaten

1. Heat oven to 350°. Coat a 6-cup ring mold with nonstick cooking spray.

2. Combine bread and milk in a large bowl; let stand 10 minutes.

3. Meanwhile, heat oil in a large nonstick skillet over medium-high heat. Add mushrooms, onion, celery, carrots and ¼ teaspoon salt; cook, stirring, 2 minutes. Add water; cover and cook over medium heat, stirring occasionally, about 10 minutes. Let cool slightly.

4. Add vegetable mixture, ground turkey, bread crumbs, egg and remaining ¾ teaspoon salt to bread mixture in bowl; stir to combine. Scrape mixture into prepared mold.

5. Bake in heated 350° oven 30 minutes or until internal temperature registers 165° on an instant-read thermometer. Invert mold onto a large round serving platter and serve.

Fast Fix

Quick Tricks with Turkey

BECAUSE TURKEY has such a neutral flavor, it takes well to pungent seasonings. Each of these recipes makes 4 servings.

Cutlets Italian-Style

► For 4 cutlets, mix 1 beaten egg, ¼ cup grated Parmesan cheese, 1 teaspoon dried basil and pinch red-pepper flakes.

► Dip cutlets into mixture and place in a lightly oiled baking dish.

► Bake at 350° degrees about 10 minutes or until cutlets are cooked through.

Burgers with Flair

► Start with 1 pound ground turkey; mix in 3 tablespoons Worcestershire sauce,

3 tablespoons finely chopped red onion and 1 teaspoon dried tarragon.

► Shape into patties and grill or broil until internal temperature registers 165° on an instant-read thermometer.

Turkey & Asparagus Roll-Ups

MAKES 6 servings

PREP 10 minutes

COOK 20 minutes

PER SERVING
227 calories, 23 g protein,
11 g fat, 9 g carbohydrate,
601 mg sodium,
53 mg cholesterol.

12 large asparagus spears, tough ends trimmed and
   stems peeled

6 turkey cutlets (1¼ pounds total)

½ teaspoon salt

¼ teaspoon black pepper

1 teaspoon poultry seasoning

1 tablespoon corn oil

1 small onion, thinly sliced

1 can (10 ¾ ounces) 98% fat-free condensed cream of
   mushroom soup

1 cup nonfat milk

¼ cup reduced-fat sour cream

1½ teaspoons dried parsley or 1 tablespoon chopped
   fresh parsley

1. Cook asparagus in ½ inch lightly salted boiling water in a large skillet 5 to 7 minutes or until tender. Drain and cool aspargus in an ice-water bath. When cool, drain and set aside.

2. Place turkey cutlets between sheets of plastic wrap. Lightly pound until ¼ inch thick.

3. Combine salt, pepper and ½ teaspoon poultry seasoning in a small bowl. Lay turkey cutlets flat; sprinkle one side of each cutlet with seasoning mixture.

4. Place 2 asparagus spears at narrow end of each cutlet. Roll up each turkey cutlet and secure with a wooden pick to hold in place.

5. Heat oil in a large nonstick skillet over medium-high heat. Add turkey rolls; sauté about 2 minutes per side or until lightly golden on all sides. Remove turkey from skillet.

6. Add onion to skillet; sauté 3 minutes. Whisk together soup, milk and remaining ½ teaspoon poultry seasoning; add to onion in skillet along with turkey roll-ups. Simmer, uncovered, over medium-low heat 8 minutes.

7. Turn turkey roll-ups over; simmer 8 minutes or until turkey is tender and cooked through. Transfer roll-ups to a serving plate.

8. Remove skillet from heat. Stir in sour cream. Sprinkle parsley over turkey. Serve sauce on the side.

Basil-Topped Turkey Cutlets

MAKES 4 servings
PREP 10 minutes
COOK 20 minutes

PER SERVING
386 calories, 27 g protein,
27 g fat, 9 g carbohydrate,
484 mg sodium,
178 mg cholesterol.

4 turkey cutlets (1 pound total)
1 cup coarsely chopped fresh basil
½ cup pitted Kalamata olives (about 18), coarsely
   chopped
2 tablespoons pine nuts, toasted (recipe, page 231)
3 tablespoons olive oil
1 tablespoon balsamic vinegar
1 tablespoon capers, drained and rinsed
1 clove garlic, finely chopped
¼ teaspoon ground red pepper (cayenne)
¼ cup all-purpose flour
¼ cup grated Parmesan cheese
1 teaspoon dried parsley
¼ teaspoon black pepper
2 eggs
2 tablespoons unsalted butter
1 small tomato, chopped
Fresh basil sprig for garnish (optional)

1. Place turkey cutlets between sheets of plastic wrap. Lightly pound until ¼ inch thick.

2. Combine basil, olives, pine nuts, 2 tablespoons oil, vinegar, capers, garlic and red pepper in a small bowl.

3. Mix flour, Parmesan, parsley and black pepper on a sheet of waxed paper. Beat eggs in a shallow dish.

4. Dip cutlets in flour mixture to coat lightly, shaking off excess. Dip in eggs.

5. Heat butter and remaining 1 tablespoon oil in a large nonstick skillet over medium heat. Working in batches if necessary, cook cutlets 2 to 3 minutes per side or until browned and cooked through. Transfer to a platter.

6. Cook tomato in same skillet over medium heat 1 to 2 minutes or until softened. Add basil mixture; cook 1 minute or until just warmed through.

7. Spoon tomato-basil mixture over cutlets. Garnish with basil sprig if desired.

Pecan-Crusted Turkey Cutlets

MAKES 6 servings

PREP 10 minutes

COOK 6 minutes

BROIL 6 minutes

PER SERVING
480 calories, 31 g protein,
23 g fat, 40 g carbohydrate,
312 mg sodium,
77 mg cholesterol.

¾ pound ramen noodles or vermicelli
½ cup honey
¼ cup reduced-sodium soy sauce
2 cups very finely ground pecans
6 turkey cutlets (about 1½ pounds total)

1. Heat broiler; coat broiler-pan rack with nonstick cooking spray and position 6 inches from heat.

2. Cook ramen noodles according to package directions, omitting seasoning packet. Alternatively, cook vermicelli in a large pot of lightly salted boiling water until al dente, firm but tender. Drain noodles well and keep warm.

3. Meanwhile, combine honey and soy sauce in a large shallow bowl or pie plate. Place ground pecans on a sheet of waxed paper. Dip turkey cutlets into honey mixture, then into ground pecans, pressing nuts firmly onto cutlets. Place cutlets on prepared broiler-pan rack.

4. Transfer remaining honey mixture to a small saucepan. Bring to boiling; boil gently 1 minute. Reserve.

5. Meanwhile, broil cutlets about 3 minutes per side or until cooked through. Transfer to a platter; spoon honey mixture on top. Serve with hot noodles.

Basil-Topped
Turkey Cutlets,
opposite

Turkey Taco Salad

MAKES 4 servings

PREP 10 minutes

COOK 10 minutes

PER SERVING
340 calories, 24 g protein,
13 g fat, 32 g carbohydrate,
944 mg sodium,
93 mg cholesterol.

1 pound lean ground turkey

1 can (4½ ounces) mild green chiles, drained

¾ ounce (½ envelope) taco seasoning mix

¼ cup water

2 cups shredded lettuce

2 medium-size tomatoes, chopped

½ cup shredded cheddar cheese

4 ounces (½ bag) baked tortilla chips

1. Cook turkey in a large nonstick skillet over high heat until browned, about 5 minutes, stirring with a wooden spoon to break up clumps. Drain any fat from skillet. Stir in chiles, seasoning mix and water; cook over high heat until liquid is evaporated.

2. Divide meat mixture among 4 plates. Top with lettuce, tomatoes and cheese. Serve with chips.

Asian Turkey Burgers with Vegetables

MAKES 4 servings

PREP 10 minutes

COOK 15 minutes

PER SERVING
312 calories, 32 g protein,
14 g fat, 16 g carbohydrate,
918 mg sodium,
103 mg cholesterol.

1¼ pounds ground turkey

2 cloves garlic, pressed

3 teaspoons grated fresh ginger

3 tablespoons soy sauce

1 bag (16 ounces) frozen Asian mixed vegetables

1. Combine turkey, half of garlic and 1 teaspoon ginger in a medium-size bowl. Rinse hands with cold water; shape mixture into 4 burgers, about ½ inch thick.

2. Heat a large nonstick skillet over medium-high heat. Add burgers; cook, uncovered, 3 minutes or until browned. Turn over; reduce heat to medium; cook, covered, 5 minutes or until internal temperature registers 165° on an instant-read thermometer. Remove from heat. Sprinkle with 1 tablespoon soy sauce, turning burgers to coat.

3. Meanwhile, combine vegetables, 2 tablespoons water and remaining garlic, remaining 2 teaspoons ginger and remaining 2 tablespoons soy sauce in a small saucepan. Bring to simmering; simmer, covered, 7 minutes. Serve alongside burgers.

Moroccan Cornish Hens

MAKES 4 servings

PREP 5 minutes

BROIL 25 minutes

———

PER SERVING
433 calories, 42 g protein,
28 g fat, 2 g carbohydrate,
747 mg sodium,
134 mg cholesterol.

2 tablespoons vegetable oil

3 cloves garlic, finely chopped

2 teaspoons curry powder

¾ teaspoon ground cumin

½ teaspoon ground coriander

½ teaspoon ground red pepper (cayenne)

½ teaspoon salt

¼ teaspoon black pepper

2 Cornish hens (1½ pounds each), halved lengthwise

1. Heat broiler; position broiler-pan rack 3 inches from heat.

2. Heat oil in a small saucepan over medium heat. Add garlic, curry powder, cumin, coriander, red pepper, salt and black pepper; sauté 3 minutes. Let mixture cool slightly. Rub spice mixture under and over skin of hens.

3. Place hens, skin side down, on broiler-pan rack. Broil 12 minutes. Turn skin side up. Broil 13 minutes or until internal temperature of thigh registers 180° on an instant-read thermometer.

Grilled Garlicky Cornish Hens

MAKES 8 servings

PREP 10 minutes

GRILL 25 minutes

———

PER SERVING
366 calories, 40 g protein,
21 g fat, 4 g carbohydrate,
649 mg sodium,
125 mg cholesterol.

4 Cornish hens (1 pound each)

3 cloves garlic, finely chopped

1 tablespoon chopped fresh thyme or 1 teaspoon dried
thyme

¾ teaspoon salt

½ teaspoon black pepper

1. Prepare a hot grill; position rack 5 inches from heat.

2. Meanwhile, remove backbone from each hen by cutting along each side of bone from tail to neck with kitchen shears.

3. Mix garlic, thyme, salt and pepper in a bowl.

4. With fingers, loosen skin on hens' breasts. Rub garlic mixture under skin. Tuck wing tips under back of each hen; tie legs together with string.

5. Place hens on grill; cover and grill 25 minutes or until internal temperature of thigh registers 180° on an instant-read thermometer; turn occasionally.

6. Remove string and cut through center of each breastbone to separate hens into halves.

Meat

Bacon Cheeseburgers

MAKES 6 servings

PREP 5 minutes

COOK 4 minutes

BROIL 16 minutes

PER SERVING
587 calories, 44 g protein,
34 g fat, 22 g carbohydrate,
747 mg sodium,
135 mg cholesterol.

6 slices bacon, diced
2¼ pounds ground beef
1 teaspoon Worcestershire sauce
¼ teaspoon garlic powder
¼ teaspoon black pepper
6 slices American cheese
6 hamburger buns
Lettuce leaves for serving (optional)
Tomato slices for serving (optional)

1. Heat broiler.

2. Heat a medium-size skillet over medium-high heat. Add bacon and cook 4 minutes or until browned. Drain on paper toweling.

3. Combine beef, Worcestershire sauce, garlic powder and pepper in a large bowl. Add bacon and mix to combine.

4. Form mixture into six ¼-inch-thick patties, hiding 1 slice cheese inside each. Broil 8 minutes per side or until internal temperature registers 160° on an instant-read thermometer.

5. Assemble burgers in buns, adding lettuce and tomato if desired.

Bacon Cheeseburger

Mediterranean-Style Burgers

MAKES 8 servings

PREP 15 minutes

BROIL OR GRILL 12 minutes

PER SERVING
333 calories, 30 g protein,
19 g fat, 10 g carbohydrate,
510 mg sodium,
90 mg cholesterol.

2 pounds lean ground beef
1 package (10 ounces) frozen chopped spinach, thawed
   and squeezed dry
2 cloves garlic, finely chopped
¼ cup grated Parmesan cheese
1 cup prepared spaghetti sauce (with seasoning of
   your choice)
½ cup dry Italian-seasoned bread crumbs

1. Prepare a hot grill or heat broiler; position grill rack or broiler-pan rack 4 inches from heat.

2. Combine beef, spinach, garlic, Parmesan, spaghetti sauce and bread crumbs in a large bowl; mix well. Divide mixture into 8 equal portions and shape each into a burger patty.

3. Broil or grill burgers 6 minutes per side for medium or until internal temperature registers 160° on an instant-read thermometer.

Beef Patties au Poivre

MAKES 4 servings

PREP 10 minutes

COOK 15 minutes

PER SERVING
WITHOUT BUN
322 calories, 24 g protein,
22 g fat, 4 g carbohydrate,
644 mg sodium,
106 mg cholesterol.

PEPPERCORN SAUCE
1 tablespoon green peppercorns in brine, drained
1 tablespoon butter
¼ cup frozen chopped onion, thawed
2 tablespoons brandy
2 tablespoons all-purpose flour
1 cup beef broth
¼ cup heavy cream

4 prepared beef patties (1 pound total), each
   ¼ inch thick
½ teaspoon salt
¼ teaspoon black pepper
4 buns for serving (optional)

1. Prepare peppercorn sauce: On a clean work surface, crush half of peppercorns with back of a spoon.

2. Melt butter in a small saucepan over medium heat. Add onion and all the peppercorns; sauté 4 to 5 minutes or until onion is browned. Carefully add brandy; scrape up any browned bits from bottom of pan with a wooden spoon; cook 30 seconds. Stir in flour; cook, stirring, 2 minutes.

3. Add broth to pan; bring to boiling, stirring. Lower heat; simmer 2 to 3 minutes. Add cream; cook, stirring, 1 to 2 minutes. Remove from heat; cover sauce to keep warm.

4. To prepare patties, heat a large nonstick skillet over medium heat. Season beef patties with salt and pepper. Add patties to skillet; cook 1 to 2 minutes per side or until internal temperature registers 160° on an instant-read thermometer.

5. Spoon sauce over each patty. Serve on buns if desired.

Beef Enchiladas

MAKES 6 servings

PREP 10 minutes

COOK 15 minutes

BAKE at 400° for 15 to 20 minutes

PER SERVING
390 calories, 25 g protein,
12 g fat, 46 g carbohydrate,
1,030 mg sodium,
59 mg cholesterol.

¾ pound lean ground beef

1 medium-size onion, chopped

1 clove garlic, finely chopped

1 can (4 ounces) chopped green chiles

2 tablespoons chili powder

¾ teaspoon salt

¼ cup water

12 corn tortillas (6-inch)

1½ cups fat-free refried beans

1 cup picante sauce

¼ cup shredded low-fat cheddar cheese (1 ounce)

2 tablespoons reduced-fat sour cream

1 medium-size tomato, diced

Chopped fresh cilantro for garnish (optional)

1. Heat oven to 400°.

2. Sauté beef, onion and garlic in a large nonstick skillet over medium-high heat 3 to 4 minutes or until beef is cooked through and no longer pink. Stir in chiles, chili powder, salt and water. Bring to boiling; cook, stirring occasionally, 10 minutes. Remove from heat.

3. Meanwhile, warm tortillas according to package directions.

4. Spread 2 tablespoons refried beans on a warm tortilla. Fill center with scant ¼ cup meat mixture. Roll up tortilla and place, seam side down, in a 13 x 9 x 2-inch baking dish. Repeat with remaining tortillas and filling, fitting them tightly in dish side by side.

5. Spread picante sauce over top. Sprinkle with cheddar.

6. Bake in heated 400° oven 15 to 20 minutes or until cheese is melted and filling is hot.

7. Top each serving with 1 teaspoon sour cream and some tomato; garnish with cilantro if desired.

Beef Sandwich
with Horseradish Sauce

quick COOK

MAKES 4 servings

PREP 15 minutes

COOK 3 to 4 minutes

PER SERVING
519 calories, 30 g protein,
30 g fat, 32 g carbohydrate,
900 mg sodium,
84 mg cholesterol.

HORSERADISH SAUCE

¼ cup sour cream

¼ cup mayonnaise

2 to 3 tablespoons bottled horseradish

2 tablespoons snipped fresh chives

1 tablespoon Dijon mustard

1 teaspoon fresh lemon juice

½ teaspoon salt

1 pound beef round steak, cut into 4 slices

¼ teaspoon salt

¼ teaspoon black pepper

2 tablespoons vegetable oil

4 large green lettuce leaves

4 onion rolls, sliced in half

1 small cucumber, peeled and sliced into coins

1 jar (7 ounces) mixed roasted peppers, drained

1. Prepare horseradish sauce: Combine sour cream, mayonnaise, horseradish, chives, mustard, lemon juice and salt in a small bowl.

2. Place each steak between sheets of plastic wrap. Lightly pound until about ¼ inch thick. Season with salt and pepper.

3. Heat oil in a large nonstick skillet over medium-high heat. Add steaks; cook 1 to 2 minutes per side, depending on thickness, or until cooked through and no longer pink in center.

4. Place a lettuce leaf on bottom half of each roll; add steak. Top each sandwich with cucumber, peppers and horseradish sauce.

Open-Face Reuben

MAKES 4 servings
PREP 10 minutes
BROIL 3 minutes

PER SERVING
571 calories, 29 g protein,
39 g fat, 22 g carbohydrate,
1,697 mg sodium,
116 mg cholesterol.

1 refrigerated bag (1 pound) sauerkraut
4 slices deli-style seeded rye bread, toasted
½ cup bottled Thousand Island dressing
½ pound thinly sliced corned beef (about 12 slices)
½ pound thinly sliced Swiss cheese (about 8 slices)

1. Heat broiler; coat broiler-pan rack with nonstick cooking spray and position 4 to 6 inches from heat.

2. Gently heat sauerkraut in a small saucepan; drain.

3. Spread each slice of bread with 1 tablespoon dressing; top with corned beef, sauerkraut and cheese, dividing equally.

4. Broil sandwiches 3 minutes or until tops are lightly browned.

5. Serve with remaining ¼ cup dressing on the side.

Beef Sandwich with
Horseradish Sauce, *opposite*

Open-Face Reuben

Great Ground Meat

ON SALE, ground meat is a bargain. Try these quick variations on classic themes.

Easiest-Ever Meat Loaf

▶ Combine 1 pound ground meat, 3 eggs, 2 cans (4½ ounces each) diced green chiles, 1 cup seasoned bread crumbs, ⅓ cup ketchup, 2 teaspoons chili powder, 1 teaspoon dried oregano and 2 tablespoons Worcestershire sauce.

▶ Place mixture in a loaf pan. Bake at 350° for 40 to 50 minutes or until cooked through.

▶ Makes 6 to 8 servings.

Asian Meatballs with Sweet Spicy Glaze

▶ Mix 1 can (8 ounces) water chestnuts, drained and chopped; 1 pound ground meat; 1 egg; 2 teaspoons hoisin sauce and 1 tablespoon chopped fresh parsley.

▶ Shape mixture into ¾-inch meatballs. Place in single layer in a shallow baking dish.

▶ Bake at 350° until browned, about 15 minutes; drain off liquid.

▶ For the glaze, heat 1 cup plum jelly, 2 teaspoons hot chili oil and 1 teaspoon dark Asian sesame oil in a small saucepan.

▶ Toss meatballs with glaze or serve it alongside and dip them.

▶ Makes 8 to 10 appetizer servings.

Pasta with Creamy Mushroom & Meat Sauce

▶ Cook 1 package egg noodles in a large pot of lightly salted boiling water until al dente, firm but tender. Drain well.

▶ Meanwhile, heat 1 tablespoon oil in a large nonstick skillet over medium heat; add 1 chopped onion and 4 ounces sliced mushrooms. Cook 5 minutes.

▶ Add 1 pound ground meat; cook 7 minutes, stirring to break up meat.

▶ Add 1 can (10¾ ounces) condensed golden mushroom soup, 1 cup milk, ½ teaspoon salt, ⅛ teaspoon black pepper and 2 tablespoons butter; heat 4 minutes.

▶ Serve with cooked egg noodles.

▶ Makes 4 to 6 servings.

Meatball Kabob

▶ Mix 1¼ pounds ground meat, 3 tablespoons prepared barbecue sauce, ⅔ cup bread crumbs, 1 egg and 1 tablespoon Worcestershire sauce.

▶ Shape mixture into 18 meatballs.

▶ Cut 1 red onion and 1 sweet green pepper into 1-inch pieces.

▶ Thread meatballs alternately with vegetables onto six 12-inch metal skewers.

▶ Brush skewers with additional barbecue sauce.

▶ Broil 3 to 4 minutes per side.

▶ Makes 4 to 6 servings.

Mini Meat Loaves

30 minutes MAX

MAKES 8 servings

PREP 10 minutes

BAKE at 475° for 20 minutes

───────────

PER SERVING
315 calories, 25 g protein,
17 g fat, 14 g carbohydrate,
619 mg sodium,
129 mg cholesterol.

1 can (14½ ounces) chili-style chunky tomatoes

2 tablespoons Worcestershire sauce

2 eggs

¼ teaspoon salt

¼ teaspoon black pepper

1 pound ground beef

1 pound ground pork

1¼ cups dry seasoned bread crumbs

½ cup ketchup

1. Place rack in upper third of oven. Heat oven to 475°. Line a 15 x 10 x 1½-inch jelly-roll pan with aluminum foil. Coat foil with nonstick cooking spray.

2. Combine tomatoes, Worcestershire sauce, eggs, salt and pepper in a large bowl. Add meat and bread crumbs, stirring until just combined. Divide mixture into 8 equal pieces; shape into mini-loaves. Place on prepared pan.

3. Bake in heated 475° oven 15 minutes. Spread ketchup over top of loaves. Bake 5 minutes more or until internal temperature registers 160° on an instant-read thermometer.

Chipotle Chili

one POT

MAKES 4 servings

PREP 8 minutes

COOK 35 minutes

───────────

PER SERVING
429 calories, 38 g protein,
25 g fat, 15 g carbohydrate,
601 mg sodium,
138 mg cholesterol.

1 tablespoon vegetable oil

1 medium-size onion, chopped

2 cloves garlic, finely chopped

1¾ pounds ground beef

2 tablespoons chili powder

1 teaspoon salt

½ teaspoon ground cumin

½ teaspoon paprika

1 can (14½ ounces) stewed tomatoes with green chiles

1 chipotle chile in adobo sauce

2 teaspoons adobo sauce

2 teaspoons ketchup

1 can (19 ounces) red kidney beans, drained

1. Heat oil in a medium-size nonstick skillet over medium heat. Add onion and garlic and sauté 8 minutes.

2. Add beef, chili powder, salt, cumin and paprika. Turn heat to medium-high; cook 7 minutes.

3. Add tomatoes, chipotle chile with its sauce, adobo sauce and ketchup; lower heat to medium and simmer 15 minutes. Add beans and cook 5 more minutes.

Steak Topped with Blue Cheese

MAKES 4 servings

PREP 5 minutes

GRILL OR BROIL about 13
minutes

————

PER SERVING
598 calories, 64 g protein,
36 g fat, 1 g carbohydrate,
870 mg sodium,
193 mg cholesterol.

4 shell steaks (about 3 pounds total)
¼ teaspoon salt
6 ounces blue cheese
2 tablespoons butter, at room temperature
1 tablespoon chopped fresh parsley

1. Prepare a medium-hot grill or heat broiler; position grill rack or broiler-pan rack 6 inches from heat.

2. Season steaks with salt.

3. Grill steaks, covered, or broil them, about 6 minutes per side for medium-rare or until internal temperature registers 145° on an instant-read thermometer.

4. Meanwhile, using a spoon, blend together blue cheese and butter in a small bowl until creamy.

5. Spread blue cheese mixture over steaks. Return pan to broiler or keep steaks on grill another 30 seconds or until butter melts. Sprinkle with parsley.

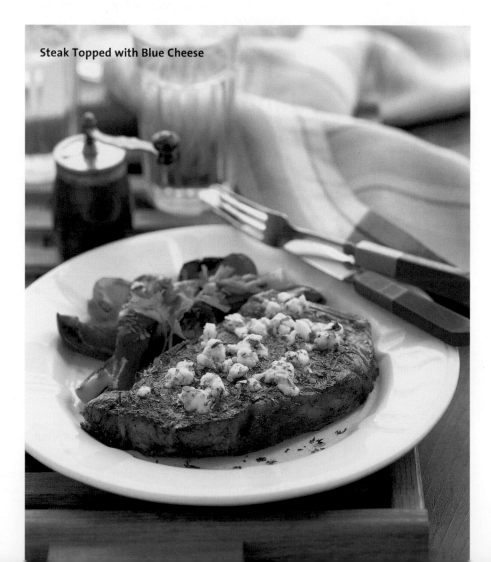

Steak Topped with Blue Cheese

Marinated Flank
Steak

Marinated Flank Steak

quick
COOK

MAKES 6 servings

PREP 10 minutes

REFRIGERATE overnight

GRILL OR BROIL 8 minutes

STAND 10 minutes

PER SERVING
252 calories, 32 g protein,
13 g fat, 0 g carbohydrate,
194 mg sodium,
78 mg cholesterol.

MARINADE

1 large bunch fresh cilantro, stemmed and coarsely
 chopped (about 1 cup)

1 jalapeño chile, seeded and coarsely chopped

3 cloves garlic, coarsely chopped

½ teaspoon grated lime rind

Juice of 2 limes (about ¼ cup)

2 tablespoons olive oil

1 teaspoon salt

½ teaspoon ground cumin

¼ teaspoon black pepper

1 flank steak, about ¾ inch thick (2 pounds)

1. Prepare marinade: Place cilantro, chile, garlic, lime rind, lime juice, oil, salt, cumin and pepper in a food processor or blender. Whirl until smooth.

2. Combine marinade and flank steak in a plastic food-storage bag and seal. Refrigerate overnight.

3. Prepare a medium-hot grill or heat broiler; coat broiler-pan rack with nonstick cooking spray and position 2 inches from heat. Remove steak from marinade. Discard marinade.

4. Grill or broil steak about 4 minutes per side for medium-rare or until internal temperature registers 145° on an instant-read thermometer, or until desired doneness.

5. Remove steak to a cutting board. Let stand 10 minutes. Cut steak diagonally into thin slices across grain.

Meat

139

Garlicky Beef Tips

MAKES 8 servings

PREP 15 minutes

COOK 10 minutes

PER SERVING
243 calories, 20 g protein,
9 g fat, 19 g carbohydrate,
337 mg sodium,
57 mg cholesterol.

8 slices white bread

2 tablespoons butter

8 cloves garlic, sliced

1 boneless sirloin steak (1¼ to 1½ pounds), trimmed and
    cut into 1-inch cubes

2 tablespoons dry sherry

½ cup beef broth

2 tablespoons all-purpose flour

¼ teaspoon salt

⅛ teaspoon black pepper

½ teaspoon Dijon mustard

1. Lightly toast bread. Cut off crusts; cut slices in half diagonally.

2. Heat butter in a large skillet over medium-high heat until lightly browned. Add garlic and sirloin; sauté until beef is cooked through, 5 minutes. Add sherry; cook 1 minute.

3. Mix broth, flour, salt, pepper and mustard in a small bowl. Add to skillet; cook 2 minutes to thicken.

4. Serve beef and sauce with toast.

Beef Fajitas

MAKES 4 servings

PREP 15 minutes

REFRIGERATE 1 hour

COOK 15 minutes

PER SERVING
334 calories, 29 g protein,
12 g fat, 30 g carbohydrate,
513 mg sodium,
59 mg cholesterol.

1 clove garlic, finely chopped

2 tablespoons red-wine vinegar

1 teaspoon salt

½ teaspoon dried oregano

¼ teaspoon black pepper

1 tablespoon olive oil

1 flank steak (1 pound), thinly sliced diagonally across
    the grain

2 large onions, thinly sliced

½ pound mushrooms, thinly sliced

3 plum tomatoes, chopped

1 pickled jalapeño chile, cored, seeded and chopped

1 teaspoon cornstarch

1 tablespoon water

8 small fat-free flour tortillas (6-inch), warmed
    according to package directions

1. Combine garlic, vinegar, ½ teaspoon salt, oregano, pepper and 1 teaspoon oil in a plastic food-storage bag. Add steak; seal. Refrigerate to marinate 1 hour.

2. Remove beef from marinade; drain well. Discard marinade. Heat 1 teaspoon oil in a large nonstick skillet over high heat. Add beef; sauté until cooked through, about 5 minutes. Transfer beef to a plate; cover to keep warm.

3. Add remaining teaspoon oil, onions and mushrooms to skillet; sauté until onions are softened and mushrooms give off their juices, about 6 minutes. Add tomatoes, chile and beef; cook until heated through, about 2 minutes.

4. Stir together cornstarch, remaining ½ teaspoon salt and water in a small bowl until smooth. Pour into skillet; cook, stirring constantly, about 2 minutes or until mixture is thickened and bubbly.

5. Spoon filling into warmed tortillas. Wrap up tortillas and serve.

Fast Fix

Three-Way Sloppy Joe

WHEN YOU'RE LOOKING for something different but as quick and family-pleasing as a burger, turn to Sloppy Joes. Here's the all-American classic, along with 2 variations from foreign shores. Each makes 6 servings and can be on the table in about half an hour.

All-American Sloppy Joes

► Cook 1½ pounds ground beef in a large nonstick skillet over medium-high heat, breaking up clumps, 8 minutes or until no longer pink. Drain off fat.

► Stir in 1 can (8 ounces) tomato sauce, ⅓ cup ketchup, 1 tablespoon Worcestershire sauce, 2 tablespoons white-wine vinegar and 2 teaspoons sugar; cook, stirring occasionally, over medium-low heat until flavors are blended, about 10 minutes.

► Divide equally among 6 hamburger buns.

Mexican Sloppy Joes

► Cook 1½ pounds ground beef and 1 tablespoon chili powder in a large nonstick skillet over medium-high heat, breaking up clumps, 8 minutes or until no longer pink. Drain off fat.

► Stir in 1 can (8 ounces) tomato sauce, ⅓ cup salsa, 1 tablespoon Worcestershire sauce, 2 tablespoons white-wine vinegar and 2 teaspoons sugar; cook, stirring occasionally, over medium-low heat until flavors are blended, about 10 minutes.

► Divide equally among 6 taco shells.

Italian Sloppy Joes

► Cook 1½ pounds ground beef, 1 teaspoon dried basil and 1 teaspoon dried oregano in a large nonstick skillet over medium-high heat, breaking up clumps, 8 minutes or until no longer pink. Drain off fat.

► Stir in 1 can (8 ounces) tomato sauce, ⅓ cup spaghetti sauce, 1 tablespoon Worcestershire sauce, 2 tablespoons white-wine vinegar and 2 teaspoons sugar; cook, stirring occasionally, over medium-low heat until flavors are blended, about 10 minutes.

► Spoon over 6 individual prepared pizza crusts. Garnish with shredded mozzarella cheese. Bake a few minutes at 400°, until cheese is melted.

Smothered Steak

MAKES 6 servings

PREP 10 minutes

COOK 27 minutes

BAKE at 350° for 15 minutes

(at same time as cooking)

———————

PER SERVING
284 calories, 31 g protein,
15 g fat, 3 g carbohydrate,
386 mg sodium,
85 mg cholesterol.

2 tablespoons butter

2 onions, sliced

2 pounds London broil

¾ teaspoon salt

½ teaspoon black pepper

½ cup dry red wine

1. Heat oven to 350°.

2. Heat butter in a large skillet over medium heat. Add onions; cook 25 minutes, stirring occasionally, until golden brown.

3. Meanwhile, heat an ovenproof skillet large enough to hold London broil over high heat. Season meat with ½ teaspoon salt and pepper. Sear meat in skillet over high heat, turning once.

4. Bake steak in heated 350° oven in skillet, uncovered, 15 minutes. Let stand 10 minutes while completing onions.

5. Once onions are golden brown, add wine and remaining ¼ teaspoon salt. Raise heat to high and cook 2 minutes. Slice steak; serve with onion sauce.

Grilled Tenderloin with Caper Mayonnaise

MAKES 8 servings

PREP 10 minutes

REFRIGERATE 2 hours

GRILL about 30 minutes

OR ROAST at 450° for 40 minutes

———————

PER SERVING
WITH 1 TABLESPOON
MAYONNAISE
332 calories, 30 g protein,
23 g fat, 1 g carbohydrate,
231 mg sodium,
93 mg cholesterol.

1 beef tenderloin (2½ to 3 pounds)

3 cloves garlic, cut into thin slivers

2 tablespoons olive oil

1 tablespoon black peppercorns, crushed

¼ teaspoon salt

CAPER MAYONNAISE

½ cup mayonnaise

1 tablespoon olive oil

2 teaspoons mustard

1 teaspoon fresh lemon juice

1 tablespoon capers, drained, rinsed and chopped

1. Pat meat dry with paper toweling. Using tip of a sharp paring knife, make small slits all over meat. Insert garlic slivers. Rub meat with oil. Press peppercorns onto meat. Sprinkle with salt. Place on a plate; cover with plastic wrap and refrigerate 2 hours.

2. Meanwhile, prepare caper mayonnaise: Whisk together mayonnaise, oil, mustard and lemon juice in a small bowl. Fold in capers. Refrigerate 1 hour.

3. Prepare a grill so it is hot on one side (see note below to roast in oven). Sear meat on all sides over direct heat, about 5 minutes total. Move to side, off direct heat, and cover grill. Grill meat about 12 minutes per side for medium-rare or until internal temperature registers 145° on an instant-read thermometer. Serve with caper mayonnaise.

Note: To roast in oven, heat oven to 450°. Coat a roasting rack with nonstick cooking spray. Place tenderloin on prepared rack. Roast 40 minutes for medium-rare or until internal temperature registers 145° on an instant-read thermometer.

Grilled Tenderloin with Caper Mayonnaise

Skillet Sensations

COOKING SLICED INGREDIENTS over high heat in a frying pan is one of the fastest techniques around. Use precut ingredients to make these dishes even quicker.

Pepper & Steak Stir-Fry

▶ Dice 1 sweet red pepper, 1 sweet green pepper, 1 red onion and enough pitted black olives to equal ½ cup.

▶ Heat 2 tablespoons olive oil in a large nonstick skillet; add diced vegetables, ½ pound sliced boneless pork or beef round steak and ½ teaspoon crushed fennel seeds.

▶ Sauté until meat is cooked through, about 5 minutes.

▶ Season with a splash of vinegar.

▶ Makes about 4 servings.

Steak & Green Bean Stir-Fry

▶ Heat 2 tablespoons vegetable oil in a large skillet; add ½ pound thin-sliced pork tenderloin or beef round steak, 1 sliced red onion, ½ pound trimmed green beans and 2 cloves finely chopped garlic.

▶ Sauté until meat is cooked through, about 5 minutes.

▶ Combine 2 tablespoons dark Asian sesame oil, 1 cup chicken broth, pinch red-pepper flakes, 1 teaspoon black bean garlic sauce, 1 tablespoon soy sauce and 1 teaspoon sugar. Add to meat.

▶ Thicken with 1 teaspoon cornstarch mixed with 1 tablespoon water.

▶ Makes about 4 servings.

Peach-Beef Stir-Fry

MAKES 4 servings

PREP 15 minutes

REFRIGERATE 30 minutes

COOK 10 minutes

———

PER SERVING
246 calories, 17 g protein,
7 g fat, 30 g carbohydrate,
807 mg sodium,
38 mg cholesterol.

3 tablespoons soy sauce

½ cup plus 2 tablespoons peach nectar

1 teaspoon grated fresh ginger

2 tablespoons cornstarch

½ pound beef top round, sliced for stir-fry

1 tablespoon vegetable oil

1 tablespoon finely chopped fresh ginger

1 tablespoon finely chopped garlic

¼ cup chopped scallions, including part of the green

⅛ teaspoon red-pepper flakes

3 to 4 ripe peaches, peeled, pitted and sliced

⅓ cup thinly sliced canned water chestnuts

½ pound snow peas, trimmed

1 tablespoon rice-wine vinegar

1. Stir together 2 tablespoons soy sauce, 2 tablespoons peach nectar, grated ginger and cornstarch in a medium-size bowl until smooth. Toss beef with soy sauce marinade to coat. Cover and refrigerate 30 minutes.

2. Heat 1 teaspoon oil in a wok or large skillet over medium-high heat. Add beef with marinade; stir-fry until cooked through and no longer pink in center, 2 to 4 minutes. Remove to a medium-size bowl, scraping out juices with a rubber spatula.

3. Add remaining 2 teaspoons oil, chopped ginger, garlic, scallions and red-pepper flakes to wok or skillet; stir-fry 1 to 2 minutes. Add peach slices, water chestnuts and snow peas; stir-fry another 2 minutes. Return beef with juices to pan. Stir in remaining 2 tablespoons soy sauce, remaining ½ cup peach nectar and vinegar.

Beef-Noodle Stir-Fry

MAKES 4 servings
PREP 15 minutes
COOK 18 minutes

———

PER SERVING
466 calories, 29 g protein,
17 g fat, 48g carbohydrate,
1,264 mg sodium,
59 mg cholesterol.

2 tablespoons cooking sesame oil
1 tablespoon chopped garlic
1 tablespoon chopped fresh ginger
1 flank steak (1 pound), thinly sliced crosswise
1 small onion, sliced
⅓ pound mushrooms, sliced
1 sweet red pepper, cored, seeded and thinly sliced
¼ teaspoon red-pepper flakes
1½ cups lower-sodium chicken broth
⅓ cup hoisin sauce
¼ cup lower-sodium soy sauce
2 tablespoons cornstarch
6 ounces snow peas, trimmed
4½ ounces maifun rice sticks
1 Jar (4½ ounces) baby corn, drained and rinsed

1. Heat 1 tablespoon oil in a large nonstick skillet over medium-high heat. Add 1 teaspoon garlic, 1 teaspoon ginger and steak; sauté 4 minutes or until almost cooked through. Transfer to a plate.

2. Heat remaining 1 tablespoon oil in same skillet. Add onion, mushrooms, sweet red pepper, red-pepper flakes, remaining 2 teaspoons garlic and remaining 2 teaspoons ginger; sauté 4 minutes.

3. Mix broth, hoisin sauce, soy sauce and cornstarch in a small bowl. Add to skillet; cook, stirring, 2 minutes. Add snow peas and rice sticks; stir-fry over medium-low heat 4 minutes or until thickened. Add sautéed beef and corn. Cover; let stand on heat 2 minutes.

Orange Beef with Cashews

MAX

MAKES 4 servings

PREP 10 minutes

MICROWAVE 2 minutes

COOK 11 minutes

PER SERVING
404 calories, 29 g protein,
22 g fat, 25 g carbohydrate,
1,070 mg sodium,
70 mg cholesterol.

1 pound beef top round, sliced for stir-fry
2 tablespoons light-brown sugar
¼ cup plus 2 tablespoons reduced-sodium soy sauce
2 tablespoons bottled chopped garlic
4 cups broccoli flowerets
2 teaspoons water
4 scallions, cut into 1-inch lengths
⅔ cup orange juice
2 tablespoons cornstarch
2 teaspoons rice-wine vinegar
2 teaspoons ground ginger
½ teaspoon red-pepper flakes
2 tablespoons peanut oil
½ cup salted cashews

1. Combine beef, brown sugar, 2 tablespoons soy sauce and garlic in a plastic food-storage bag and seal. Turn to coat meat and let stand briefly.

2. Meanwhile, place broccoli and water in a microwave-safe dish. Cover tightly with plastic wrap. Microwave at 100% power 2 minutes.

3. Stir together scallions, orange juice, remaining ¼ cup soy sauce, cornstarch, vinegar, ginger and red-pepper flakes in a small bowl.

4. Heat oil in a wok or large skillet over high heat. Add beef with marinade; stir-fry 1 to 3 minutes. Add broccoli; stir-fry 1 to 2 minutes or until heated through. Add cashews; cook 1 minute. Stir in scallion–orange juice mixture; cook 2 to 3 minutes or until thickened.

Orange Beef with Cashews

Steak with
Mushroom Sauce

Steak with Mushroom Sauce

MAKES 4 servings

PREP 10 minutes

COOK 20 minutes

PER SERVING
247 calories, 26 g protein,
13 g fat, 7 g carbohydrate,
647 mg sodium,
64 cholesterol.

MUSHROOM SAUCE

2 teaspoons vegetable oil

½ cup chopped onion

1 cup coarsely chopped mushrooms

2 cloves garlic, finely chopped

¾ cup beef broth

1 large tomato, chopped

¼ cup dry red wine

8 Kalamata olives, pitted and chopped

2 teaspoons chopped fresh thyme

4 club steaks (1 pound total)

½ teaspoon salt

¼ teaspoon black pepper

Watercress sprigs for garnish (optional)

1. Prepare mushroom sauce: Heat oil in a medium-size skillet over medium heat. Add onion and cook until softened, 5 minutes. Add mushrooms and garlic; cook until very tender, 5 minutes. If too dry, add broth, ¼ cup at a time. Stir in tomato, wine, olives and remaining broth. Simmer, uncovered, 10 minutes. Add thyme; keep warm.

2. Meanwhile, coat a large nonstick skillet with nonstick cooking spray; heat over medium-high heat. Season steaks with salt and pepper. Add to skillet; brown 4 minutes per side for medium-rare or until internal temperature registers 145° on an instant-read thermometer, or until desired doneness.

3. Transfer steaks to a platter. Spoon sauce over. Garnish with watercress if desired.

Chicken-Fried Steak with Gravy

quick
COOK

MAKES 4 servings
PREP 5 minutes
REFRIGERATE 20 minutes
COOK 10 minutes

———————

PER SERVING
493 calories, 31 g protein,
32 g fat, 20 g carbohydrate,
759 mg sodium,
187 mg cholesterol.

1 pound beef round steak, cut into 4 slices
⅔ cup plus 1 tablespoon all-purpose flour
1 teaspoon salt
½ teaspoon paprika
½ teaspoon black pepper
2 eggs
⅔ cup vegetable oil
1¼ cups milk
1 can (7 ounces) mushrooms with pieces and stems,
   drained
1 teaspoon Worcestershire sauce
2 tablespoons chopped fresh parsley for garnish
   (optional)

1. Place each steak between sheets of plastic wrap. Lightly pound until ¼ inch thick.

2. Combine ⅔ cup flour, ½ teaspoon salt, paprika and ¼ teaspoon pepper on a sheet of waxed paper. Beat eggs slightly in a shallow dish.

3. Dip steaks in flour mixture to coat lightly, shaking off excess; dip into egg, then back into flour mixture, coating both sides. Refrigerate coated beef on a wire rack set over a baking sheet 20 minutes.

4. Heat oil in a large nonstick skillet over medium heat. Add beef, working in batches, if necessary; cook 2 minutes per side or until cooked through and no longer pink in center. Transfer beef to a platter; keep warm.

5. Pour off all but 3 tablespoons fat from skillet. Stir remaining 1 tablespoon flour into hot fat in skillet until flour forms a paste, about 20 seconds. Stir in milk, mushrooms and Worcestershire sauce. Bring to boiling; lower heat to medium; cook 2 to 3 minutes or until thickened. Season with remaining ½ teaspoon salt and ¼ teaspoon pepper.

6. Spoon sauce over beef. Garnish with parsley if desired.

Teriyaki Cube Steaks

MAX

MAKES 4 servings
PREP 10 minutes
COOK 20 minutes

PER SERVING
422 calories, 30 g protein,
9 g fat, 51 g carbohydrate,
854 mg sodium,
59 mg cholesterol.

1 can (14¾ ounces) beef broth
1 cup water
1 cup long-grain white rice
1 teaspoon grated lime rind
1 teaspoon ground ginger
2 tablespoons fresh lime juice
2 tablespoons teriyaki sauce
½ teaspoon red-pepper flakes
4 cube steaks (1 pound total)
2 teaspoons vegetable oil
2 sweet green peppers, cored, seeded and sliced
1 red onion, sliced

1. Combine 1 cup broth and water in a medium-size saucepan. Bring to boiling. Add rice, lime rind and ½ teaspoon ginger. Cover; lower heat and simmer 20 minutes or until rice is tender.

2. Meanwhile, combine remaining broth, lime juice, 1 tablespoon teriyaki sauce, remaining ½ teaspoon ginger and red-pepper flakes in a small bowl; set aside.

3. Brush steaks with remaining 1 tablespoon teriyaki sauce. Heat oil in a large nonstick skillet over medium heat. Add steaks and cook 2 minutes per side or until cooked through. Transfer to a plate; keep warm.

4. Add peppers and onion to skillet; sauté 8 minutes, adding broth mixture as needed to prevent sticking. Return beef and broth mixture to skillet; cook until heated through.

Fast Fix

Pot Roast Power

LEFTOVER POT ROAST translates into no-fuss main courses. No leftovers? You'll find pot roast (and various other cuts of meat) fully cooked in the supermarket meat case, ready for microwave reheating, or to go straight into this "homemade" winner.

Beef Stroganoff Casserole

▶ Cook 1 pound medium egg noodles and 1 large sliced onion in a large pot of lightly salted water until noodles are al dente, firm but tender; drain.

▶ Cut 1½ pounds cooked pot roast into ½-inch cubes.

▶ Whisk together 2 cans (10¾ ounces each) condensed golden mushroom soup, 2 cups milk, ½ pint sour cream, 2 tablespoons fresh lemon juice, ½ teaspoon salt and ¼ teaspoon pepper in a medium-size bowl.

▶ Place noodles and onion in a 4-quart casserole. Fold in cubed pot roast along with any gravy. Pour soup mixture over noodles; stir to combine completely.

▶ Bake in a heated 350° oven 30 minutes.

▶ Makes 10 servings.

Greek-Style Beef Kabobs

Greek-Style Beef Kabobs

quick
COOK

MAKES 6 servings

PREP 25 minutes

GRILL OR BROIL 10 minutes

2 cloves garlic, finely chopped

¼ cup lemon juice

1 teaspoon grated lemon rind

1 teaspoon dried oregano, crumbled

½ cup olive oil

12 cherry tomatoes

12 medium-size mushrooms

1 sweet green pepper, cut into 1-inch squares

1½ pounds top sirloin, cut against the grain into
   ½-inch-thick strips

½ teaspoon salt

¼ teaspoon black pepper

Fresh mint sprigs for garnish (optional)

Lemon wedges for garnish (optional)

1. Prepare a medium-hot grill or heat broiler; position grill rack or broiler-pan rack 6 inches from heat.

2. Whisk together garlic, lemon juice, lemon rind and oregano in a small bowl. Slowly whisk in oil.

3. Thread tomatoes onto 1 metal skewer. Repeat with mushrooms, green pepper and meat. Brush all skewers with lemon juice mixture.

4. Grill or broil kabobs: If grilling, cover grill while cooking. Grill or broil green pepper 2 minutes. Add mushrooms; grill or broil 2 minutes. Then turn peppers and mushrooms. Add tomatoes and beef; grill or broil 3 minutes per side or until beef is cooked through.

5. Transfer all skewers to a platter. Season with salt and black pepper. Garnish with fresh mint and lemon wedges if desired.

Asian Beef Kabobs

MAKES 6 servings
PREP 15 minutes
REFRIGERATE 4 to 6 hours
COOK 3 minutes
GRILL 12 minutes
OR BROIL 10 minutes

PER SERVING
417 calories, 30 g protein,
26 g fat, 17 g carbohydrate,
1,435 mg sodium,
75 mg cholesterol.

MARINADE
½ cup soy sauce
½ cup cooking sesame oil
½ cup rice-wine vinegar
2 tablespoons sesame seeds
2 tablespoons sugar
6 cloves garlic, finely chopped
⅔ teaspoon red-pepper flakes

1½ pounds boneless sirloin steak, cut into 1-inch cubes
2 ears fresh corn, shucked
2 small zucchini
4 large scallions

1. Prepare marinade: Whisk soy sauce, oil, vinegar, sesame seeds, sugar, garlic and red-pepper flakes in a small bowl.

2. Place half of marinade in a large plastic food-storage bag; add steak cubes. Seal; turn bag to coat meat well. Refrigerate 4 to 6 hours. Reserve remainder of marinade to use as dipping sauce.

3. Prepare a medium-hot grill or heat broiler. Position grill rack or broiler-pan rack 6 inches from heat.

4. Meanwhile, cut corn and zucchini into 1-inch pieces. Cut each scallion into 3 pieces, each piece about 1½ inches long.

5. Boil enough water to cover corn. Add corn and cook 3 minutes. Drain.

6. Thread meat cubes onto six 12-inch metal skewers, alternating meat pieces with corn, zucchini and scallions. Brush once with marinade from plastic bag.

7. Grill or broil kabobs, turning occasionally, 10 to 12 minutes for medium-rare. If grilling, cover grill while cooking. If broiling, brush occasionally with marinade from plastic bag.

8. Serve kabobs with reserved marinade for dipping.

Meat

Pork & Veggies

MAKES 4 servings

PREP 10 minutes

COOK 35 minutes

———————

PER SERVING
473 calories, 30 g protein,
28 g fat, 27 g carbohydrate,
1,185 mg sodium,
90 mg cholesterol.

2 tablespoons flour

1 teaspoon salt

½ teaspoon black pepper

4 boneless pork chops (1 pound total)

2 tablespoons vegetable oil

1 small onion, sliced

2 cloves garlic, sliced

1 teaspoon curry powder

¾ pound red new potatoes, unpeeled, quartered

1 cup chicken broth

1 cup sour cream

¼ cup half-and-half

1 box (10 ounces) frozen peas

1. Combine flour, salt and pepper on a sheet of waxed paper. Dip pork chops in flour mixture to coat lightly, shaking off excess.

2. Heat 1 tablespoon oil in a medium-size nonstick skillet with a cover over medium-high heat. Add pork; sauté 5 minutes per side or until internal temperature registers 160° on an instant-read thermometer. Transfer pork to a plate; keep warm.

3. Add remaining 1 tablespoon oil to skillet. Stir in onion and garlic; sauté 8 minutes. Add curry powder, potatoes and broth; cook, covered, 12 minutes.

4. Reduce heat to low. Stir in sour cream, half-and-half and peas. Cook, stirring constantly, about 3 minutes. Add pork to skillet, heat another minute.

Maple-Nut Pork Chops

quick
PREP

MAKES 4 servings

PREP 5 minutes

BAKE at 400° for 25 minutes

COOK about 12 minutes

(at same time as baking)

———————

PER SERVING
410 calories, 30 g protein,
24 g fat, 22 g carbohydrate,
413 mg sodium,
75 mg cholesterol.

3 tablespoons maple syrup

1 tablespoon light-brown sugar

2 teaspoons Dijon mustard

¼ teaspoon dried thyme

½ teaspoon salt

¼ teaspoon black pepper

4 pork chops, each ¾ inch thick (about 1¾ pounds total)

¾ cup chopped walnuts

1 tablespoon butter

3 zucchini, sliced into coins

1. Heat oven to 400°. Coat a baking dish large enough to hold chops in a single layer with nonstick cooking spray.

2. Combine 2 tablespoons maple syrup, brown sugar, mustard, thyme, salt and pepper in a small bowl. Spread over both sides of pork chops. Put ½ cup walnuts on a sheet of waxed paper and press both sides of chops into nuts to coat.

3. Place chops in prepared baking dish and bake in heated 400° oven 25 minutes or until internal temperature registers 160° on an instant-read thermometer.

4. Meanwhile, melt butter in large nonstick skillet over medium-high heat. Add zucchini; cook 10 minutes. Add remaining 1 tablespoon maple syrup and ¼ cup walnuts. Cook another minute or so to heat through. Serve over pork chops.

Spicy Pork with Pineapple

MAKES 4 servings

PREP 10 minutes

COOK 6 minutes

PER SERVING
262 calories, 19 g protein,
9 g fat , 27 g carbohydrate,
561 g sodium,
52 mg cholesterol.

1 teaspoon ground cumin

½ teaspoon garlic powder

½ teaspoon ground ginger

½ teaspoon ground allspice

½ teaspoon salt

⅛ teaspoon black pepper

¾ pound pork loin, cut into 1-inch cubes

2 teaspoons vegetable oil

1 cup chicken broth

2 tablespoons cornstarch

1 can (20 ounces) juice-packed pineapple chunks

Cooked jasmine, Texmati or basmati rice for serving
  (optional)

1 scallion, chopped, including part of the green,
  for garnish (optional)

1 tablespoon finely chopped fresh cilantro for garnish
  (optional)

1. Combine cumin, garlic powder, ginger, allspice, ¼ teaspoon salt and pepper in a large plastic food-storage bag; mix ingredients thoroughly. Add pork cubes to bag; seal and toss to coat pork evenly.

2. Heat oil in a large nonstick skillet over medium-high heat. When hot but not smoking, add pork; stir-fry 5 minutes or until cooked through.

3. Meanwhile, stir broth into cornstarch in a small bowl until mixture is smooth. Add broth mixture, pineapple with its juice and remaining ¼ teaspoon salt to pork in skillet; cook, stirring, 1 minute or until mixture is thickened and heated through.

4. If desired, serve pork mixture over rice, garnished with scallions and cilantro.

Roast Pork & Vegetables

Roast Pork & Vegetables

MAKES 6 servings

PREP 10 minutes

ROAST at 475° for 15 minutes

154

PER SERVING
318 calories, 22 g protein,
15 g fat, 23 g carbohydrate,
983 mg sodium,
56 mg cholesterol.

Family Circle Quick & Easy Recipes

1 bag (14 ounces) frozen small whole red potatoes,
    thawed, larger potatoes halved
1 bag (1 pound) frozen sweet pepper stir-fry, thawed
    and drained
2 jars (6½ ounces each) marinated artichoke hearts
2 teaspoons bottled chopped garlic
1 teaspoon dried Italian seasoning
½ teaspoon salt
¼ teaspoon black pepper
1 pork tenderloin (¾ pound), trimmed
3 to 4 links hot Italian sausage (½ pound total),
    casings removed
½ cup drained pitted black ripe olives

1. Heat oven to 475°.

2. Combine potatoes, pepper stir-fry, artichoke hearts, garlic, Italian seasoning, salt and black pepper in a large bowl. Let stand 5 minutes.

3. Meanwhile, cut pork into ½-inch cubes. Crumble sausage. Add pork, sausage and olives to bowl. Spoon mixture onto a 15 x 10-inch jelly-roll pan.

4. Roast, uncovered, in heated 475° oven 15 minutes or until meat is cooked through.

Pork with Cider Sauce

MAKES 4 servings

PREP 10 minutes

COOK 20 minutes

PER SERVING
413 calories, 23 g protein,
20 g fat, 37 g carbohydrate,
317 mg sodium,
72 mg cholesterol.

4 boneless pork chops (1 pound total)

¼ cup all-purpose flour

1 teaspoon dried thyme

½ teaspoon salt

¼ teaspoon black pepper

2 tablespoons vegetable oil

2 tablespoons unsalted butter

1 small onion, chopped

2 cups apple cider

½ cup mixed dried fruit, chopped

2 tablespoons cider vinegar

1 teaspoon ground ginger

1. Place pork between sheets of plastic wrap. Lightly pound until ¼ inch thick.

2. Combine flour, thyme, salt and pepper in a large plastic food-storage bag. Add pork; seal bag and shake to coat.

3. Heat oil and 1 tablespoon butter in a large nonstick skillet over medium heat. Add pork, working in batches if necessary, and cook about 4 minutes per side or until cooked through. Transfer pork to a platter; keep warm.

4. Heat remaining 1 tablespoon butter in same skillet, scraping up any browned bits from bottom of skillet. Add onion; cook 2 minutes or until slightly softened.

5. Add apple cider, dried fruit, vinegar and ginger to skillet. Boil about 12 minutes or until slightly thickened. Spoon sauce over pork.

Pork with Cider Sauce

Chutney-Topped Pork Medallions

quick **COOK**

MAKES 6 servings

PREP 5 minutes

BROIL 5 minutes

———————

PER SERVING
199 calories, 26 g protein,
7 g fat, 7 g carbohydrate,
242 mg sodium,
67 mg cholesterol.

1 pork tenderloin (1½ pounds)
¼ teaspoon salt
¼ teaspoon black pepper
1 tablespoon Dijon mustard
⅓ cup chutney
¼ cup unsalted peanuts
2 tablespoons chopped fresh parsley

1. Heat broiler. Spray broiler-pan rack with nonstick cooking spray.

2. Slice pork into medallions, each about ⅓ inch thick. Flatten each medallion slightly and sprinkle both sides with salt and pepper.

3. Broil medallions 2 minutes. Turn meat; broil 1 more minute. Remove pan from broiler and leave broiler on.

4. Brush tops of medallions with mustard. Spoon chutney on top, dividing equally. Sprinkle with peanuts.

5. Broil 2 minutes or until pork is cooked through. Transfer to a serving platter. Sprinkle with parsley.

Barbecued Pork Tenderloin

5 ingredients or **LESS**

MAKES 4 servings

PREP 10 minutes

BROIL OR GRILL 5 minutes

———————

PER SERVING
164 calories, 18 g protein,
3 g fat, 16 g carbohydrate,
402 mg sodium,
50 mg cholesterol.

½ cup ketchup
3 tablespoons cider vinegar
2 tablespoons packed light-brown sugar
¼ teaspoon red-pepper flakes
1 pork tenderloin (¾ pound)

1. Prepare a hot grill or heat broiler; coat grill rack or broiler-pan rack with nonstick cooking spray and position 4 inches from heat.

2. Combine ketchup, vinegar, brown sugar and red-pepper flakes in a small bowl until well blended.

3. Slice pork crosswise into ½-inch-thick medallions. Thread medallions onto 4 metal skewers, dividing equally.

4. Reserve ½ cup ketchup mixture. Brush remainder over pork on skewers.

5. Broil or grill 5 minutes or until cooked through and no longer pink in center; turn once after 3 minutes. Serve with reserved ketchup mixture.

Pork Tenderloin Plus!

ADD ANY OF THESE simple glazes and no-fuss sauces to pork tenderloin for a delicious—and lean—main dish. To serve 4, begin with 2 tenderloins (about 1½ pounds total). Heat oven to 425° or prepare a hot grill. Trim any fat and remove silver skin from pork, then rub with 1 tablespoon olive oil and season with salt and pepper. Place in a roasting pan or on grill, add a sauce or glaze as directed below and roast or grill 20 minutes (if grilling, turn to brown each side) or until internal temperature registers 160° on an instant-read thermometer.

Pineapple Sauce

► Combine one 8-ounce can crushed pineapple, ½ cup sugar, ¼ cup ketchup, ⅓ cup cider vinegar, 2 tablespoons soy sauce and 1 clove finely chopped garlic in a small saucepan; heat over low heat.

► Thicken with 1 tablespoon cornstarch mixed with ¼ cup water.

► Serve alongside roast tenderloin—tasty on grilled pork chops, too.

► Makes about 1½ cups.

Indonesian Peanut Dip

► Combine 1 cup smooth peanut butter with 2 tablespoons each soy sauce, sherry, sugar, Worcestershire sauce and dark Asian sesame oil.

► Add 1 tablespoon each finely chopped garlic and ginger.

► Serve alongside roast or grilled pork.

► Makes about 1½ cups.

Sweet & Savory Glaze

► Mix ¼ cup apricot jam and ¼ cup Italian salad dressing.

► Brush over pork tenderloin.

► Grill or bake; brush occasionally with additional glaze during cooking.

► Makes ½ cup.

Mustard-Honey Soy Glaze

► Combine 1 tablespoon mustard and 2 tablespoons honey. Add ½ cup soy sauce and 1 clove finely chopped garlic.

► Brush glaze over pork tenderloin before roasting.

► Makes scant ¾ cup.

Orange-Balsamic Glaze

► Mix 2 cloves finely chopped garlic, ½ cup orange juice, ¼ cup balsamic vinegar and 1 teaspoon ground cumin.

► Brush over tenderloin before or after grilling.

► Makes about ¾ cup.

Horseradish Sauce

► Mix 1 to 2 tablespoons bottled horseradish, ¼ cup chopped chives and 1 cup sour cream.

► Serve alongside roast tenderloin—good on grilled pork chops, too.

► Makes about 1¼ cups.

Apricot-Glazed Pork Skewers

MAKES 8 servings

PREP 15 minutes

BROIL OR GRILL 6 minutes

———

PER SERVING
214 calories, 19 g protein,
6 g fat, 20 g carbohydrate,
528 mg sodium,
51 mg cholesterol.

¾ cup apricot preserves
3 tablespoons chopped scallions, including part of
   the green
3 tablespoons Dijon mustard
1 tablespoon reduced-sodium soy sauce
1 clove garlic, finely chopped
1 teaspoon salt
1 teaspoon black pepper
2 pork tenderloins (about 1½ pounds total), trimmed

1. Prepare a hot grill or heat broiler; position grill rack or broiler-pan rack 6 inches from heat.

2. Whisk preserves, scallions, mustard, soy sauce, garlic, ½ teaspoon salt and ½ teaspoon pepper in a small bowl.

3. Thinly slice pork on diagonal. Thread onto eight 10-inch skewers. Season with remaining ½ teaspoon salt and remaining ½ teaspoon pepper.

4. Place skewers on grill or broiler-pan rack and brush with glaze, reserving leftover glaze. Broil or grill 3 minutes per side or until cooked through. Transfer skewers to a platter.

5. Boil remaining glaze in a saucepan 1 minute. Spoon over pork.

Roasted Pepper & Pork Sandwich

MAKES 4 servings

PREP 10 minutes

BROIL meat 20 minutes,
bread 3 to 4 minutes

———

PER SERVING
245 calories, 22 g protein,
7 g fat, 23 g carbohydrate,
468 mg sodium,
52 mg cholesterol.

2 teaspoons chopped fresh thyme
½ teaspoon salt
¼ teaspoon black pepper
1 clove garlic, finely chopped
1 teaspoon olive oil
1 pork tenderloin (about ¾ pound), trimmed

GARLIC TOAST
1 teaspoon olive oil
1 clove garlic, mashed
2 teaspoons chopped fresh oregano
4 slices bread

1 jar (12 ounces) roasted red peppers, drained
Fresh thyme sprigs for garnish (optional)

1. Heat broiler; position broiler-pan rack 6 inches from heat.

2. Combine thyme, salt, pepper, garlic and oil in a small bowl. Rub over pork.

3. Broil pork 20 minutes or until internal temperature registers 160° on an instant-read thermometer. Remove meat from broiler and let stand 10 minutes; leave broiler on.

4. Meanwhile, prepare garlic toast: Combine oil, garlic and oregano in a small bowl; rub on 1 side of each slice bread. Place bread on a baking sheet, flavored side up, and broil a few minutes or until browned.

5. Place toasted bread on plates. Thinly slice pork; arrange with roasted red peppers on bread. Garnish with thyme sprigs if desired.

Roasted Pepper & Pork Sandwich,
opposite

Apricot-Glazed Pork Skewers,
opposite

Pork Marsala

MAKES 4 servings

PREP 10 minutes

COOK 10 minutes

___

PER SERVING
273 calories, 33 g protein,
12 g fat, 4 g carbohydrate,
69 mg sodium,
92 mg cholesterol.

4 boneless pork loin chops (about 1¼ pounds total)

1 tablespoon olive oil

1 small red onion, chopped

⅓ cup dry Marsala wine

Cooked white rice for serving (optional)

1. Place pork between sheets of plastic wrap. Lightly pound until ¼ inch thick.

2. Heat oil in a large skillet over medium-high heat. Add pork; cook until browned on both sides and cooked through, about 6 minutes, turning once. Transfer to a platter; keep warm.

3. Add onion to same skillet on medium-high heat, cooking until golden and tender, 2 to 3 minutes. Add wine; bring to boiling, scraping up any browned bits from bottom of skillet. Remove skillet from heat. Spoon sauce over pork. Serve with rice if desired.

Curried Pork with Pear & Apricots

MAKES 4 servings

PREP 20 minutes

COOK 45 minutes

___

PER SERVING
547 calories, 28 g protein,
20 g fat, 65 g carbohydrate,
738 mg sodium,
75 mg cholesterol.

1 tablespoon olive oil

4 boneless pork chops (about 1¼ pounds total), each about ½ inch thick

1 teaspoon curry powder

1¾ cups water

2 tablespoons balsamic vinegar

1 cup brown rice

⅓ cup chopped dried apricots

1¼ teaspoons salt

¼ cup fresh orange juice

¼ cup apricot jam

1 firm pear, peeled, cored and finely chopped

2 scallions, chopped, including part of the green, for garnish (optional)

1. Heat oil in a large nonstick skillet over medium-high heat. Add pork; brown on both sides, about 6 minutes.

2. Stir in curry powder; cook 30 seconds. Add water, vinegar, rice, apricots and salt. Bring to boiling. Lower heat; cover and cook 30 to 35 minutes or until rice is tender.

3. Push pork to side of skillet. Stir orange juice, jam and pear into rice. Arrange chops on top of rice. Cook, uncovered, another 5 minutes or until heated through. Garnish with scallions if desired.

Cajun Pork with Spicy Beans

MAKES 4 servings

PREP 10 minutes

COOK 14 minutes

—————

PER SERVING
401 calories, 37 g protein,
14 g fat, 44 g carbohydrate,
871 mg sodium,
71 mg cholesterol.

2 teaspoons Cajun spice mix

4 boneless pork chops (about 1¼ pounds total), each
   about ½ inch thick

1 tablespoon olive oil

1 medium-size red onion, chopped

1 sweet red pepper, cored, seeded and chopped

1 can (19 ounces) black beans, drained but not rinsed

1 can (8 ounces) no-salt-added corn niblets, drained

2 tablespoons prepared barbecue sauce

1. Sprinkle 1 teaspoon spice mix on both sides of chops.

2. Heat oil in a large nonstick skillet over medium heat. Add chops; cook 3 minutes.

3. Turn chops over. Add onion and pepper around meat in skillet; cover and cook 7 minutes.

4. Stir in remaining 1 teaspoon spice mix; cook 1 minute. Add beans, corn and barbecue sauce; simmer 2 to 3 minutes or until heated through and internal temperature of pork registers 160° on an instant-read thermometer.

Honey-Lemon Pork Chops

MAKES 4 servings

PREP 15 minutes

REFRIGERATE 4 hours

GRILL OR BROIL 10 to 12

minutes

—————

PER SERVING
341 calories, 44 g protein,
13 g fat, 9 g carbohydrate,
398 mg sodium,
125 mg cholesterol.

2 tablespoons honey

Finely grated rind of 1 lemon

2 tablespoons fresh lemon juice

1 tablespoon olive oil

1 tablespoon chopped fresh mint or ½ teaspoon dried
   mint, crushed

½ teaspoon salt

¼ teaspoon ground red pepper (cayenne)

4 rib pork chops (about 1¾ pounds total), each ¾ inch thick

1. Whisk together honey, lemon rind, lemon juice, oil, mint, salt and red pepper in a small glass measuring cup.

2. Place chops in a glass baking dish. Pour marinade over; turn chops to coat. Cover; refrigerate at least 4 hours or overnight, turning occasionally.

3. Prepare a hot grill or heat broiler; position grill rack or broiler-pan rack 4 inches from heat. Grill or broil 5 to 6 minutes per side or until internal temperature registers 160° on an instant-read thermometer.

Kielbasa Strata

MAKES 6 servings

PREP 10 minutes

BAKE at 375° for 30 minutes

PER SERVING
560 calories, 31 g protein,
30 g fat, 41 g carbohydrate,
1,108 mg sodium,
282 mg cholesterol.

6 eggs

1½ cups milk

2 tablespoons mustard

½ teaspoon dried sage

¼ teaspoon salt

¼ teaspoon black pepper

12 thick slices white bread

½ pound kielbasa, cut into ½-inch-thick slices

1 package (10 ounces) frozen chopped spinach, thawed
and squeezed dry

2 cups shredded Swiss cheese

1. Heat oven to 375°. Coat a 13 x 9 x 2-inch baking dish with nonstick cooking spray.

2. Whisk eggs, milk, mustard, sage, salt and pepper in a large bowl. Add bread slices and press down gently to submerge. Remove 6 slices, letting excess drip back into bowl, and lay them in bottom of prepared baking dish. Top with half of kielbasa, half of spinach and half of cheese. Place remaining bread on top and repeat layering with remaining kielbasa, spinach and cheese. Pour egg mixture over the top.

3. Bake, covered, in heated 375° oven 15 minutes. Uncover; bake 15 minutes.

Easy Sausage Bake

MAKES 6 servings

PREP 10 minutes

BAKE at 350° for 40 to
45 minutes

PER SERVING
420 calories, 15 g protein,
15 g fat, 53 g carbohydrate,
979 mg sodium,
31 mg cholesterol.

1 tablespoon garlic-flavored olive oil

4 links hot or sweet Italian sausage (¾ pound total),
cooked

1 cup frozen pepper strips (about 4 ounces)

1 cup frozen chopped onion

2 cups chicken broth

1½ cups arborio rice

1 cup prepared spaghetti sauce

½ cup grated Parmesan cheese

1. Heat oven to 350°.

2. Cut sausages into ½-inch-thick slices; cut peppers into ½-inch pieces. Toss together sausage, peppers, onion and oil in a shallow 2-quart baking dish.

3. Bring broth to boiling. Add to dish along with rice and spaghetti sauce; stir to combine. Add ¼ cup Parmesan; stir. Cover dish with aluminum foil.

4. Bake in heated 350° oven 30 to 35 minutes or until liquid is absorbed. Uncover; stir. Sprinkle with remaining ¼ cup Parmesan. Bake, uncovered, 10 minutes.

Polenta & Sausage

MAKES 4 servings

PREP 10 minutes

COOK 22 minutes

BROIL 2 minutes

PER SERVING
382 calories, 17 g protein,
16 g fat, 43 g carbohydrate,
987 mg sodium,
45 mg cholesterol.

1 box (6 ounces) polenta

1 pound hot or sweet Italian sausage, cut into ¼-inch-
   thick slices

1 onion, chopped

2 cloves garlic, chopped

1 can (16 ounces) plum tomatoes

1. Prepare polenta according to package directions; spoon into a 9-inch pie plate; smooth top.

2. Coat a medium-size nonstick skillet with nonstick cooking spray; heat over medium heat. Add sausage, onion and garlic; sauté until sausage is no longer pink, about 8 minutes. Add tomatoes; cook, breaking up tomatoes with a wooden spoon, 14 minutes or until slightly thickened.

3. Heat broiler.

4. Cut polenta into 4 wedges. Place on broiler-pan rack. Broil 1 minute per side or until lightly browned. Serve topped with sauce.

Polenta & Sausage

Ham Skewers with Pink Aioli

quick **COOK**

MAKES 6 servings
PREP about 25 minutes
COOK 7 minutes
GRILL 3 minutes

───────

PER SERVING
303 calories, 9 g protein,
25 g fat, 11 g carbohydrate,
778 mg sodium,
34 mg cholesterol.

¾ pound red or white new potatoes, quartered

3 cloves garlic, pressed or mashed

¾ cup mayonnaise

1 teaspoon olive oil

1 tablespoon lemon juice

Pinch black pepper

1 jar (7 ounces) roasted red peppers, drained

½ pound ham (whole piece) cut into 1-inch cubes

1. Prepare a hot grill; place grill rack 6 inches from heat. Place eighteen 8-inch wooden skewers in a container of warm water to soak.

2. Place potatoes in a medium-size saucepan with enough water to cover. Bring to boiling; cook 7 minutes or until barely tender. Drain and rinse. Allow to cool to prevent pieces from splitting when threaded onto skewers.

3. Meanwhile, to make pink aioli, combine garlic, mayonnaise, oil, lemon juice and black pepper in a food processor or blender. Chop about 3 tablespoons roasted peppers and add to container. Whirl until mixture is smooth. Pour into a serving bowl.

4. Slice remaining peppers into 1-inch squares.

5. When potatoes are cool, remove skewers from water. Thread each with 1 cube ham, 1 piece pepper and 1 piece potato. Grill or broil skewers 3 minutes, turning once. Serve with pink aioli.

Fast Fix

Easy-on-You Ham

HERE IS THE LOW-DOWN on warming a ham, plus ideas for glazes in a hurry. Begin with a fully cooked 12- to 16-pound bone-in or boneless ham. Place, fat side up, in a roasting pan, brush with one of the glazes and roast at 325° for 15 minutes per pound or until internal temperature registers 140° on an instant-read thermometer. Brush occasionally with glaze.

Tart-Sweet Mix

▶ Combine ½ cup whole-berry cranberry sauce and ½ cup applesauce in a small bowl, mashing with back of a spoon until spreadable.

▶ Makes about 1 cup.

Hot-Sweet Mix

▶ Mix 1 can (8 ounces) crushed pineapple with 1 finely chopped jalapeño chile and 2 tablespoons chopped fresh cilantro in a small bowl.

▶ Makes about 1 cup.

One-Step Glazes

▶ Use any of the following, straight from the jar: maple syrup, orange marmalade, apricot preserves, ginger preserves, honey mustard.

Lamb Keftedes

quick PREP

MAKES 8 servings

PREP 10 minutes

BAKE at 375° for 12 to 15 minutes

BROIL 6 minutes

———————

PER SERVING
245 calories, 21 g protein,
16 g fat, 4 g carbohydrate,
290 mg sodium,
102 mg cholesterol.

2 pounds ground lamb, meat loaf mix or ground beef

⅔ cup fresh bread crumbs

2 cloves garlic, finely chopped

1 medium-size onion, finely chopped

2 tablespoons red-wine vinegar

1 teaspoon dried oregano

1 teaspoon dried mint

¾ teaspoon salt

¼ teaspoon black pepper

1 egg, slightly beaten

Tzatziki for serving (optional, recipe follows)

1. Heat oven to 375°.

2. Combine lamb, bread crumbs, garlic, onion, vinegar, oregano, mint, salt, pepper and egg in a large bowl.

3. Scoop heaping 1 tablespoonful from the mixture; form into a 2-inch ball with your hands. Repeat. (You should have about 32 balls.) Place on 2 ungreased rimmed baking sheets, dividing equally.

4. Bake in heated 375° oven 15 minutes. Remove baking sheets from oven and increase oven temperature to broil.

5. Run meatballs under broiler to brown slightly; about 3 minutes per pan or until cooked through. Transfer to a platter. If desired, serve with wooden picks and tzatziki.

Tzatziki

no COOK

MAKES 2½ cups

PREP 10 minutes

REFRIGERATE 1 hour

———————

PER ¼ CUP
33 calories, 3 g protein,
1 g fat, 4 g carbohydrate,
86 mg sodium,
3 mg cholesterol.

1 container (16 ounces) plain low-fat yogurt

1 medium-size seedless cucumber, peeled

2 cloves garlic, peeled

1½ tablespoons snipped fresh dill or 1½ teaspoons dried dillweed

2 tablespoons red-wine vinegar

¼ teaspoon salt

⅛ teaspoon black pepper

1. Line a strainer with paper toweling or cheesecloth. Spoon in yogurt; refrigerate up to 1 hour to drain liquid.

2. Meanwhile, grate cucumber into a medium-size bowl using large holes on a grater. Grate garlic into bowl using small holes on grater.

3. Add drained yogurt, dill, vinegar, salt and pepper; stir to blend.

Vegetables

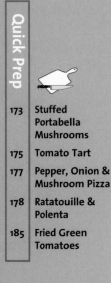

Basil Stuffed Eggplant

MAKES 6 servings
PREP 10 minutes
BROIL 14 minutes

PER SERVING
324 calories, 15 g protein,
13 g fat, 38 g carbohydrate,
724 mg sodium,
38 mg cholesterol.

1 large eggplant (about 1½ pounds)
½ teaspoon salt
½ teaspoon black pepper
1 tablespoon grated Parmesan cheese
1 jar (12 ounces) roasted red peppers, drained and
   patted dry
4 ounces thinly sliced Fontina or mozzarella cheese
¾ cup ricotta cheese
6 fresh basil leaves
12 slices seeded Italian bread, toasted

1. Heat broiler; coat broiler-pan rack with nonstick cooking spray and position 6 inches from heat.

2. Cut eggplant lengthwise into 12 equal slices. Season with salt and pepper. Place on prepared broiler-pan rack.

3. Broil eggplant until golden, about 5 minutes per side. Sprinkle top with Parmesan.

4. Layer each slice with red peppers, Fontina, ricotta and basil. Roll up each slice jelly-roll fashion. Place on pan, seam side down.

5. Broil until heated through and cheese is melted, about 4 minutes. Place each roll on 1 slice toast.

Basil Stuffed Eggplant

Vegetables

Roasted Asparagus

MAKES 6 servings

PREP 5 minutes

ROAST at 350° for 25 minutes

───────────

PER SERVING
31 calories, 1 g protein,
2 g fat, 2 g carbohydrate,
93 mg sodium,
0 mg cholesterol.

1 pound asparagus, tough ends trimmed and
   stems peeled
½ teaspoon grated lemon rind
1 tablespoon fresh lemon juice
1 tablespoon olive oil
¼ teaspoon salt
⅛ teaspoon freshly ground black pepper
2 cloves garlic, crushed

1. Heat oven to 350°.

2. Mix asparagus, lemon rind, lemon juice, oil, salt and pepper in a 12 x 8-inch glass baking dish. Arrange asparagus in a single layer. Place garlic on top.

3. Bake in heated 350° oven 25 minutes or until fork-tender. Before serving, remove and discard garlic.

Sautéed Green Beans

MAKES 6 servings

PREP 5 minutes

COOK 12 minutes

───────────

PER SERVING
71 calories, 2 g protein,
5 g fat, 6 g carbohydrate,
547 mg sodium,
0 mg cholesterol.

1 pound green beans, trimmed
2 tablespoons olive oil
3 cloves garlic, cut in half
¼ teaspoon salt
1 tablespoon sliced almonds or chopped walnuts

1. Cook green beans in a large pot of lightly salted boiling water 5 to 8 minutes or until crisp-tender. Drain; cool under cold running water or submerge in an ice bath until well chilled. Drain; shake off excess water.

2. Heat oil in a large skillet over low heat. Add garlic; cook 5 minutes. Add green beans, salt and almonds; heat through, 2 minutes. Before serving, remove and discard garlic.

Glazed Baby Carrots

MAKES 6 servings

PREP 2 minutes

COOK 8 to 10 minutes

————

PER SERVING
52 calories, 1 g protein,
2 g fat, 8 g carbohydrate,
72 mg sodium,
5 mg cholesterol.

1 bag (1 pound) fresh baby carrots
1 tablespoon butter
1 tablespoon dark-brown sugar
⅛ teaspoon ground cinnamon
⅛ teaspoon salt

1. Cook carrots in a medium-size pot of boiling water 8 to 10 minutes or until fork-tender.

2. Drain carrots and return to hot pot. Add butter, sugar, cinnamon and salt; stir to coat carrots evenly. Heat through.

Minted Peas & Carrots

MAKES 8 servings

PREP 10 minutes

————

PER SERVING
81 calories, 5 g protein,
2 g fat, 12 g carbohydrate,
166 mg sodium,
4 mg cholesterol.

2 tablespoons reduced-fat mayonnaise
2 tablespoons reduced-fat sour cream
1½ teaspoons cider vinegar
½ teaspoon sugar
4 cups frozen peas, thawed
1 medium-size carrot, shredded
2 tablespoons chopped fresh mint
2 slices turkey bacon, cooked and crumbled

Mix mayonnaise, sour cream, vinegar and sugar in a medium-size bowl. Add peas, carrot and mint; stir to combine. Top with bacon.

Smoky Black-Eyed Peas

MAKES 8 servings

PREP 5 minutes

STAND 30 minutes

(or refrigerate 24 hours)

————

PER SERVING
218 calories, 20 g protein,
9 g fat, 13 g carbohydrate,
190 mg sodium,
47 mg cholesterol.

1½ pounds cooked barbecued pork ribs
2 cans (15 ounces each) black-eyed peas, drained
2 cups chunky-style salsa

1. Pull meat from rib bones and place in a large bowl. Add peas and salsa; stir to combine.

2. Cover bowl; let stand 30 minutes or refrigerate up to 24 hours to blend flavors. Serve at room temperature.

Vegetable Stir-Fry

Vegetable Stir-Fry

MAKES 4 servings

PREP 15 minutes

COOK 10 minutes

PER SERVING
162 calories, 10 g protein,
7 g fat, 16 g carbohydrate,
670 mg sodium,
0 mg cholesterol.

⅔ cup beef broth

¼ cup red-wine vinegar

¼ cup reduced-sodium soy sauce

2 tablespoons sugar

1 tablespoon cornstarch

2 teaspoons dark Asian sesame oil

1 tablespoon vegetable oil

4 cloves garlic, finely chopped

1 teaspoon ground ginger

3 Japanese eggplants, quartered lengthwise

3 scallions, cut into 3-inch pieces

16 ounces firm tofu, drained and cut into chunks

8 radishes, halved

1. Whisk together broth, vinegar, soy sauce, sugar, cornstarch and sesame oil in a large bowl.

2. Heat 1 teaspoon vegetable oil in a large nonstick skillet. Add garlic and ginger and stir-fry over medium-high heat until softened and lightly browned, 2 minutes. Transfer garlic mixture to bowl with beef broth mixture.

3. Heat remaining 2 teaspoons vegetable oil in same skillet over medium-high heat. Add eggplant and scallions; stir-fry until eggplant and scallions are just tender, about 8 minutes. Add tofu and radishes; add broth-garlic mixture. Stir gently over high heat until sauce boils and thickens.

Veggie Burger

30 minutes **MAX**

MAKES 6 burgers

PREP 10 minutes

COOK 4 minutes

GRILL OR BROIL 10 minutes

———

PER SERVING
266 calories, 14 g protein,
9 g fat, 35 g carbohydrate,
354 mg sodium,
46 mg cholesterol.

1 tablespoon vegetable oil

½ cup chopped onion

2 cups shredded zucchini

1 cup chopped mushrooms

1 cup sodium-free dry seasoned bread crumbs

1 teaspoon dried Italian seasoning

1 clove garlic, finely chopped

1 egg, slightly beaten

3 tablespoons prepared pizza sauce

1 cup shredded low-fat cheese (4 ounces)

6 whole-wheat rolls

1 bunch watercress

6 thick tomato slices

1. Prepare a medium-hot grill or heat broiler; lightly coat grill rack or broiler-pan rack with nonstick cooking spray and position 4 inches from heat.

2. Heat oil in a medium-size nonstick skillet over medium-low heat. Add onion; sauté 4 minutes or until softened. Remove from heat.

3. Squeeze excess moisture from zucchini. Combine zucchini with cooked onion, mushrooms, bread crumbs, Italian seasoning, garlic, egg and pizza sauce in a large bowl. Stir in cheese. Shape into 6 equal patties.

4. Grill or broil patties 10 minutes or until internal temperature registers 160° on an instant-read thermometer, turning once.

5. Line each roll with watercress. Add a patty and top with a tomato slice.

Veggie Burger

Broccoli with Red-Pepper Butter

5 ingredients or LESS

MAKES 4 servings
PREP 10 minutes
COOK 20 minutes

PER SERVING
113 calories, 4 g protein,
9 g fat, 7 g carbohydrate,
165 mg sodium,
23 mg cholesterol.

2 cups broccoli flowerets
3 tablespoons butter
1 sweet red pepper, cored, seeded and cut into
   thin strips
¼ teaspoon salt
⅛ teaspoon black pepper

1. Cook broccoli in a medium-size pot of lightly salted boiling water 5 to 6 minutes or until tender. Drain; keep warm.

2. Meanwhile, heat 2 tablespoons butter in a medium-size nonstick skillet over medium heat. Add red pepper; reduce heat to medium-low; cook, stirring occasionally, 20 minutes. Remove from heat. Add remaining tablespoon butter, salt and black pepper.

3. Place broccoli in a serving bowl. Pour butter over top.

Fast Fix

Side Dishes 1, 2, 3!

EVERYONE'S LOOKING for quick and tasty ways to accentuate a main-course meat dish. Here they are.

Zesty Roast Onions

▶ Spray a baking dish with nonstick cooking spray.

▶ Add 4 quartered medium-size onions, 3 tablespoons Worcestershire sauce and ½ teaspoon dried thyme; toss to coat.

▶ Bake at 350° until tender, about 45 minutes.

▶ Sprinkle with salt.

▶ Makes 4 to 6 servings.

Summertime Tomatoes

▶ Halve 2 ripe tomatoes; sprinkle with 2 cloves finely chopped garlic, 1 teaspoon chili powder and salt and black pepper to taste.

▶ Place on a baking sheet. Bake at 400° until tomatoes are slightly soft, about 15 minutes.

▶ Top tomatoes with ¾ cup Mexican shredded 4-cheese blend. Broil briefly to melt cheese.

▶ Makes 4 servings.

Zucchini Salsa Stir-Fry

▶ Heat 1 tablespoon vegetable oil in a large nonstick skillet; add 2 chopped medium-size zucchini and 1 diced small onion. Sauté over high heat about 5 minutes.

▶ Stir in 2 cups fresh or frozen corn kernels and ⅔ cup salsa. Heat through.

▶ Makes 4 to 6 servings.

172

Family Circle **Quick & Easy** Recipes

Cheesy Broccoli

MAKES 10 servings

PREP 15 minutes

BAKE at 350° for 20 minutes

───────

PER SERVING
117 calories, 8 g protein,
8 g fat, 4 g carbohydrate,
183 mg sodium,
25 mg cholesterol.

8 cups broccoli flowerets

2 cups shredded cheddar cheese (8 ounces)

2 tablespoons grated Parmesan cheese

½ teaspoon black pepper

1. Heat oven to 350°. Lightly coat a 2½-quart shallow baking dish with nonstick cooking spray.

2. Cook broccoli in a large pot of lightly salted boiling water 5 to 6 minutes or until just crisp-tender. Drain; cool under running cold water. Blot dry.

3. Place half of broccoli in prepared baking dish. Sprinkle half of cheddar, Parmesan and pepper on top. Repeat, using remaining broccoli, cheddar, Parmesan and pepper.

4. Bake in heated 350° oven 20 minutes or until heated through.

Note: Recipe can be prepared ahead through step 3 and refrigerated, covered, up to 1 day. Increase the cooking time by about 10 minutes when baking.

Stuffed Portabella Mushrooms

MAKES 4 servings

PREP 5 minutes

COOK 6 minutes

BAKE at 375° for 20 minutes

───────

PER SERVING
416 calories, 31 g protein,
24 g fat, 26 g carbohydrate,
988 mg sodium,
79 mg cholesterol.

11 portabella mushrooms (about 2½ pounds total)

3 links hot Italian sausage (½ pound total), casings
   removed

1 large onion, diced

¼ teaspoon salt

¼ teaspoon black pepper

¾ teaspoon dried basil

1⅓ cups fresh bread crumbs

1¼ cups shredded Fontina cheese

1. Chop 3 mushrooms; you should have about 4 cups. Trim small stems from remaining mushrooms and add to chopped mushrooms. Set aside chopped mushrooms and remaining 8 mushroom caps.

2. Heat oven to 375°.

3. Sauté sausage and onion in a large nonstick skillet over medium-high heat 3 minutes, breaking up sausage with a wooden spoon. Add chopped mushrooms and cook 3 minutes, stirring occasionally. Remove from heat. Stir in salt, pepper, basil, bread crumbs and Fontina.

4. Turn reserved portabella caps upside down. Press sausage mixture into caps, dividing equally.

5. Place filled caps on a baking sheet. Bake in heated 375° oven 20 minutes.

Grilled Pepper & Zucchini Sandwich

MAKES 6 servings
PREP 5 minutes
MARINATE 20 minutes
BROIL 13 minutes

———

PER SERVING
334 calories, 14 g protein,
15 g fat, 36 g carbohydrate,
568 mg sodium,
30 mg cholesterol.

2 medium-size zucchini, each cut lengthwise
   into 6 slices
2 sweet red peppers, each cored, seeded and cut
   lengthwise into 6 pieces
½ cup bottled Italian salad dressing
12 slices Italian bread
12 thin slices mozzarella cheese (about 8 ounces)

1. Combine zucchini and peppers in a large plastic food-storage bag; add 5 tablespoons dressing, seal and let stand 20 minutes.

2. Heat broiler; coat broiler-pan rack with nonstick cooking spray and position 4 inches from heat.

3. Remove vegetables from marinade. Place vegetables on broiler-pan rack and broil 12 minutes, turning once. Remove from broiler; keep broiler on.

4. Meanwhile, toast bread, then brush 6 slices with remaining 3 tablespoons dressing.

5. Divide broiled vegetables among the 6 brushed slices; top each with 2 slices mozzarella. Broil 1 minute to melt cheese. Top with remaining bread.

Tomato Tart, *opposite*

Tomato Tart

MAKES 8 servings

PREP 10 minutes

CHILL 30 minutes

BAKE crust at 400° for 20 minutes; tart at 400° for 30 minutes

STAND 10 minutes

———————

PER SERVING
276 calories, 6 g protein, 19 g fat , 21 g carbohydrate, 326 mg sodium, 46 mg cholesterol.

3 medium-size tomatoes, all red or a mix of red and yellow (about 1 pound total)

1 refrigerated ready-to-use piecrust

¼ teaspoon dried thyme

¼ teaspoon dried basil

¼ teaspoon dried rosemary, crushed

1 egg white

2 tablespoons prepared or homemade pesto (recipe, page 231)

½ cup crumbled feta cheese (3 ounces)

⅛ teaspoon salt

Pinch black pepper

1 tablespoon olive oil

Fresh basil leaves for garnish (optional)

1. Thinly slice tomatoes. Place on paper toweling to drain for about 30 minutes; turn slices over after 15 minutes.

2. Heat oven to 400°.

3. On a lightly floured surface, roll piecrust into a 13-inch round. Sprinkle thyme, basil and rosemary over crust and pat in with rolling pin. Press into bottom and up sides of an 11-inch tart pan with a removable bottom. Prick bottom of crust with a fork; line shell with aluminum foil. Fill with pie weights or dried beans.

4. Bake crust in bottom third of heated 400° oven 15 minutes. Remove from oven; remove foil. Brush crust with egg white. Bake in oven 5 minutes. Transfer pan to a wire rack to cool. Leave oven on.

5. Spread crust with pesto. Sprinkle with cheese. Decoratively arrange tomato slices in concentric circles. Sprinkle with salt and pepper.

6. Bake in heated 400° oven 30 minutes or until tomatoes are soft and crust is golden brown.

7. Remove tart from oven and brush with oil. Cool on a wire rack 10 minutes. Remove pan sides. Garnish with basil leaves if desired.

Steamed Vegetables Mornay

MAKES 6 servings

PREP 5 minutes

COOK 16 minutes

_____

PER SERVING
124 calories, 6 g protein,
7 g fat, 10 g carbohydrate,
357 mg sodium,
22 mg cholesterol.

1 tablespoon butter

1½ tablespoons flour

1½ cups milk

½ teaspoon salt

¼ teaspoon black pepper

Pinch ground nutmeg

⅓ cup shredded Gruyère cheese (1½ ounces)

2 tablespoons grated Parmesan cheese

2 teaspoons Dijon mustard

Pinch ground red pepper (cayenne)

1 bag (1 pound) precut assorted raw vegetables

1. Melt butter in a medium-size saucepan over medium heat. Whisk in flour and cook 1 minute. Add half of milk and whisk until thickened, about 2 minutes. Add remaining milk. Bring to boiling over medium-high heat, whisking constantly. Cook, continuing to whisk, 2 to 3 minutes or until thickened. Remove from heat and whisk in salt, black pepper, nutmeg, cheeses, mustard and red pepper.

2. Meanwhile, steam vegetables in a steamer basket in a covered large pot over gently boiling water until tender, about 10 minutes.

3. Remove vegetables to a serving bowl. Pour sauce over vegetables.

Spinach & Shallot Frittata

MAKES 6 servings

PREP 10 minutes

COOK 18 minutes

BROIL 2 minutes

_____

PER SERVING
168 calories, 15 g protein,
10 g fat, 4 g carbohydrate,
501 mg sodium,
228 mg cholesterol.

6 eggs

6 egg whites

½ teaspoon salt

¼ teaspoon black pepper

¼ teaspoon ground nutmeg

½ cup shredded Fontina cheese

3 slices bacon, diced

1 shallot, finely chopped

1 package (10 ounces) frozen chopped spinach,
    thawed and squeezed dry

2 tablespoons grated Parmesan cheese

1. Heat broiler; position oven rack 6 inches from heat.

2. Whisk together eggs, egg whites, salt and pepper in a large bowl. Stir in nutmeg and Fontina.

3. Cook bacon in a large ovenproof nonstick skillet over medium heat until crispy, 3 to 4 minutes. Remove bacon to paper toweling; reserve. Wipe excess bacon fat from skillet.

4. Add shallot to skillet; cook over medium heat 3 minutes, adding a teaspoon of water if necessary to prevent sticking. Add spinach; cook 1 minute. Pour in egg mixture. Stir in reserved bacon. Cook over low heat, stirring occasionally, until eggs are firm and set, about 10 minutes. Remove from heat. Sprinkle top of frittata with Parmesan.

5. Broil in skillet until golden, about 2 minutes. Cut into wedges.

Pepper, Onion & Mushroom Pizza

quick
PREP

MAKES 4 servings

PREP 10 minutes

COOK sauce 8 minutes

BAKE al 450° for 22 minutes

PER SERVING
369 calories, 11 g protein,
11 g fat, 45 g carbohydrate,
1,078 mg sodium,
25 mg cholesterol.

2 sweet green peppers, cored, seeded and thinly sliced

1 large red or yellow onion, sliced

1 can (15 ounces) reduced-sodium stewed tomatoes

1 teaspoon tomato paste

2 teaspoons chopped fresh sage or ¾ teaspoon
   dried sage (optional)

½ teaspoon dried basil

½ teaspoon dried oregano

1 package (10 ounces) refrigerated pizza dough

1½ cups shredded part-skim mozzarella cheese
   (6 ounces)

1 cup sliced mushrooms

2 tablespoons grated Parmesan cheese

1. Combine peppers, onion, stewed tomatoes, tomato paste, sage if desired, basil and oregano in a large skillet. Bring to simmering and cook, covered, 5 minutes. Uncover; cook 3 minutes or until sauce is thickened. Allow to cool.

2. Meanwhile, heat oven to 450°. Lightly coat a 12-inch pizza pan with nonstick cooking spray.

3. Roll dough out to 13-inch round on a floured surface. Fit into prepared pizza pan. Bake in heated 450° oven 10 minutes.

4. Remove crust from oven and spread sauce mixture evenly on top, leaving a 1-inch border. Sprinkle with mozzarella, mushrooms and Parmesan. Return pizza to oven. Bake 12 minutes or until golden.

Ratatouille & Polenta

quick PREP

MAKES 8 servings
PREP 10 minutes
COOK 30 minutes
BROIL polenta 3 minutes

———————

PER SERVING
218 calories, 6 g protein,
5 g fat, 39 g carbohydrate,
453 mg sodium,
0 mg cholesterol.

2 tablespoons olive oil

1 large onion, sliced

4 cloves garlic, finely chopped

2 sweet green peppers, cored, seeded and cut into chunks

2 medium-size zucchini, cut into chunks

1 eggplant (about 1 pound), cut into chunks

1 can (28 ounces) peeled tomatoes, drained and chopped

½ cup dry white wine

1 teaspoon dried oregano

1 teaspoon salt

½ teaspoon black pepper

1 bay leaf

2 tablespoons chopped fresh parsley

1 package (1 pound) ready-to-heat polenta

1. Heat oil in a large saucepan. Add onion; cook over medium-high heat until softened, about 3 minutes. Add garlic, green peppers, zucchini, eggplant, tomatoes, wine, oregano, salt, black pepper and bay leaf. Bring to boiling; cover and simmer 15 minutes. Uncover; cook 10 minutes more or until liquid is reduced by half. Remove from heat; stir in parsley.

2. Heat broiler; position oven rack 4 inches from heat. Coat a baking dish with nonstick cooking spray. Cut polenta into 8 rounds; arrange in prepared dish.

3. Broil polenta until it is lightly golden, about 3 minutes. Transfer to a platter. Remove bay leaf from ratatouille; spoon over polenta.

Ratatouille & Polenta

Salsa, Bean & Cheese Pizza

MAKES 4 servings

PREP 10 minutes

COOK 5 minutes

BAKE at 425° for 8 minutes

———

PER SERVING
419 calories, 24 g protein,
6 g fat, 52 g carbohydrate,
817 mg sodium,
30 mg cholesterol.

1 can (15 ounces) black beans, drained and rinsed

1 can (14¾ ounces) salsa-style tomatoes, drained

1 ready-to-use thin-crust pizza shell (12-inch, 1 pound)

1 cup shredded Monterey Jack cheese (4 ounces)

4 scallions, chopped, including part of the green

1. Heat oven to 425°.

2. Cook beans and tomatoes in a medium-size saucepan over medium heat until heated through, about 5 minutes.

3. Sprinkle pizza crust with half of cheese and all the scallions. Spoon bean mixture on top; spread to cover entire surface. Sprinkle evenly with remaining cheese.

4. Bake in heated 425° oven 8 minutes or until pizza is heated through.

Veggie-Hummus Wrap

MAKES 4 servings

PREP 15 minutes

———

PER SERVING
297 calories, 8 g protein,
9 g fat, 46 g carbohydrate,
903 mg sodium,
2 mg cholesterol.

2 cups coarsely chopped seedless cucumber

1½ cups seeded, diced tomato

¼ cup pitted, diced Kalamata olives

¼ teaspoon salt

½ teaspoon black pepper

½ cup plain low-fat yogurt

1 teaspoon chopped fresh mint

8 low-fat flour tortillas (6-inch)

½ cup prepared hummus

1 cup alfalfa sprouts or shredded green-leaf lettuce

1. Mix cucumber, tomato, olives, salt, pepper, yogurt and mint in a medium-size bowl.

2. Warm tortillas according to package directions.

3. Spread each tortilla with 1 tablespoon hummus. Add 2 tablespoons sprouts and ½ cup cucumber mixture to each; roll up.

Scallion-Potato Pancakes

MAKES 12 pancakes

PREP 15 minutes

COOK about 8 minutes

———

PER PANCAKE
88 calories, 2 g protein,
5 g fat, 8 g carbohydrate,
103 mg sodium,
36 mg cholesterol.

1 all-purpose potato (¾ pound), peeled
1 sweet potato (½ pound), peeled
1 tablespoon fresh lemon juice
5 scallions, sliced lengthwise into 3-inch
   matchstick strips
2 eggs, slightly beaten
½ teaspoon salt
¼ teaspoon black pepper
¼ teaspoon dried tarragon
3 tablespoons all-purpose flour
1 cup vegetable oil

1. Grate both potatoes into a large bowl. Mix in lemon juice, scallions, eggs, salt, pepper, tarragon and flour.

2. Heat oil in a large nonstick skillet over medium-high heat. Using ¼ cup batter for each pancake (for a total of 12), drop potato mixture into oil; cook in batches if necessary. Flatten each dollop into a 4-inch pancake. Cook 4 minutes per side or until cooked through. Adjust heat to prevent burning. Use a slotted spoon to transfer pancakes to paper toweling to drain.

Scalloped Potatoes

MAKES 6 servings

PREP 15 minutes

BAKE at 450° for 40 minutes

———

PER SERVING
200 calories, 12 g protein,
5 g fat, 28 g carbohydrate,
340 mg sodium,
18 mg cholesterol.

2 pounds all-purpose potatoes, peeled and thinly sliced
1 tablespoon vegetable oil
½ teaspoon salt
⅛ teaspoon black pepper
1 cup low-fat (1%) milk
1 jar (6 ounces) roasted red peppers, drained and chopped
¼ cup chopped fresh parsley
1 cup shredded reduced-fat Jarlsberg cheese (4 ounces)
¼ cup grated Parmesan cheese

1. Heat oven to 450°. Coat an 8 x 8 x 2-inch or an 11 x 7 x 2-inch baking dish with nonstick cooking spray.

2. Arrange potato slices in overlapping rows in prepared baking dish. Drizzle with oil; sprinkle with salt and black pepper.

3. Bake in heated 450° oven 15 minutes. Remove from oven; keep oven on.

4. Meanwhile, heat milk in a small saucepan to a slow boil.

5. Pour milk over potatoes and sprinkle with roasted red peppers, parsley and cheeses. Bake 25 minutes more or until potatoes are tender and cheese is golden brown.

Vegetable & Egg Duets

ALMOST NOTHING is easier to make than eggs. And these variations show just how versatile this incredible ingredient can be when paired with zucchini, peppers, broccoli and more.

Western Omelets

▶ Heat 2 teaspoons vegetable oil in a medium-size skillet. Add 1 chopped medium-size zucchini, ¼ pound chopped mushrooms and 1 chopped small onion; sauté until tender. Stir in 3 tablespoons marinara sauce.

▶ Whisk together 8 eggs, ½ cup water, ½ teaspoon salt and a pinch black pepper.

▶ Melt 1 tablespoon butter in each of 2 medium-size skillets over medium heat. Add half of egg mixture to each. Cook until no longer runny.

▶ Spoon vegetables over eggs, dividing equally. Fold each omelet in half.

▶ Makes 4 servings.

Breakfast Burrito

▶ Heat 1 tablespoon vegetable oil in a small skillet. Add 1 chopped small sweet red or green pepper and 1 chopped small red onion; sauté until tender.

▶ Whisk together 4 eggs, 1 tablespoon water, ¼ teaspoon salt and sautéed vegetables in a medium-size bowl.

▶ Heat a nonstick skillet over medium heat. Add egg mixture and scramble until set.

▶ Meanwhile, heat 4 large flour tortillas according to package directions.

▶ Spread each tortilla with 2 tablespoons salsa, one-quarter of the eggs and 1 tablespoon shredded cheddar cheese; roll up.

▶ Place in a microwave-safe baking dish and heat in microwave at 100% power about 1 minute.

▶ Makes 4 servings.

Broccoli-Pasta Soufflé

▶ Following package directions and reserving cheese mix, prepare a 7.25-ounce box of macaroni and cheese. After 3 minutes of cooking, add 1 cup chopped broccoli to pot. Continue cooking until macaroni and broccoli are just tender; drain.

▶ Meanwhile, combine 2 egg yolks, 1 tablespoon mustard, ½ cup milk, ¼ cup butter, reserved cheese mix and 3 ounces diced smoked ham in a large bowl.

▶ Add hot macaroni to egg yolk mixture.

▶ Beat 2 egg whites in a medium-size bowl until stiff peaks form; fold into macaroni mixture.

▶ Pour into a buttered 2-quart baking dish. Bake at 350° about 20 minutes.

▶ Makes 6 servings.

Party Asparagus

▶ Thinly slice 8 to 10 trimmed asparagus spears.

▶ Heat 2 tablespoons oil in a large skillet over medium heat; add asparagus and cook 5 to 6 minutes or until tender.

▶ Cut ¼ pound smoked salmon into thin strips.

▶ Whisk together 4 whole eggs and 6 egg whites; stir in 1 to 2 teaspoons horseradish and the salmon.

▶ Add egg mixture to pan with asparagus. Scramble until eggs are set.

▶ Makes 4 servings.

Vegetables

Vegetarian Quesadillas

MAKES 6 servings

PREP 5 minutes

BROIL 1½ to 2 minutes

PER SERVING
535 calories, 20 g protein,
19 g fat, 71 g carbohydrate,
1358 mg sodium,
36 mg cholesterol.

12 flour tortillas (8-inch)
1 can (11 ounces) Mexicali corn, drained
1 can (15 ounces) small red or black beans, drained,
   rinsed and lightly mashed
2 cups taco-flavored shredded cheese (8 ounces)
1 can (4 ounces) diced green chiles

1. Heat broiler. Coat broiler-pan rack with nonstick cooking spray.

2. Place 6 tortillas on prepared rack. Lightly coat with nonstick cooking spray; flip over. Spread with corn, beans, cheese and chiles, dividing equally. Season with salt. Top with remaining 6 tortillas. Coat with nonstick cooking spray.

3. Broil 45 to 60 seconds on each side or until lightly browned. Turn broiler off; move pan to cooler part of oven. Let sit, with oven door ajar, 1 to 2 minutes, to be sure cheese is completely melted.

4. To serve, cut each quesadilla into quarters.

Vegetarian Quesadillas

Kielbasa-Topped Baked Potato

MAKES 4 servings

PREP 5 minutes

MICROWAVE 8 minutes

COOK 5 minutes

———

PER SERVING
341 calories, 16 g protein,
8 g fat, 68 g carbohydrate,
373 mg sodium,
47 mg cholesterol.

4 baking potatoes (about 9 ounces each), unpeeled,
   scrubbed and pricked several times with a fork
2 teaspoons olive oil
2 medium-size onions, chopped
2 sweet green peppers, cored, seeded and chopped
½ pound reduced-fat turkey kielbasa, coarsely chopped

1. Microwave potatoes at 100% power 8 minutes or until fork-tender, turning at least once.

2. Meanwhile, heat oil in a large nonstick skillet. Add onions, peppers and kielbasa and sauté over medium-high heat until onion is softened and mixture is heated through, 5 minutes.

3. Split top of each potato open. Spoon kielbasa mixture over top of each.

Crunchy Potato "Fries"

MAKES 4 servings

PREP 3 minutes

BAKE at 450° for 20 to 25 minutes

———

PER SERVING
225 calories, 6 g protein,
0 g fat, 51 g carbohydrate,
379 mg sodium,
0 mg cholesterol.

2 pounds baking potatoes
1 egg white
½ teaspoon salt
¼ teaspoon black pepper
¼ cup cornflake crumbs

1. Heat oven to 450°. Coat a baking sheet with nonstick cooking spray.

2. Cut potatoes into 3½ x ½ x ½-inch strips.

3. Beat egg white slightly in a medium-size bowl. Stir in salt and pepper. Dip potatoes in egg white. Place on prepared sheet. Sprinkle with crumbs.

4. Bake in heated 450° oven 20 to 25 minutes or until crisp and golden.

Tomato Mashed Potatoes

one POT

MAKES 6 servings

PREP 15 minutes

COOK 20 minutes

———

PER SERVING
195 calories, 4 g protein,
8 g fat, 28 g carbohydrate,
310 mg sodium,
22 mg cholesterol.

2 pounds Yukon gold potatoes or all-purpose potatoes,
   unpeeled and scrubbed
¾ teaspoon salt
3 tablespoons butter or margarine
⅓ cup milk
¼ cup shredded cheddar cheese (1 ounce)
6 to 8 dry-pack sun-dried tomatoes, chopped

1. Coarsely chop potatoes. Place in a large saucepan and add water to cover. Bring to boiling; boil 20 minutes or until fork-tender.

2. Drain potatoes; return to pot over low heat. Add salt, butter and milk; mash to desired consistency.

3. Add cheddar cheese and sun-dried tomatoes; mash well. Serve warm.

Fast Fix

Potato Power

THERE'S ALWAYS ROOM FOR POTATOES, especially when they are as easy to make as these recipes.

Barely Hot Potatoes

► Cut 1½ pounds red boiling potatoes into chunks. Toss in a microwave-safe baking dish with 2 tablespoons olive oil.

► Cover and microwave at 100% power 8 minutes, stirring once.

► Stir in 2 tablespoons hot pepper jelly; microwave 30 seconds more to blend flavors. Sprinkle with ¼ teaspoon salt.

► Makes about 4 servings.

Savory Topped Potatoes

► Microwave 4 baking potatoes at 100% power 10 minutes.

► Mix ½ cup sour cream; 3 chopped scallions, including part of the green; 2 tablespoons chopped pimientos and 2 tablespoons finely chopped pitted ripe black olives in a small bowl.

► Cut an X in each potato and fill with sour cream mixture.

► Sprinkle chili powder on top for color and flavor.

► Makes 4 servings.

Warm or Cold Italian Potatoes

► Boil 2 pounds red boiling potatoes 15 to 20 minutes or until tender. Drain; cut in half and place in a large bowl.

► Combine 3 slices cooked bacon, chopped; ½ cup Italian salad dressing and 2 tablespoons sugar in a cup.

► Stir dressing mixture into potatoes. Sprinkle chopped parsley on top. Toss; let stand briefly or refrigerate for a few hours to blend flavors.

► Makes about 6 servings.

Pepper-Jack Mashed Potatoes

MAKES 8 servings

PREP 5 minutes

COOK 25 minutes

PER SERVING
249 calories, 8 g protein,
13 g fat, 26 g carbohydrate,
264 mg sodium,
38 mg cholesterol.

2½ pounds Yukon gold or all-purpose potatoes,
   unpeeled and coarsely chopped
½ cup milk
¼ cup (½ stick) unsalted butter
1 cup shredded pepper-Jack cheese (4 ounces)
½ teaspoon salt
¼ teaspoon black pepper

1. Bring a large pot of lightly salted water to boiling. Add potatoes; cook 20 minutes or until fork-tender. Drain and return to pot.

2. Add milk and butter to potatoes. Mash potatoes, leaving lumps if desired. Add cheese, salt and pepper, blending well.

Fried Green Tomatoes

MAKES 6 servings

PREP 10 minutes

COOK about 30 minutes

PER SERVING
235 calories, 6 g protein,
15 g fat, 20 g carbohydrate,
363 mg sodium,
73 mg cholesterol.

3 large green tomatoes
Pinch salt
⅓ cup all-purpose flour
2 eggs
½ cup cornmeal
2 tablespoons grated Parmesan cheese
Pinch ground red pepper (cayenne)
¾ teaspoon salt
⅛ teaspoon black pepper
⅓ cup vegetable oil

1. Core tomatoes; slice each into four ¾-inch-thick slices. Drain slightly on paper toweling. Season with salt.

2. Place 3 shallow dishes on a work surface. Spread flour in one dish. Lightly beat eggs in second dish. In third dish, mix cornmeal, Parmesan, red pepper, salt and black pepper.

3. Heat oven to 200°. Line 2 baking sheets with paper toweling.

4. Dip each tomato slice first in flour to coat lightly, shaking off excess, then into egg and last into cornmeal mixture to coat.

5. Heat 3 tablespoons oil in a large skillet over medium-high heat. Working in batches, add tomato slices to skillet; cook 3 to 4 minutes per side or until coating is golden and crispy and tomatoes are tender. Add more oil as needed to prevent sticking. Transfer cooked tomato slices to prepared baking sheets; keep warm in heated 200° oven until all slices are cooked.

Vegetarian Chili

one POT

MAKES 8 servings

PREP 15 minutes

COOK 53 minutes

———

PER SERVING
205 calories, 6 g protein,
10 g fat, 26 g carbohydrate,
708 mg sodium,
0 mg cholesterol.

⅓ cup olive oil

2 cups chopped onion

2 cups chopped sweet green pepper

1 cup chopped carrot

4 cloves garlic, finely chopped

2 cups sliced mushrooms

½ teaspoon red-pepper flakes

2 teaspoons ground cumin

2 tablespoons chili powder

1 teaspoon dried oregano

1 teaspoon salt

1 can (28 ounces) diced tomatoes, undrained

1 can (14 ounces) diced tomatoes, undrained

1 cup cooked bulgur

1 can (15½ ounces) red kidney beans, drained and rinsed

1. Heat oil briefly in a large pot over high heat. Add onion, green pepper, carrot, garlic, mushrooms, red-pepper flakes, cumin, chili powder, oregano and salt and cook over high heat 5 minutes, stirring constantly.

2. Add both cans of tomatoes with their liquid. Bring to boiling, then reduce heat to medium-low. Simmer 45 minutes.

3. Add bulgur and beans to vegetable mixture; stir to combine. Simmer 3 minutes or until beans and bulgur are heated.

Tomatoes with Grilled Mozzarella

30 minutes MAX

MAKES 12 slices

PREP 10 minutes

BROIL 4 minutes

———

PER SERVING
126 calories, 8 g protein,
9 g fat, 3 g carbohydrate,
189 mg sodium,
30 mg cholesterol.

3 large tomatoes, cut into ½-inch-thick slices

1 tablespoon olive oil

¼ teaspoon salt

¼ teaspoon black pepper

24 basil leaves

1 pound fresh mozzarella, cut into ¼-inch-thick slices,
   or 1 package (16 ounces) shredded mozzarella

1. Heat broiler; coat broiler-pan rack with nonstick cooking spray and position 6 inches from heat.

2. Spread tomato slices on broiler-pan rack. Brush slices with oil; sprinkle with salt and pepper. Coarsely chop basil leaves; sprinkle over tomatoes. Distribute cheese over tomatoes, dividing evenly.

3. Broil 4 minutes or until cheese begins to melt and bubble.

Stuffed Cherry Tomatoes

MAKES 12 servings

PREP 20 minutes

PER SERVING
66 calories, 2 g protein,
5 g fat, 3 g carbohydrate,
89 mg sodium,
8 mg cholesterol.

24 cherry tomatoes
6 tablespoons light cream cheese
1 ounce blue cheese, crumbled
2 tablespoons mayonnaise
1 tablespoon milk
Pinch salt
Pinch black pepper
¼ cup shelled pistachios, chopped

1. Line a baking sheet with paper toweling. Slice tops off tomatoes; remove stems and reserve tops. Using a melon baller, hollow out tomatoes. Invert tomatoes on paper toweling to drain.

2. Blend cream cheese, blue cheese, mayonnaise, milk, salt and pepper in a medium-size bowl; don't blend totally smooth. Add pistachios. Chop reserved tomato tops; add to cheese mixture.

3. Spoon cheese mixture into a large pastry bag without a tip. Pipe into tomatoes. Alternatively, use a small spoon. Cover and refrigerate until ready to serve.

Vegetarian Chili, *opposite*

Black Bean Chili

MAKES 6 servings

PREP 5 minutes

COOK 30 minutes

───────────

PER SERVING
171 calories, 12 g protein,
9 g fat, 15 g carbohydrate,
589 mg sodium,
32 mg cholesterol.

1 tablespoon olive oil

1 large onion, finely chopped

1 sweet green pepper, cored, seeded and diced

1 clove garlic, finely chopped

½ pound ground turkey

¼ cup chili powder

1 tablespoon ground cumin

¾ teaspoon salt

½ teaspoon ground allspice

1 can (16 ounces) stewed tomatoes

1 cup water

2 medium-size zucchini, diced

1 can (19 ounces) black beans, drained and rinsed

1 can (4 ounces) chopped green chiles

¼ cup shredded cheddar cheese

¼ cup chopped scallions, including part of the green

1. Heat oil in a large skillet over medium-low heat. Add onion, pepper and garlic; sauté until softened, 8 minutes. Add ground turkey; sauté, breaking up turkey with a wooden spoon, 4 minutes or until no longer pink.

2. Stir in chili powder, cumin, salt and allspice; sauté 1 minute. Add tomatoes and water; simmer 7 minutes.

3. Stir in zucchini, beans and chiles; simmer, stirring occasionally, 10 minutes or until zucchini is tender.

4. Transfer to a serving dish. Sprinkle with cheese and scallions.

Note: Prepare chili a day ahead for maximum flavor. Refrigerate, covered. Reheat over low heat, stirring occasionally, 15 to 20 minutes.

Tex-Mex Zucchini

MAKES 8 servings

PREP 15 minutes

COOK 25 minutes

———

PER SERVING
173 calories, 10 g protein,
12 g fat, 8 g carbohydrate,
723 mg sodium,
30 mg cholesterol.

4 slices bacon, thinly sliced crosswise

6 medium-size zucchini, chopped

½ teaspoon onion powder

2 teaspoons chili powder

¼ teaspoon ground red pepper (cayenne)

¾ teaspoon salt

1½ cups salsa

1½ cups Mexican shredded 4-cheese blend
    (6 ounces)

1. Cook bacon in a large nonstick skillet over medium-high heat 6 to 7 minutes or until crisp.

2. Add zucchini, onion powder, chili powder, red pepper, salt and salsa; stir to combine. Bring to simmering over medium-high heat; cook 15 minutes, stirring occasionally.

3. Add 1 cup cheese; stir and cook 1 minute more.

4. Sprinkle top with remaining ½ cup cheese; cover and cook over low heat 2 minutes.

Marinated Zucchini & Mushrooms

MAKES 4 servings

PREP 5 minutes

COOK 2 minutes

REFRIGERATE overnight

———

PER SERVING
88 calories, 2 g protein,
7 g fat, 6 g carbohydrate,
5 mg sodium,
0 mg cholesterol.

¼ cup water

¼ cup cider vinegar

¼ cup olive oil

½ teaspoon dried Italian seasoning

½ teaspoon sugar

1 pound zucchini, sliced into coins

¼ pound mushrooms, halved

½ small red onion, thinly sliced

1. Combine water, vinegar, oil, Italian seasoning and sugar in a medium-size saucepan. Stir to combine. Add zucchini and mushrooms; stir and bring to simmering over medium-high heat. Simmer 2 minutes.

2. Remove pan from heat. Let cool, then refrigerate overnight.

3. When ready to serve, transfer zucchini mixture to a platter; scatter onion slices on top.

Desserts

Key Lime Pie

MAKES 8 servings

PREP 10 minutes

REFRIGERATE 4 hours

───────────

PER SERVING
184 calories, 5 g protein,
12 g fat, 17 g carbohydrate,
270 mg sodium,
5 mg cholesterol.

1 package (8 ounces) nonfat cream cheese, at room
   temperature
1 teaspoon grated lime rind
⅓ cup fresh lime juice (about 3 limes)
Sugar substitute to equal ¼ cup sugar
1 container (8 ounces) light frozen nondairy whipped
   topping, thawed
1 prepared graham cracker piecrust (8½-inch, 6 ounces)
8 thin lime slices for garnish (optional)

1. Place cream cheese, lime rind, lime juice and sugar substitute in a large bowl; beat with mixer on medium speed until fluffy, 3 to 4 minutes. Fold in whipped topping. Spoon evenly into piecrust.

2. Refrigerate 4 hours or until filling is firm. Garnish with lime slices if desired.

Key Lime Pie

Instant Strawberry Cheesecake Parfait

5 ingredients or **LESS**

MAKES 4 servings

PREP 10 minutes

PER SERVING
182 calories, 11 g protein,
2 g fat, 29 g carbohydrate,
451 mg sodium,
12 mg cholesterol.

8 ounces whipped nonfat cream cheese

2 tablespoons sugar

½ cup vanilla low-fat yogurt

2 cups fresh strawberries, hulled and sliced

4 reduced-fat chocolate graham crackers, crushed

1. Mix cream cheese and sugar in a small bowl. Gently stir in yogurt.

2. In each of 4 wine glasses, alternate layers of strawberries, yogurt mixture, crumbs, yogurt mixture and strawberries. Serve at once or refrigerate, covered, up to 8 hours.

Ricotta Tarts

quick PREP

MAKES 12 tarts

PREP 10 minutes

BAKE at 375° for 30 minutes

PER TART
238 calories, 8 g protein,
9 g fat, 30 g carbohydrate,
270 mg sodium,
30 mg cholesterol.

1 container (15 ounces) part-skim ricotta cheese

⅔ cup nonfat half-and-half

¼ cup nonfat cream cheese

1 egg

1 teaspoon grated lemon rind

1 teaspoon vanilla

½ cup sugar

⅓ cup all-purpose flour

Pinch ground nutmeg

2 packages (4 ounces each) graham cracker tart shells
   (12 shells total)

Fat-free frozen nondairy whipped topping, thawed, for
   garnish (optional)

Fresh raspberries for garnish (optional)

1. Heat oven to 375°.

2. Beat together ricotta, half-and-half and cream cheese with mixer on low speed in a large bowl until smooth, about 1 minute. Add egg, lemon rind and vanilla; beat until blended. Beat in sugar, flour and nutmeg.

3. Arrange 12 tart shells on a baking sheet. Divide cheese filling equally among tart shells.

4. Bake in heated 375° oven 30 minutes or until internal temperature of filling registers 160° on an instant-read thermometer.

5. Transfer tarts to a wire rack to cool. (Filling will deflate when removed from oven.) Garnish with a dollop of whipped topping and raspberries if desired.

Mandarin Crepes

MAKES 6 servings

PREP 20 minutes

COOK 10 minutes

———

PER SERVING
199 calories, 6 g protein,
8 g fat, 27 g carbohydrate,
91 mg sodium,
72 mg cholesterol.

CREPES

2 eggs

¾ cup skim milk

½ cup cornstarch

1 tablespoon vegetable oil

2 teaspoons sugar

¾ teaspoon baking powder

Or 12 purchased crepes

FILLING

2 cans (11 ounces each) Mandarin oranges in light syrup

2 teaspoons cornstarch, dissolved in 1 tablespoon water

1 tablespoon sugar

⅛ teaspoon ground cloves

6 tablespoons finely chopped toasted walnuts (recipe,
  page 231)
Fresh mint leaves for garnish (optional)

1. Prepare crepes: Whisk together eggs, milk, cornstarch, oil, sugar and baking powder in a small bowl until very smooth.

2. Heat a 6-inch nonstick skillet over medium heat until very hot. Pour 2 tablespoons crepe batter into skillet. Rotate to coat skillet; cook 30 seconds or until crepe is lightly browned on bottom and dry around edges on top. Use a thin metal spatula to turn crepe over. Cook 5 seconds more. Transfer to paper toweling. Repeat with remaining batter, stacking crepes with paper toweling between them, for a total of 12 crepes.

3. Prepare filling: Drain mandarin oranges, pouring syrup into a medium-size nonstick skillet. Stir in cornstarch mixture, sugar and cloves; cook over medium heat until thickened, 1 to 2 minutes. Stir in mandarin oranges; cook until heated through, about 1 minute.

4. To serve, place 2 open crepes on each dessert plate. Fill each with about 2 tablespoons orange mixture. Fold crepes in half, then in half again. Spoon another tablespoon orange mixture over each serving and sprinkle with 1 tablespoon walnuts. Serve warm. Garnish with mint leaves if desired.

Note: Crepes can be made up to 1 week ahead. Layer them between sheets of waxed paper, slide into a plastic food-storage bag, and refrigerate overnight or freeze up to 1 week; thaw at room temperature. To heat, microwave on 100% power 30 to 45 seconds, or warm in a heated 225° oven about 5 minutes.

Desserts

Chocolate-Walnut Tart

MAKES 8 servings

PREP 10 minutes

BAKE at 350° for 30 or 45 minutes (depending on size)

———

PER SERVING
405 calories, 7 g protein, 23 g fat, 49 g carbohydrate, 144 mg sodium, 96 mg cholesterol.

1 refrigerated ready-to-use piecrust
1 cup semisweet chocolate pieces
1 cup coarsely chopped walnuts
¼ cup (½ stick) salted butter
½ cup packed light-brown sugar
¾ cup dark corn syrup
3 eggs
1 teaspoon vanilla
Whipped cream for serving (optional)

1. Heat oven to 350°. Place oven rack in lower third of oven.

2. Fit piecrust into an 11- or 9-inch tart pan. Sprinkle chocolate and walnuts evenly over crust.

3. Microwave butter in a large glass measure, covered, at 100% power 40 seconds. Beat in brown sugar, corn syrup, eggs and vanilla until smooth. Pour into crust.

4. Bake in heated 350° oven, 30 minutes for 11-inch tart, 45 minutes for 9-inch tart. Let cool on a wire rack. Serve with whipped cream if desired.

Phyllo Pockets

MAKES 8 servings

PREP 20 minutes

BAKE at 400° for 6 to 8 minutes

———

PER SERVING
471 calories, 4 g protein, 23 g fat, 64 g carbohydrate, 327 mg sodium, 93 mg cholesterol.

1 purchased pound cake (10¾ ounces)
⅓ cup seedless raspberry jam, melted
½ pint raspberries
½ cup (1 stick) butter
8 sheets frozen phyllo dough, thawed according to package directions
1½ cups confectioners' sugar
4 squares (1 ounce each) bittersweet chocolate, finely chopped and divided into 8 equal portions

1. Cut cake horizontally into four ⅓-inch-thick slices. Using a cookie cutter, cut each slice into two 2½-inch rounds. Brush jam over each round and top with 5 raspberries. Reserve remainder of cake for another use.

2. Melt butter in a small saucepan over very low heat.

3. Place phyllo sheets on a work surface. Cover with a damp cloth. Remove 1 sheet; brush lightly with melted butter, starting from center and working toward edges to coat completely. Dust with 2 tablespoons confectioners' sugar.

4. Cut buttered phyllo in half crosswise; stack the pieces, rotating one piece slightly. Place 1 cake round in center; sprinkle with a portion of chopped chocolate. Fold phyllo up around cake; pinch together at top. Brush top and sides with butter.

5. Place phyllo pocket in freezer on a baking sheet. Assemble 7 more pockets in the same way.

6. Heat oven to 400°. Coat a baking sheet with nonstick cooking spray. Place pockets on prepared baking sheet.

7. Bake in heated 400° oven until phyllo begins to brown, 6 to 8 minutes. Remove from oven. Dust with remaining confectioners' sugar. Serve warm.

Chocolate-Walnut Tart,
opposite

Phyllo Pockets,
opposite

Nutty Choco Pumpkin Ice Cream Pie

MAKES 8 servings

PREP 10 minutes

FREEZE 6 hours or overnight

PER SERVING
345 calories, 4 g protein,
20 g fat, 40 g carbohydrate,
265 mg sodium,
32 mg cholesterol.

4 milk chocolate butter toffee candy bars (1.4 ounces each), coarsely chopped (1⅓ cups)

1½ pints vanilla ice cream, softened

1 prepared chocolate cookie-crumb crust (9-inch)

½ cup canned pumpkin puree (not pie filling)

2 tablespoons sugar

½ teaspoon ground cinnamon

¼ teaspoon ground nutmeg

1. Combine half of candy-bar pieces and 1 pint ice cream in a small bowl. Spoon into prepared crust, smoothing top. Freeze until hardened, about 3 hours.

2. Mix together remaining ice cream, pumpkin, sugar, cinnamon and nutmeg in a small bowl. Spread over top of frozen ice cream. Return to freezer for 1 hour.

3. Press remaining candy-bar pieces to top of pie along rim. Return to freezer for 2 more hours or overnight. To serve, let stand at room temperature 15 minutes to soften.

Apple Tart

MAKES 6 servings

PREP 10 minutes

BAKE 30 minutes

PER SERVING
299 calories, 4 g protein,
17 g fat, 33 g carbohydrate,
119 mg sodium,
35 mg cholesterol.

2 Granny Smith apples, peeled and cored

1 tablespoon lemon juice

2 tablespoons sugar

1 sheet frozen puff pastry (9 ounces), thawed

1 egg, beaten

1 tablespoon apple jelly

1. Heat oven to 375°.

2. Cut apples into ⅛-inch-thick slices. Toss with lemon juice and sugar in a large bowl.

3. Roll puff pastry to a 10 x 7-inch rectangle. Cut a strip about 2½ inches wide from one long edge.

4. Place larger pastry piece on a baking sheet; prick with a fork. Cut smaller piece lengthwise into ¾-inch-wide strips. Brush borders of larger piece with beaten egg. Place strips over brushed borders to make a rim; brush with egg.

5. Overlap apple slices in 2 rows down length of pastry. Bake in heated 375° oven 30 minutes.

6. Transfer baking sheet to a wire rack; let cool briefly, then transfer tart to rack. Meanwhile, melt jelly in a small saucepan over low heat. Brush tart with jelly.

Spicy Apple Crepes with Maple Cream

MAKES 10 servings

PREP 10 minutes

REFRIGERATE 30 minutes

COOK 16 minutes

MICROWAVE crepes

30 to 45 seconds

———

PER SERVING
147 calories, 3 g protein,
1 g fat, 32 g carbohydrate,
115 mg sodium,
6 mg cholesterol.

MAPLE CREAM

½ cup low-fat cottage cheese

¼ cup plain nonfat yogurt

¼ cup maple syrup

FILLING

2 tart cooking apples, such as Granny Smith

1 tablespoon lemon juice

½ cup apple cider or water

⅓ cup raisins or dried cherries

¼ cup sugar

½ teaspoon ground cinnamon

¼ teaspoon ground nutmeg

¼ cup red-currant jelly or apple jelly

10 crepes (9-inch), packaged or homemade (recipe, page 193)

1. Prepare maple cream: Whirl cottage cheese and yogurt in a food processor or blender until very smooth, about 2 minutes. Stir in maple syrup. Refrigerate at least 30 minutes.

2. Meanwhile, prepare filling: Peel, core and chop apples into ¼-inch dice. Toss with lemon juice in a medium-size skillet. Add cider, raisins, sugar, cinnamon and nutmeg.

3. Bring to boiling over medium-high heat. Lower heat; simmer, stirring occasionally, 10 minutes or until apples are just tender. Stir in jelly; cook 5 minutes.

4. Meanwhile, warm crepes in a microwave oven at 100% power 30 to 45 seconds (or warm in a heated 225° oven about 5 minutes).

5. For each serving, place a crepe on a dessert plate. Spread 3 tablespoons filling over one half of each crepe; fold crepe over. Spoon 1½ tablespoons maple cream over each.

Desserts

Apple Crescents

MAKES 12 servings

PREP 10 minutes

COOK 5 minutes

BAKE at 375° for 10 to 12
minutes

―――――

PER SERVING
144 calories, 2 g protein,
8 g fat, 16 g carbohydrate,
223 mg sodium,
3 mg cholesterol.

1 tablespoon unsalted butter

2 Rome or Jonagold apples, peeled, cored and chopped

2 tablespoons chopped walnuts

1 tablespoon packed light-brown sugar

¼ teaspoon ground cinnamon

3 tubes (4 ounces each) refrigerated crescent-roll dough

Confectioners' sugar for dusting

1. Heat oven to 375°.

2. Melt butter in a small nonstick skillet over medium heat. Add apples, walnuts, brown sugar and cinnamon; cook, stirring, 4 minutes or until apples are tender. Let cool.

3. Unroll dough; separate into triangles. Place 1 tablespoon apple mixture on wide end of each triangle. Roll up each. Gently pinch edges together. Place on an ungreased baking sheet.

4. Bake in heated 375° oven 10 to 12 minutes or until golden. Transfer to a wire rack to cool slightly. Dust with confectioners' sugar.

Chocolate Nut Danish

MAKES 16 Danish

PREP 15 minutes

BAKE at 375° for 12 minutes

―――――

PER DANISH
197 calories, 4 g protein,
12 g fat, 19 g carbohydrate,
231 mg sodium,
17 mg cholesterol.

½ cup plus 8 unblanched almonds

2 tablespoons butter

2 tablespoons packed light-brown sugar

2 tablespoons light corn syrup

½ cup mini chocolate pieces

1 teaspoon vanilla

4 tubes (4 ounces each) refrigerated crescent-roll dough

1 egg, slightly beaten with 1 tablespoon water

1 teaspoon granulated sugar

1. Combine ½ cup almonds, butter, brown sugar and corn syrup in a food processor. Pulse until almonds are chopped. Stir in chocolate and vanilla.

2. Heat oven to 375°.

3. Unroll 1 tube of dough; separate into 4 rectangles. Cut each rectangle in half to make 2 squares. Pinch together any holes in dough. Stretch 2 opposite corners of each square slightly to lengthen dough, forming flaps.

4. Transfer squares to 2 ungreased baking sheets. Spoon scant 1 tablespoon filling across each square between the unstretched corners. Fold up 1 flap over filling; fold up second flap over first. Repeat with remaining dough and filling.

5. Chop remaining almonds. Brush Danish with egg-water mixture. Sprinkle with almonds and granulated sugar.

6. Bake in heated 375° oven 12 minutes or until golden. Transfer Danish to a wire rack to cool slightly. Serve warm.

Apple Crescents and Chocolate Nut Danish, *opposite*

Sliced Apples with Caramel Dip

quick COOK

MAKES 60 slices with dip

PREP 10 minutes

COOK 5 minutes

─────────

PER SLICE WITH
1 TEASPOONS DIP
73 calories, 1 g protein,
2 g fat, 14 g carbohydrate,
17 mg sodium,
6 mg cholesterol.

½ cup (1 stick) butter

1½ cups packed light-brown sugar

¾ cup light corn syrup

1 can (14 ounces) sweetened condensed milk

1 teaspoon vanilla

¼ teaspoon ground cinnamon

Pinch salt

6 different types of snacking apples, each cored and cut
    into 10 slices

1. Combine butter, brown sugar, corn syrup and condensed milk in a medium-size saucepan. Heat over medium heat, stirring to dissolve sugar, 5 minutes. Stir in vanilla, cinnamon and salt.

2. Pour into a dipping bowl. Serve with apple slices.

Maple Baked Bananas

30 minutes MAX

MAKES 4 servings

PREP 10 minutes

BAKE at 375° for 12 minutes

─────────

PER SERVING
236 calories, 1 g protein,
9 g fat, 41 g carbohydrate,
81 mg sodium,
16 mg cholesterol.

2 tablespoons butter

2 tablespoons maple syrup

2 tablespoons packed light-brown sugar

1 tablespoon fresh lime juice

½ teaspoon ground allspice

4 medium-size bananas, halved crosswise and
    lengthwise

2 tablespoons sweetened flake coconut

Vanilla frozen yogurt

1. Heat oven to 375°. Place butter in 9 x 9 x 2-inch-square baking pan. Place in oven to melt.

2. Remove pan from oven; leave oven on. Stir in maple syrup, brown sugar, lime juice and allspice. Arrange bananas, cut side up, in pan. Sprinkle with coconut.

3. Bake in heated 375° oven 12 minutes, turning bananas over after 6 minutes and basting with liquid in pan.

4. Place bananas in 4 dessert bowls. Top with frozen yogurt. Spoon sauce from baking pan over bananas and yogurt.

Honeyed Peach à la Mode

MAKES 4 servings

PREP 5 minutes

BROIL 10 minutes

PER SERVING
125 calories, 3 g protein,
3 g fat, 23 g carbohydrate,
30 mg sodium,
3 mg cholesterol.

2 freestone peaches, halved and pitted, or 4 canned
   peach halves, drained
2 tablespoons honey
1 cup vanilla low-fat frozen yogurt or light ice cream
2 tablespoons chopped toasted almonds or walnuts
   (recipe, page 231)

1. Heat toaster oven to broil.

2. Place peach halves, cut side up, on broiler tray; drizzle with half of honey.

3. Broil peach halves 8 to 10 minutes or until lightly browned. Transfer to small dessert bowls.

4. Top each half with ¼ cup frozen yogurt. Sprinkle with toasted nuts. Drizzle with remaining honey and serve.

Fast Fix

Saucy Desserts

WHEN YOU WANT SOMETHING SWEET without a lot of work, turn to fruit and try these luscious, but quick, ideas.

Raspberry Brownie à la Mode

► Puree 2 cups thawed frozen raspberries with confectioners' sugar to taste.

► Flavor with orange liqueur to taste.

► Reserve ¼ cup sauce; divide remainder among 4 dessert plates.

► Place a brownie on sauce; top with a scoop of ice cream or frozen yogurt.

► Drizzle reserved sauce over ice cream.

► Makes 4 servings.

Creamy Fruit Dip

► Melt ¼ cup hot pepper jelly in a small saucepan over low heat.

► Stir in 2 tablespoons honey.

► Cool slightly; stir into 1 cup sour cream.

► Use as a dip for sliced fruit.

► Makes about 1¼ cups dip.

Raspberried Strawberries

► Divide 1 pound sliced hulled strawberries among 4 dessert bowls.

► Stir together 2 tablespoons raspberry jam, 1 tablespoon balsamic vinegar and 1 tablespoon red wine in a small saucepan over low heat.

► Drizzle sauce over berries.

► Top with toasted sweetened flake coconut.

► Makes 4 servings.

Desserts

201

Blushing Berries

MAKES 4 servings

PREP 10 minutes

COOK 1 minute

REFRIGERATE 3 hours

───────

PER SERVING
152 calories, 2 g protein,
0 g fat, 32 g carbohydrate,
6 mg sodium,
0 mg cholesterol.

½ cup sugar

1 envelope unflavored gelatin

1⅓ cups cold water

½ cup rosé wine or blush wine

3 tablespoons orange juice

2 cups strawberries, hulled and thinly sliced

1. Sprinkle sugar and gelatin over ⅔ cup water in a small saucepan; let stand 1 minute to soften. Stir over low heat until sugar and gelatin are dissolved, about 1 minute. Pour into a large bowl.

2. Add remaining ⅔ cup water, wine and orange juice to gelatin. Refrigerate until mixture mounds slightly, about 1 hour. For a quick set, place gelatin mixture over a bowl of iced water; stir frequently.

3. Fold berries into gelatin mixture. Spoon into goblets. Chill until set, 2 hours.

Frozen Orange Soufflé

MAKES 8 servings

PREP 20 minutes

FREEZE 3 hours

───────

PER SERVING
95 calories, 1 g protein,
6 g fat, 12 g carbohydrate,
17 mg sodium,
0 mg cholesterol.

1 pint nonfat orange sorbet, sherbet or frozen yogurt, softened

1 container (8 ounces) light frozen nondairy whipped topping, thawed

¼ cup egg white powder (see note below)

¾ cup warm water

1 tablespoon grated orange rind (optional)

1. Make a collar for a shallow (2¼-inch-deep) 1-quart soufflé dish: Cut a piece of waxed paper 3 inches wide and long enough to go around dish, overlapping ends of paper slightly. Fold paper lengthwise in half. Wrap around outside of dish, pulling tight so filling cannot run down between paper and dish. Secure ends of paper together with tape.

2. Gently stir together sorbet and whipped topping in a large bowl until blended.

3. Stir together egg white powder and warm water in a medium-size bowl 2 minutes or until completely dissolved. Beat with mixer on medium-high speed until soft peaks form.

4. Gently fold beaten whites into sorbet mixture. Spoon into prepared dish. Freeze until firm, about 3 hours. Let stand at room temperature 10 minutes before serving. Garnish with orange rind if desired.

Note: Egg white powder is found in the baking section of supermarkets. Because of health concerns about eating raw eggs, be sure to use it for this uncooked soufflé.

Raspberry-Peach Tart

quick
COOK

MAKES 12 servings

PREP 15 minutes

BAKE crust at 450° for
9 to 11 minutes

―――――

PER SERVING
151 calories, 2 g protein,
7 g fat, 21 g carbohydrate,
216 mg sodium,
5 mg cholesterol.

1 refrigerated ready-to-use piecrust

1 box (3.4 ounces) vanilla instant pudding-and-pie-
   filling mix

1¾ cups milk

2 small peaches, peeled and pitted

1½ cups raspberries

2 tablespoons peach jelly

1. Heat oven to 450°.

2. Unfold pastry; it should be an 11-inch round; roll to 11 inches if necessary. Press into a 9-inch tart pan with a removable bottom. Trim edge of pastry. Blind-bake pastry according to package directions for single-crust pie. Transfer to a wire rack to cool.

3. Meanwhile, prepare pudding mix according to package directions for pie, using the 1¾ cups milk.

4. Once tart has cooled, spread 1 cup pudding over bottom. Reserve remaining pudding for another use. Cut peaches into total of 12 to 13 wedges. Fan 4 or 5 peach slices decoratively in center of tart. Place 1 raspberry in center. Line perimeter of tart with remaining peach slices. Fill in remaining spaces with raspberries.

5. Melt jelly in a small dish in microwave at 100% power 25 seconds or in a small saucepan over medium heat. Gently brush peaches and raspberries with jelly. Let set.

Frozen Orange Soufflé,
opposite

Raspberry-Peach Tart

Triple-Play Shortcake

MAX

MAKES 8 servings
PREP shortcakes 10 minutes,
sauces about 10 minutes
each
BAKE at 425° for 20 minutes
(while preparing a sauce)

———

PER SERVING
WITH SAUCE
297 calories, 4 g protein,
13 g fat, 42 g carbohydrate,
230 mg sodium,
34 mg cholesterol.

2 cups all-purpose flour
¼ cup plus 1½ teaspoons sugar
1 tablespoon baking powder
¼ teaspoon salt
½ cup (1 stick) butter, in pieces
¾ cup plus 1½ teaspoons milk
Strawberry-Ginger, Strawberry-Orange or Strawberry-
Raspberry Sauce (recipes follow)
Whipped cream for garnish (optional)

1. Heat oven to 425°.

2. Combine flour, ¼ cup sugar, baking powder and salt in a medium-size bowl. Cut in butter until mixture resembles coarse crumbs. Make a well in center; add ¾ cup milk; stir to make a soft dough.

3. Drop dough by heaping ¼ cupfuls onto an ungreased baking sheet, making a total of 8 mounds. Pat to flatten each into a ¾-inch-thick round.

4. Brush tops of rounds with remaining 1½ teaspoons milk; sprinkle with remaining 1½ teaspoons sugar. Bake in heated 425° oven 20 minutes or until lightly browned. Transfer shortcakes to a wire rack to cool.

5. Split shortcakes in half. Assemble on plates, using your choice of sauce. Serve with whipped cream if desired.

Fast Fix

Strawberry Sauces

FRESH STRAWBERRIES can easily be transformed into wonderful sauces. To make enough for 8 servings of shortcake, begin with 3 cups hulled strawberries.

Strawberry-Ginger Sauce

► Mix ⅓ cup sugar, 1 tablespoon raspberry vinegar, 1 tablespoon honey, 2 teaspoons finely chopped crystallized ginger and a pinch black pepper in a medium-size bowl.

► Add ½ cup strawberries; mash well with a fork.

► Cut remaining berries into quarters; stir into mixture.

Strawberry-Orange Sauce

► Mix ⅓ cup sugar, 1 tablespoon raspberry vinegar, 1 tablespoon thawed frozen orange juice concentrate, 1 tablespoon sieved orange marmalade and a pinch black pepper in a medium-size bowl.

► Add ½ cup strawberries; mash well with a fork.

► Cut remaining berries into quarters; stir into mixture.

Strawberry-Raspberry Sauce

► Mix ⅓ cup sugar, 2 tablespoons seedless raspberry jam, 1 tablespoon raspberry vinegar, 1 tablespoon raspberry liqueur and a pinch black pepper in a medium-size bowl.

► Add ½ cup strawberries; mash well with a fork.

► Cut remaining berries into quarters; stir into mixture.

Orange-Pecan Angelfood Cake

MAKES 12 servings

PREP 10 minutes

BAKE at 350° for 45 to 50 minutes

————

PER SERVING
241 calories, 4 g protein,
5 g fat, 47 g carbohydrate,
325 mg sodium,
0 mg cholesterol.

CAKE

⅔ cup finely chopped pecans

2 tablespoons granulated sugar

1 tablespoon light corn syrup

1½ teaspoons ground cinnamon

1½ teaspoons grated orange rind

½ teaspoon orange extract

1 box (18.25 ounces) angelfood cake mix

GLAZE

½ cup confectioners' sugar

2 teaspoons milk

1. Heat oven to 350°.

2. Prepare cake: Combine pecans, granulated sugar, corn syrup, cinnamon, orange rind and orange extract in a medium-size bowl.

3. Prepare cake mix according to package directions, beating in a large bowl on medium-high speed. Spoon half of batter into an ungreased 10-inch tube pan. Sprinkle a ring of pecan mixture on top of batter; keep mixture away from pan sides and tube. Top with remaining batter.

4. Bake in heated 350° oven 45 to 50 minutes or until crust is golden and cracked, looks dry and is firm.

5. Invert pan onto its legs to cool, about 1½ hours. If pan has no legs extending above rim, invert onto a wine or similar weighted bottle, placing center of tube over neck of bottle. Loosen edges of cooled cake and remove from pan.

6. Prepare glaze: Stir together confectioners' sugar and milk in a small bowl. Drizzle over cake.

Desserts

Miniature Lemon Cheesecake Tarts

Miniature Lemon Cheesecake Tarts

MAX

MAKES 30 tarts

PREP 15 minutes

BAKE at 375° for 8 minutes

———

PER TART
75 calories, 1 g protein,
3 g fat, 10 g carbohydrate,
34 mg sodium,
14 mg cholesterol.

Family Circle **Quick & Easy** Recipes

2 packages (2.1 ounces each) mini phyllo dough shells
   (30 shells total)
4 ounces cream cheese, at room temperature
⅓ cup sugar
1 egg
½ cup lemon curd
2 teaspoons lemon juice
Fresh raspberries for garnish

1. Heat oven to 375°. Place 3 mini muffin pans (twelve 1¾ x 1-inch cups each) on a large baking sheet.

2. Place each phyllo shell in a muffin cup, dividing equally among pans.

3. Beat cream cheese and sugar with mixer on low speed in a medium-size bowl until very smooth, 2 minutes. Beat in egg. Beat in lemon curd and lemon juice just until blended. Transfer mixture to a large glass measuring cup and pour into phyllo shells, filling each about seven-eighths full.

4. Bake in heated 375° oven 8 minutes or until slightly puffed; do not overbake. Transfer pans to a wire rack and let cool completely. Refrigerate tarts in pans until ready to serve.

5. To serve, remove each tart from pan and top each with a fresh raspberry.

Blackberry Jelly Roll

MAKES 8 servings

PREP 15 minutes

BAKE at 375° for
12 to 15 minutes

———

PER SERVING
285 calories, 5 g protein,
3 g fat, 62 g carbohydrate,
169 mg sodium,
106 mg cholesterol.

¼ cup confectioners' sugar

1 cup all-purpose flour

1 teaspoon baking powder

¼ teaspoon salt

4 eggs

¾ cup granulated sugar

2 teaspoons grated lemon rind

¼ cup fresh lemon juice

1 teaspoon vanilla

1 jar (12 ounces) blackberry jam

1. Heat oven to 375°. Coat a 15 x 10 x 1½-inch jelly-roll pan with nonstick cooking spray. Line with waxed paper; coat paper with spray. Dust a kitchen towel with 2 tablespoons confectioners' sugar.

2. Whisk together flour, baking powder and salt in a small bowl. In a medium-size bowl, beat eggs with mixer on medium speed until thick and lemon colored, about 5 minutes. Gradually add granulated sugar until well blended. Beat in lemon rind, lemon juice and vanilla. Gently fold in flour mixture until well combined. Scrape batter into prepared pan, spreading until level.

3. Bake in heated 375° oven 12 to 15 minutes or until center springs back when lightly pressed with fingertip.

4. Immediately invert cake onto sugar-dusted cloth. Remove paper; roll up cloth and cake together from a long side. Let cool completely on a wire rack. Unroll. Spread evenly with jam; reroll from long side. Dust with remaining 2 tablespoons confectioners' sugar.

Blackberry Jelly Roll

Citrus Roll

MAX

MAKES 10 servings
PREP 15 minutes
BAKE at 400° for 8 to
10 minutes

PER SERVING
118 calories, 3 g protein,
4 g fat, 19 g carbohydrate,
107 mg sodium,
85 mg cholesterol.

4 eggs, separated
¼ teaspoon salt
⅓ cup granulated sugar
¼ cup all-purpose flour
½ teaspoon baking powder
½ teaspoon lemon extract

CITRUS FILLING
1 cup light frozen nondairy whipped topping, thawed
⅓ cup lemon curd
1 can (11 ounces) Mandarin oranges in light syrup,
    drained and patted dry, 5 sections reserved

Confectioners' sugar for dusting
Fresh mint sprigs for garnish (optional)

1. Heat oven to 400°. Coat a 15½ x 10½ x 1-inch jelly-roll pan with nonstick cooking spray. Line bottom of pan with aluminum foil, leaving a 2-inch overhang on short edges. Lightly coat foil with nonstick cooking spray. Place a sheet of aluminum foil on a wire rack large enough to hold cake. Coat foil with nonstick cooking spray.

2. Beat egg whites and salt with mixer on medium speed in a large bowl until fluffy. Gradually beat in sugar until stiff, but not dry, peaks form.

3. Sift together flour and baking powder onto waxed paper.

4. Beat yolks and lemon extract in a medium-size bowl until thick and lemon colored, about 3 minutes. Using a spatula, fold ½ cup beaten whites into yolks. Fold in remaining whites and flour mixture. Scrape batter into prepared pan, spreading until level.

5. Bake in heated 400° oven 8 to 10 minutes or until top is golden and center springs back when lightly pressed with a fingertip. Loosen cake around edges; invert onto foil on rack. Remove pan; peel foil from bottom. Let cake cool.

6. Prepare filling: Gently fold together whipped topping and lemon curd in a small bowl. Coarsely chop all but the 5 reserved Mandarin orange sections. Fold chopped oranges into lemon curd mixture.

7. Transfer foil with cake to a work surface. Spread filling over entire cake. Using foil as an aid, roll up cake from a short edge. Place, seam side down, on a serving platter. Sift confectioners' sugar over top of cake. Garnish with reserved Mandarin orange sections and mint.

Family Circle **Quick & Easy** Recipes

Sweet Soufflé Omelet

MAX

MAKES 6 servings
PREP 10 minutes
COOK 5 minutes
BAKE at 375° for 5 minutes

———

PER SERVING
130 calories, 5 g protein,
3 g fat, 20 g carbohydrate,
92 mg sodium,
108 mg cholesterol.

3 egg yolks
3 tablespoons granulated sugar
6 egg whites
Pinch salt
1 teaspoon unsalted butter
1½ cups reduced-sugar cherry pie filling
1 tablespoon confectioners' sugar
Strips of orange rind (optional)

1. Heat oven to 375°.

2. Whisk yolks and sugar in a large bowl. Beat whites and salt in a second large bowl until stiff peaks form. Fold into egg yolk mixture.

3. Melt butter in a 10-inch nonstick ovenproof skillet over medium-low heat. Spread egg mixture in skillet. Cook 5 minutes or until mixture is set on bottom. Transfer to heated 375° oven; bake 5 minutes or until puffed.

4. Meanwhile, warm pie filling in a small saucepan over low heat.

5. When omelet is done, dust with confectioners' sugar. Serve immediately, topped with pie filling. Garnish with orange rind if desired.

Fast Fix

Pound Cake Perfection

START WITH A FROZEN or bakery pound cake and the sky's the limit.

Toasted Ice-Cream Sundae

▶ Cut a 12-ounce pound cake into 8 slices, each 1 inch thick; place on a broiler-pan rack.

▶ Broil slices briefly, turning to toast both sides.

▶ Place each slice on a dessert plate.

▶ Top each with a scoop of ice cream or frozen yogurt.

▶ Stir 1 teaspoon grated orange rind and 2 teaspoons orange-flavored liqueur into 1 cup prepared fudge sauce in a small saucepan.

▶ Heat sauce over medium heat, then drizzle over sundaes.

▶ Makes 8 servings.

Dreamy Pudding-Cake Combo

▶ Dissolve 1 tablespoon instant coffee granules in 1¾ cups milk in a measuring cup.

▶ Use this flavored milk to prepare 1 box instant vanilla pudding.

▶ Cut a 12-ounce pound cake into 16 slices, each ½ inch thick.

▶ Place 1 slice on each of 8 dessert plates; top with ¼ cup pudding and a second slice of cake.

▶ Combine 1 cup heavy cream, ¼ teaspoon ground cinnamon, 2 tablespoons sugar and 1 teaspoon vanilla in a medium-size bowl; whip until stiff.

▶ Top each serving of cake with whipped cream; dust with sifted cocoa powder.

▶ Makes 8 servings.

Desserts

Mocha Sour Cream Cake

MAKES 12 servings

PREP 10 minutes

BAKE at 325° for 30 to 32 minutes

PER SERVING
476 calories, 8 g protein,
30 g fat, 47 g carbohydrate,
393 mg sodium,
88 mg cholesterol.

CAKE

3 tablespoons instant espresso powder

¼ cup coffee-flavored liqueur or strong brewed coffee

1 box (18.25 ounces) chocolate cake mix

4 eggs

1 cup sour cream

⅓ cup canola oil or vegetable oil

FROSTING

10 squares (1 ounce each) semisweet chocolate, chopped

1 cup sour cream

1 teaspoon instant espresso powder

½ teaspoon ground cinnamon

Whipped cream for garnish (optional)

Chocolate-covered espresso beans for garnish (optional)

1. Heat oven to 325°. Coat two 9-inch round layer cake pans with nonstick cooking spray.

2. Prepare cake: Mix espresso powder and liqueur in a small bowl. Beat together cake mix, eggs, sour cream, oil and espresso mixture with mixer on low speed in a large bowl until blended. Increase mixer speed to medium and beat 2 minutes. Scrape batter into prepared pans.

3. Bake in heated 325° oven 30 to 32 minutes or until a wooden pick inserted in centers comes out clean and cakes begin to pull away from sides. Let cakes cool in pans on wire racks 10 minutes. Turn out cakes onto racks to cool completely.

4. Prepare frosting: In a glass bowl, microwave chocolate at 100% power 90 seconds or until spreadable. Stir in sour cream, espresso powder and cinnamon.

5. Place 1 cake layer on a serving plate. Spread with half of frosting. Top with second cake layer. Spread remaining frosting on top of cake. Serve garnished with whipped cream and chocolate-covered espresso beans if desired.

Raspberry Crumb Bars

quick PREP

MAKES 24 bars

PREP 10 minutes

BAKE at 375° for 22 minutes

STAND 10 to 15 minutes

———

PER BAR
183 calories, 3 g protein,
9 g fat, 24 g carbohydrate,
70 mg sodium,
24 mg cholesterol.

2 cups all-purpose flour

1 teaspoon baking powder

½ teaspoon salt

1 cup almonds (about 4 ounces)

¾ cup (1½ sticks) unsalted butter, at room temperature

1 teaspoon vanilla

⅔ cup sugar

1 egg

1 jar (12 ounces) raspberry preserves

1. Heat oven to 375°. Coat a 13 x 9 x 2-inch baking pan with nonstick cooking spray.

2. Combine flour, baking powder and salt in a small bowl.

3. Whirl almonds in a food processor until finely ground. Add butter and vanilla. Whirl until well blended. Add flour mixture and sugar. Whirl to mix.

4. Remove ½ cup mixture and reserve for topping. Add egg to remaining flour mixture in food processor. Whirl until well combined and a dough forms.

5. Press dough over bottom of prepared baking pan. Bake in heated 375° oven 10 minutes or until lightly browned. Transfer pan to a wire rack to cool slightly, 10 to 15 minutes; leave oven on.

6. Spread raspberry preserves over dough. Sprinkle diagonal stripes of reserved crumb mixture across top. Return pan to heated 375° oven and bake 12 minutes or until top is golden brown. Let cool in pan on wire rack. Cut into bars.

Raspberry Crumb Bars

Mochaccino Pudding

MAKES 6 servings

PREP 10 minutes

COOK 15 minutes

REFRIGERATE several hours

PER SERVING
228 calories, 6 g protein,
7 g fat, 37 g carbohydrate,
113 mg sodium,
123 mg cholesterol.

¾ cup sugar

¼ cup unsweetened cocoa powder

3 tablespoons cornstarch

½ teaspoon ground cinnamon

⅛ teaspoon salt

3 cups milk

3 egg yolks

2 teaspoons instant espresso coffee powder, dissolved
   in 1 tablespoon boiling water

1 tablespoon brandy (optional)

1 teaspoon vanilla

1. Combine sugar, cocoa powder, cornstarch, cinnamon and salt in a large saucepan. Gradually stir in 1 cup milk until cornstarch is dissolved. Beat in egg yolks, remaining milk and espresso powder.

2. Bring slowly to boiling, stirring constantly, about 15 minutes; boil 30 seconds or until thickened enough to mound slightly when dropped from a spoon. Remove from heat. Stir in brandy if desired and vanilla.

3. Cover surface with plastic wrap. Refrigerate several hours or until set.

Neapolitan Mousse

MAKES 10 servings

PREP 20 minutes

REFRIGERATE 1 hour

PER SERVING
167 calories, 3 g protein,
5 g fat, 29 g carbohydrate,
120 mg sodium,
7 mg cholesterol.

1 package (3.1 ounces) instant chocolate mousse mix

3 tablespoons chocolate syrup

1½ pints raspberries

2 tablespoons confectioners' sugar

2 packages (2.7 ounces each) instant vanilla mousse
   mix

1. Prepare chocolate mousse according to package directions. Fold in chocolate syrup. Set mousse aside in refrigerator.

2. Combine 1 cup raspberries and confectioners' sugar in a food processor or blender. Whirl until pureed. Strain through a fine sieve into a small bowl to remove seeds.

3. Prepare instant vanilla mousse according to package directions. Transfer half of mousse to another small bowl and fold raspberry puree into it.

4. Arrange mousses and berries in layers as follows, dividing each layer equally among ten 8-ounce glass dessert glasses or filling one 10-cup glass serving dish: chocolate mousse, ½ cup raspberries, raspberry-vanilla mousse, ½ cup raspberries, remaining plain vanilla mousse.

5. Refrigerate 1 hour before serving. Garnish with remaining 1 cup berries.

Pumpkin Spice Cake

MAKES 12 servings

PREP 10 minutes

BAKE at 325° for 35 to 40 minutes

———

PER SERVING
510 calories, 5 g protein,
22 g fat, 74 g carbohydrate,
357 mg sodium,
85 mg cholesterol.

CAKE

1 box (18.25 ounces) yellow cake mix

2½ teaspoons ground cinnamon

2½ teaspoons ground ginger

1 cup canned pumpkin puree (not pie filling)

½ cup water

⅓ cup canola oil or vegetable oil

3 eggs

FROSTING

1 package (8 ounces) cream cheese

¼ cup (½ stick) butter, at room temperature

1 teaspoon vanilla

½ teaspoon ground ginger

1 box (1 pound) confectioners' sugar

Strips of orange rind for garnish (optional)

1. Place oven rack at top of lower third of oven. Heat oven to 325°. Coat a 13 x 9 x 2-inch baking pan with nonstick cooking spray.

2. Prepare cake: Beat together cake mix, cinnamon, ginger, pumpkin, water, oil and eggs with mixer on low speed in a medium-size bowl until blended. Increase mixer speed to medium; beat 2 minutes. Scrape batter into prepared baking pan.

3. Bake in heated 325° oven 35 to 40 minutes or until a wooden pick inserted in center comes out clean. Let cake cool in pan on a wire rack 10 minutes. Turn out cake onto rack to cool completely.

4. Prepare frosting: Beat together cream cheese, butter and vanilla with mixer on low speed in a large bowl until smooth. Add ginger and confectioners' sugar, 1 cup at a time, beating until blended and a good spreading consistency.

5. Place cake on a serving platter. Spread frosting over cake. Garnish with orange rind if desired.

Pecan Cookie Turtles

MAKES 2½ dozen cookies

PREP 15 minutes

MICROWAVE caramel for
45 seconds; chocolate for
1 minute

REFRIGERATE 45 minutes

———

PER COOKIE
141 calories, 2 g protein,
9 g fat, 15 g carbohydrate,
47 mg sodium,
1 mg cholesterol.

30 mini (1½-inch) chocolate chip cookies or other mini
 cookies
1 package (9 ounces) soft and chewy caramels
120 pecan halves (about 2 cups)
1 package (6 ounces) semisweet chocolate pieces (1 cup)
¼ cup chopped pecans

1. Cover 2 baking sheets with waxed paper; coat with nonstick cooking spray. Arrange cookies on paper.

2. Combine caramels and 4 teaspoons water in a large microwave-safe glass measuring cup. Microwave, uncovered, at 100% power 30 seconds. Stir to mix. Microwave 15 seconds more.

3. Top each cookie with ½ teaspoon caramel mixture. Press 4 pecan halves into caramel mixture on each cookie to resemble turtle feet.

4. Place chocolate in a clean microwave-safe bowl. Microwave at 100% power about 1 minute or until melted. Stir until smooth. Spoon 1 teaspoon chocolate over pecans on each cookie. Sprinkle some chopped pecans over soft chocolate.

5. Refrigerate at least 45 minutes to set chocolate.

Rocky Road Cookies

MAKES 1 dozen cookies

PREP 15 minutes

FREEZE 1¼ hours

———

PER COOKIE
349 calories, 5 g protein,
17 g fat, 50 g carbohydrate,
189 mg sodium,
26 mg cholesterol.

2 cups wheat-and-barley cereal bits
¼ cup unsweetened cocoa powder
½ cup chopped pecans
½ cup chocolate-covered raisins
½ cup sweetened flake coconut
½ cup mini marshmallows
2 envelopes liquid baking chocolate
¼ cup (½ stick) unsalted butter, melted
½ cup light corn syrup
1 tablespoon warm water
4 cups (2 pints) chocolate ice cream or vanilla ice cream

1. Whirl 1 cup cereal in a food processor 1 minute or until finely crushed. Add cocoa powder; pulse to blend. Combine in a large bowl with remaining cereal, pecans, raisins, coconut and marshmallows.

2. Mix liquid chocolate, butter, syrup and water in a small bowl. Pour over cereal mixture; stir.

3. Using half of marshmallow batter, place 1 heaping tablespoonful into each of twelve 2¾ x 1¼-inch muffin cups. Press into cups to cover bottom. Place in freezer.

4. Cover a baking sheet with waxed paper. Divide remaining batter, making 12 equal mounds on the paper. Top with a second sheet of waxed paper or plastic wrap; flatten each mound with bottom of a glass. Remove top paper; gently pat "cookies" into rounds that are the same size as top of muffin cups. Place in freezer to chill along with muffin cups, 15 minutes.

5. Meanwhile, let ice cream stand at room temperature 15 minutes to soften slightly. Fill each muffin cup with ⅓ cup ice cream and top with a cookie. Freeze at least 1 hour or until solid. Unmold and serve.

Rocky Road Cookies,
opposite

Pecan Cookie Turtles,
opposite

Chocolate Peanut Butter Squares

quick COOK

MAKES 40 squares

PREP 10 minutes

COOK 10 minues

REFRIGERATE 30 minutes

STAND 3 hours

SHOWN ON PAGE 7.

PER SQUARE
303 calories, 7 g protein,
13 g fat, 41 g carbohydrate,
206 mg sodium,
7 mg cholesterol.

2 packages (10 ounces each) peanut butter pieces
⅓ cup butter or margarine
2 cans (14 ounces each) sweetened condensed milk
2 cups finely ground honey graham cracker crumbs
   (15 whole crackers)
1½ cups unsalted peanuts, finely chopped
1 package (12 ounces) semisweet chocolate pieces

1. Line a 13 x 9 x 2-inch baking pan with aluminum foil.

2. Melt peanut butter pieces and butter in top of a double boiler over barely simmering, not boiling, water, stirring until smooth. Spoon into a large bowl. Whisk in condensed milk.

3. Gradually stir in crumbs and ½ cup peanuts (use hands if necessary to mix thoroughly). Pat mixture evenly into prepared pan. Refrigerate until firm, about 30 minutes.

4. Melt chocolate pieces in top of a double boiler over barely simmering water, stirring until smooth. Spread over top of peanut mixture. Sprinkle with remaining peanuts. Set aside until firm, about 3 hours. Cut into squares.

Peanutty Chocolate Chip Cookies

30 minutes MAX

MAKES about 3½ dozen
cookies

PREP 15 minutes

BAKE at 350° for 10 minutes

PER COOKIE
148 calories, 3 g protein,
9 g fat, 16 g carbohydrate,
98 mg sodium,
16 mg cholesterol.

2¼ cups all-purpose flour
1 teaspoon baking soda
½ teaspoon salt
½ cup (1 stick) unsalted butter, at room temperature
¾ cup creamy peanut butter
⅓ cup granulated sugar
⅓ cup packed light-brown sugar
2 eggs
1 teaspoon vanilla
¾ cup peanut butter pieces
1 package (12 ounces) semisweet chocolate pieces
   (2 cups)
½ cup chopped peanuts

1. Heat oven to 350°.

2. Sift flour, baking soda and salt into a small bowl.

3. Beat butter and peanut butter with mixer on medium-high speed in a large bowl until smooth and creamy. Add granulated sugar and brown sugar and beat until light and fluffy. Add eggs, one at a time, beating well after each addition. Beat in vanilla until blended.

4. Beat in flour mixture with mixer on low speed until blended. Using a spatula, fold in peanut butter pieces, chocolate pieces and peanuts until evenly distributed throughout batter.

5. Scoop about 1 heaping tablespoonful dough into your hands; gently flatten into a 2-inch disc. Transfer to an ungreased baking sheet. Continue making discs with remaining dough and set 1 inch apart on baking sheet.

6. Bake in heated 350° oven 10 minutes or until lightly golden and firm. Let cool on sheet on a wire rack 2 minutes. Transfer cookies to rack to cool completely.

Mocha Granola Bars

quick COOK

MAKES 3 dozen bars

PREP 15 minutes

COOK 5 minutes

REFRIGERATE crust 30 minutes, filling 3 hours, bars 3 hours

PER BAR
151 calories, 1 g protein, 9 g fat, 16 g carbohydrate, 40 mg sodium, 11 mg cholesterol.

CRUST

2 cups chocolate wafer cookie crumbs (30 to 36 cookies)

1 cup finely chopped pecans

3 tablespoons granulated sugar

½ cup (1 stick) butter or margarine, melted

FILLING

2 tablespoons milk

2 tablespoons instant espresso powder

2 cups sifted confectioners' sugar

¼ cup (½ stick) butter or margarine, at room temperature

1 teaspoon vanilla

1 cup granola, crushed

TOPPING

½ cup semisweet chocolate pieces

2 tablespoons solid vegetable shortening

4 ounces white chocolate candy bar

1. Coat a 13 x 9 x 2-inch baking pan with nonstick cooking spray.

2. Prepare crust: Mix together cookie crumbs, pecans, granulated sugar and butter in a medium-size bowl until well combined. Press mixture in an even layer over bottom of prepared pan. Refrigerate until firm, about 30 minutes.

3. Prepare filling: Measure milk into a small bowl. Sprinkle espresso powder on top; stir to dissolve. Add confectioners' sugar, butter and vanilla, beating with mixer on medium speed until well blended and smooth.

4. Spread filling evenly over crust. Sprinkle evenly with granola. Refrigerate several hours or until firm.

5. Prepare topping: Melt semisweet chocolate pieces and 1 tablespoon shortening in top of a double boiler over barely simmering, not boiling, water, stirring until smooth. Drizzle over top of filling layer. Repeat with white chocolate and remaining 1 tablespoon shortening.

6. Cover pan; refrigerate 3 hours or until chocolate has hardened. Cut into bars.

Mocha Brownies

MAKES 30 brownies

PREP 8 minutes

MICROWAVE 2 minutes

BAKE at 350° for 30 minutes

———

PER BROWNIE
132 calories, 1 g protein,
7 g fat, 18 g carbohydrate,
6 mg sodium,
27 mg cholesterol.

¾ cup (1½ sticks) unsalted butter

4 squares (1 ounce each) unsweetened chocolate

2 cups sugar

1 tablespoon instant coffee powder, dissolved in
   2 tablespoons hot water

1 cup all-purpose flour

2 eggs

1½ cups chopped walnuts (optional)

1. Heat oven to 350°. Lightly coat a 13 x 9 x 2-inch baking pan with nonstick cooking spray.

2. Microwave butter and chocolate in a large glass bowl at 100% power 1 minute; stir, then microwave 1 minute more. Remove bowl from microwave.

3. Stir chocolate again, then beat in sugar and dissolved coffee with mixer. Stir in flour, then beat in eggs until smooth. Add 1 cup walnuts if using, and stir just until combined. Scrape into prepared pan. Sprinkle with remaining walnuts.

4. Bake in heated 350° oven 30 minutes or until a wooden pick inserted in center comes out clean. Let cool completely in pan on a wire rack. Cut into bars.

Bourbon Balls

MAKES about 2 dozen cookies

PREP 20 minutes

REFRIGERATE 24 hours

———

PER COOKIE
108 calories, 1 g protein,
3 g fat, 18 g carbohydrate,
51 mg sodium,
0 mg cholesterol.

2½ cups (about 10 ounces) finely crushed vanilla wafer
   cookies (70 cookies)

1¼ cups confectioners' sugar

2 tablespoons finely ground hazelnuts

¼ cup bourbon

2 tablespoons unsweetened cocoa powder

3 tablespoons corn syrup

⅓ cup granulated sugar

1. Mix crumbs, confectioners' sugar, hazelnuts, bourbon, cocoa powder and corn syrup in a medium-size bowl. Press all ingredients together in bowl to form a large ball.

2. Shape level tablespoonfuls of dough into balls; place on waxed paper.

3. Place granulated sugar in a small shallow dish. Roll balls in sugar to coat. Place in a tightly covered container at least 24 hours for flavors to develop.

Ginger-Pignoli Shortbread

MAKES 24 cookies

PREP 10 minutes

BAKE at 350° for 20 to 25 minutes

———

PER COOKIE
133 calories, 2 g protein,
8 g fat, 14 g carbohydrate,
46 mg sodium,
21 mg cholesterol.

¾ cup confectioners' sugar
⅓ cup crystallized ginger
½ teaspoon salt
2¼ cups all-purpose flour
1 cup (2 sticks) chilled unsalted butter, cut into pats
6 tablespoons pine nuts (pignoli)

1. Heat oven to 350°. Lightly coat two 9-inch round layer cake pans with nonstick cooking spray.

2. Combine confectioners' sugar, crystallized ginger and salt in a food processor. Whirl until ginger is finely chopped, about 10 seconds. Add flour and whirl until combined. Add butter and pulse until butter is finely chopped. Then whirl again until mixture just starts to come together.

3. Crumble mixture into prepared pans, dividing equally. Press mixture evenly over bottoms of pans, using the flat bottom of a glass measure to compact and level dough. Sprinkle on pine nuts and pat lightly into dough.

4. Bake in heated 350° oven 20 to 25 minutes or until shortbread is golden. Let cool in pans on wire racks 10 minutes. While still warm, cut shortbread in each pan into 12 wedges.

Ginger-Pignoli
Shortbread

Ricotta Cookies

quick
COOK

MAKES 6½ dozen cookies

PREP 10 minutes

REFRIGERATE overnight

BAKE at 350° for 10 minutes

———

PER COOKIE
67 calories, 1 g protein,
2 g fat, 11 g carbohydrate,
61 mg sodium,
10 mg cholesterol.

4 cups all-purpose flour

2 teaspoons baking powder

1 teaspoon baking soda

1 teaspoon salt

½ cup (1 stick) unsalted butter

1½ cups granulated sugar

2 eggs

2 teaspoons vanilla

1 container (15 ounces) part-skim ricotta cheese

GLAZE

2 cups confectioners' sugar, sifted

3 tablespoons orange juice

Colored sprinkles (optional)

1. Combine flour, baking powder, baking soda and salt in a medium-size bowl.

2. Beat together butter and granulated sugar with mixer on medium speed in a large bowl until light and fluffy, about 3 minutes. Beat in eggs, vanilla and ricotta until well blended.

3. Stir in flour mixture until well blended. Cover and refrigerate overnight.

4. Heat oven to 350°. Lightly coat 2 baking sheets with nonstick cooking spray.

5. Shape level tablespoonfuls of dough into balls; place at least 1 inch apart on prepared baking sheets.

6. Bake in heated 350° oven 10 minutes or until bottoms are lightly brown. Do not overbake. Transfer cookies to a wire rack to cool slightly.

7. Meanwhile, prepare glaze: Stir together confectioners' sugar and orange juice in a small bowl until smooth and a good glazing consistency. If too thick, add additional orange juice, drop by drop, until desired consistency. Drizzle glaze evenly over each cookie. Garnish with sprinkles if desired. Let stand until hardened.

Baker's Tip

Store them right

CHANCES ARE, they'll be eaten before they get stale. But to keep cookies at their best, follow these tricks.

Soft cookies

▶ Store at room temperature in a container with a tight-fitting cover.

Crisp cookies

▶ Store at room temperature in a container with a loose-fitting cover.

Bars

▶ Store, tightly covered, in the baking pan. Refrigerate fudgy varieties; store others at room temperature.

Mint Chocolate Chip Cookies

quick COOK

MAKES about 4½ dozen
cookies
PREP 20 minutes
BAKE at 375° for 9 to 11
minutes

———————

PER SERVING
131 calories, 1 g protein,
6 g fat, 18 g carbohydrate,
39 mg sodium,
18 mg cholesterol.

2 cups all-purpose flour
¾ cup unsweetened cocoa powder
1 teaspoon baking soda
¼ teaspoon salt
1 cup (2 sticks) unsalted butter, at room temperature
1 cup packed light-brown sugar
¾ cup granulated sugar
2 eggs
2 teaspoons vanilla
¼ teaspoon mint extract, if using semisweet
   chocolate pieces
2 cups mint chocolate pieces or semisweet
   chocolate pieces

GLAZE
¾ cup confectioners' sugar
2 drops mint extract
3½ teaspoons water

1. Heat oven to 375°.

2. Sift flour, cocoa powder, baking soda and salt into a medium-size bowl.

3. Beat butter with mixer on medium speed in a large bowl until creamy. Add brown sugar and granulated sugar; beat until fluffy. Beat in eggs, one at a time, beating well after each addition. Beat in vanilla and mint extract if needed.

4. Beat in flour mixture with mixer on low speed. Using a spatula, gently fold in chocolate pieces.

5. Drop dough by heaping teaspoonfuls, about 2 inches apart, onto ungreased baking sheets. Bake in heated 375° oven 9 to 11 minutes or until crisp. Let cool on sheet on a wire rack 2 minutes. Transfer to wire rack to cool completely.

6. Prepare glaze: Stir together confectioners' sugar, mint extract and water in a small bowl until smooth. Transfer to a plastic food-storage bag; snip off 1 corner of bag. Drizzle over cooled cookies. Let stand until glaze is set.

Desserts

221

Peppermint Chiffon Pie

Peppermint Chiffon Pie

MAKES 8 servings

PREP 15 minutes

REFRIGERATE 1 hour

———

PER SERVING
314 calories, 3 g protein,
17 g fat, 36 g carbohydrate,
330 mg sodium,
30 mg cholesterol.

2 cups crushed chocolate wafer cookies (30 to 36 cookies)
6 tablespoons (¾ stick) butter, softened
1 package (3.4 ounces) white chocolate instant pudding-and-pie-filling mix
1½ cups milk
3 drops red food coloring
¼ teaspoon peppermint extract
2½ cups frozen nondairy whipped topping, thawed
6 red and white mint candies

1. Measure 1½ cups cookie crumbs into a medium-size bowl. Stir in butter until well blended. Press mixture over bottom and up sides of a 9-inch pie plate.

2. Place pudding-and-pie-filling mix in a large bowl. Whisk in milk, food coloring and peppermint extract.

3. Fold in whipped topping. Pour one-third of mixture into pie shell. Layer with remaining cookie crumbs. Top with remaining filling. Refrigerate at least 1 hour or until set.

4. Unwrap and crush mint candies. Sprinkle around edge of pie. Serve chilled.

Holiday Trifle

MAKES 16 servings

PREP 15 minutes

REFRIGERATE 1 hour or
overnight

———

PER SERVING
402 calories, 6 g protein,
25 g fat, 39 g carbohydrate,
224 mg sodium,
99 mg cholesterol.

1 can (5 ounces) evaporated milk

1 can (14 ounces) sweetened condensed milk

2 all-butter pound cakes (12 ounces each), cut into 1-
inch cubes

2 cups heavy cream, whipped, or 4 cups frozen nondairy
whipped topping, thawed

1 cup sweetened flake coconut

Fresh raspberries for garnish (optional)

1. Combine evaporated milk and condensed milk in a small bowl.

2. Arrange half of cake cubes in a 3- to 4-quart straight-sided glass bowl. Pour half of milk mixture over cake cubes. Spread whipped cream or topping on top. Sprinkle with half of coconut.

3. Repeat layering with remaining ingredients.

4. Refrigerate at least 1 hour or overnight. Garnish with berries if desired.

Holiday Trifle

Double Ginger Scones

MAKES 12 scones

PREP 10 minutes

BAKE at 400° for 12 to 15 minutes

———————

PER SERVING
192 calories, 5 g protein,
3 g fat, 38 g carbohydrate,
355 mg sodium,
6 mg cholesterol.

2¾ cups all-purpose flour

½ cup packed light-brown sugar

1 tablespoon finely chopped crystallized ginger

1 tablespoon baking powder

1 teaspoon baking soda

1 teaspoon ground ginger

¾ teaspoon salt

¼ cup unsweetened applesauce

2 tablespoons butter or margarine, cut into pieces

1 cup vanilla low-fat yogurt

½ cup golden raisins

1 egg white, lightly beaten

1 tablespoon granulated sugar

1. Heat oven to 400°. Coat a large baking sheet with nonstick cooking spray.

2. Combine flour, brown sugar, crystallized ginger, baking powder, baking soda, ground ginger and salt in a large bowl. Add applesauce and butter; mix with fingers or a fork until mixture resembles coarse crumbs. Stir in yogurt and raisins.

3. Turn dough out onto a floured surface. Gather into a ball and pat into a 9-inch round. Using a sharp knife coated with nonstick cooking spray, cut into 12 equal wedges. Arrange wedges on prepared baking sheet, 2 inches apart. Brush with egg white; sprinkle with granulated sugar.

4. Bake in heated 400° oven 12 to 15 minutes or until golden brown. Remove to a wire rack to cool slightly. Serve warm or at room temperature.

Pecan Logs

MAKES 2½ dozen logs

PREP 15 minutes

BAKE at 350° 12 to 14 minutes

———————

PER LOG
89 calories, 1 g protein,
6 g fat, 9 g carbohydrate,
20 mg sodium,
8 mg cholesterol.

1¼ cups all-purpose flour

⅓ cup ground pecans

¼ teaspoon salt

½ cup (1 stick) butter, at room temperature

⅓ cup sugar

1 teaspoon vanilla

½ cup finely chopped pecans

½ cup semisweet chocolate pieces

1. Heat oven to 350°. Coat a large baking sheet with nonstick cooking spray.

2. Combine flour, ground pecans and salt in a small bowl.

3. Beat together butter, sugar and vanilla with mixer on medium speed in a medium-size bowl until creamy and smooth, about 2 minutes. Stir in flour mixture.

4. Fill a small bowl with water. Place chopped pecans on waxed paper. Pinch off pieces of dough in rounded teaspoonfuls. Roll into logs, dip into water and roll in finely chopped pecans to coat. Place on prepared baking sheet.

5. Bake in heated 350° oven 12 to 14 minutes; let cool on sheet on a wire rack.

6. Meanwhile, melt chocolate in top of a double boiler over barely simmering water, stirring until smooth. Dip one end of each cooled log into melted chocolate; place on waxed paper until firm.

Frozen Coconut Dream Pie

quick COOK

MAKES 12 servings

PREP 30 minutes

BAKE crust at 425° for 10 to 12 minutes

COOK filling 8 minutes

FREEZE 4 hours

———

PER SERVING
193 calories, 1 g protein, 12 g fat, 21 g carbohydrate, 62 mg sodium, 13 mg cholesterol.

CRUST

1²/₃ cups crushed animal crackers (about 60 crackers)

5 tablespoons butter, melted

1 tablespoon honey

FILLING

1 tablespoon sugar

¼ cup cornstarch

1 can (11.8 ounces) sweetened coconut water

3 tablespoons sweetened flake coconut

1 teaspoon coconut extract

1 container (8 ounces) frozen nondairy whipped topping, thawed

Grated lime rind for garnish (optional)

1. Heat oven to 425°.

2. Prepare crust: Combine cracker crumbs, melted butter and honey in a small bowl. Press crumb mixture evenly over bottom and sides of a 10-inch pie plate.

3. Bake crust in heated 425° oven 10 to 12 minutes or until slightly golden around edges. Transfer pie plate to a wire rack to cool.

4. Prepare filling: Mix sugar and cornstarch in a small saucepan. Stir in coconut water and coconut. Cook over medium heat until thickened and bubbly, 8 minutes. Add coconut extract. Let cool to room temperature, about 15 minutes.

5. Fold whipped topping into cooled coconut mixture. Spread filling evenly in prepared pie shell. Freeze at least until firm, about 4 hours.

6. To serve, let stand at room temperature to soften, about 1 hour if frozen solid. Garnish with grated lime rind if desired.

Chocolate Strawberry-Cream Pizza

quick COOK

MAKES 12 servings
PREP 20 minutes
COOK coconut 3 minutes
REFRIGERATE 1¼ hours

PER SERVING
415 calories, 6 g protein,
32 g fat, 32 g carbohydrate,
85 mg sodium,
21 mg cholesterol.

1½ cups plus 2 tablespoons semisweet
    chocolate pieces
2 tablespoons solid vegetable shortening
2 cups finely chopped nuts
½ cup sweetened flake coconut
1 package (8 ounces) cream cheese,
    at room temperature
2 tablespoons seedless strawberry jam
1 teaspoon vanilla
¾ cup red and green candy-coated chocolate pieces
½ ounce white chocolate baking bar, grated

1. Line a 14-inch pizza pan with heavy-duty aluminum foil.

2. Melt 1½ cups semisweet chocolate pieces and 1½ tablespoons (4½ teaspoons) shortening in top of a double boiler over barely simmering, not boiling, water, stirring until smooth. Add nuts.

3. Using a thin metal spatula, spread chocolate mixture over bottom of prepared pan. Refrigerate 1 hour, until firm.

4. Meanwhile, toast coconut in a large skillet over medium heat, stirring occasionally, until lightly golden, 3 minutes. Remove to paper toweling.

5. Invert chilled chocolate "crust" onto a flat tray or serving plate. Peel off foil, being careful not to break crust.

6. Beat cream cheese, jam and vanilla in a medium-size bowl. Carefully spread over crust, leaving a ½-inch border. Sprinkle with candy-coated chocolate pieces and coconut. Return to refrigerator.

7. Melt remaining 2 tablespoons semisweet chocolate pieces and ½ tablespoon (1½ teaspoons) shortening in top of a double boiler over barely simmering, not boiling, water, stirring until smooth.

8. Remove cheese-topped "crust" from refrigerator. Drizzle with melted chocolate; sprinkle with grated white chocolate. Serve immediately or refrigerate until ready to serve.

Chocolate Fondue

MAKES 6 servings

PREP 20 minutes

COOK 8 minutes

PER SERVING
192 calories, 3 g protein,
5 g fat, 39 g carbohydrate,
158 mg sodium,
1 mg cholesterol.

2 thin slices angelfood cake, cut into cubes

2 kiwis, peeled, halved lengthwise and cut crosswise
into ¼-inch-thick slices

1 banana, cut into ¼-inch-thick slices

1 pear, cored and sliced lengthwise into 6 wedges

½ cup evaporated skim milk

Scant ⅔ cup reduced-fat semisweet chocolate pieces
(4 ounces)

¼ teaspoon mint extract

1. Skewer cake, kiwi, banana and pear onto wooden picks. Arrange on outer edge of a serving plate. Cover with plastic wrap; refrigerate while making fondue.

2. Combine evaporated milk and chocolate in a small nonstick saucepan. Cook over medium heat, stirring often, 3 to 4 minutes or until mixture is bubbly. Continue to heat 3 to 4 minutes longer or until chocolate is melted and mixture is smooth and thick. Stir in mint extract. Pour into a small dipping cup.

3. Place chocolate in center of fruit plate. Serve immediately.

Note: You can use any fruit of your choice for this fondue.

Chocolate
Strawberry-Cream
Pizza, *opposite*

Mango Chiffon in Raspberry Sauce

CHIFFON

1 envelope unflavored gelatin

⅓ cup plus 2 tablespoons mango nectar

½ cup liquid egg substitute

¼ cup sugar

1 container (8 ounces) plain low-fat yogurt, stirred until
   very smooth

RASPBERRY SAUCE

½ pint fresh raspberries

2 tablespoons sugar, plus additional if desired

2 tablespoons water

Raspberries for garnish (optional)
Fresh mint for garnish (optional)

1. Prepare chiffon: Sprinkle gelatin over 2 tablespoons mango nectar in a small microwave-safe bowl or a saucepan; let stand 1 minute to soften. Microwave at 100% power 20 seconds or heat over low heat, stirring, to dissolve gelatin completely.

2. Beat egg substitute and sugar in a small bowl until light colored and thickened, about 5 minutes. Add remaining ⅓ cup mango nectar.

3. Add gelatin mixture; stir to combine. Fold in yogurt. Divide chiffon equally among six ⅔-cup custard cups or molds. Freeze overnight or until set.

4. Prepare sauce: Combine raspberries, sugar and water in a small saucepan. Cook over medium heat until raspberries are softened, about 5 minutes. Strain through a fine-mesh sieve into a small bowl, forcing mixture through with back of a spoon or rubber spatula; discard seeds. Taste; add more sugar to puree if too tart.

5. To serve: Run warm water over bottoms of custard cups until chiffons loosen. Carefully unmold onto dessert plates. Spoon sauce over chiffons. Garnish with raspberries and fresh mint if desired.

Caramel Bonbons

MAKES 20 cookies

PREP 15 minutes

BAKE at 350° 12 to 14 minutes

PER COOKIE
110 calories, 2 g protein,
6 g fat, 12 g carbohydrate,
40 mg sodium,
23 mg cholesterol.

1¼ cups all-purpose flour

⅓ cup unblanched almonds, finely chopped

¼ teaspoon salt

½ cup (1 stick) butter, at room temperature

⅓ cup sugar

1 egg, separated, white lightly beaten

½ teaspoon vanilla

½ teaspoon almond extract

5 small caramel candies

Red and green coarse decorating sugar crystals

1. Heat oven to 350°. Coat a large baking sheet with nonstick cooking spray.

2. Combine flour, almonds and salt in a small bowl.

3. Beat together butter, sugar, egg yolk, vanilla and almond extract with mixer on medium speed in a medium-size bowl until creamy and smooth, about 2 minutes. Stir in flour mixture.

4. Cut caramel candies into quarters. Divide dough into 20 equal balls. In palm of your hand, flatten 1 ball into a 2-inch round. Press a piece of caramel into center of dough; securely pinch dough closed. Reshape into a ball and place on baking sheet. Repeat with remaining caramel and dough, arranging balls 2 inches apart on baking sheet.

5. Brush tops of balls with egg white; sprinkle with sugar crystals. Bake in heated 350° oven 12 to 14 minutes or until lightly colored; be careful not to overbake or bonbons will split. Transfer to a wire rack to cool.

Chocolate Nut & Fruit Clusters

MAKES about 3 dozen candies

PREP 20 minutes

STAND 2 hours

PER CANDY
81 calories, 1 g protein,
4 g fat, 11 g carbohydrate,
26 mg sodium,
2 mg cholesterol.

1 package (12 ounces) milk chocolate pieces (2 cups)

¾ cup coarsely chopped cashews, almonds or
    macadamia nuts

¾ cup dark raisins

½ cup dried cranberries or chopped dried apricots

1. Line 2 baking sheets with waxed paper.

2. Melt chocolate in top of a double boiler over barely simmering water, stirring until smooth. Remove from heat. Stir in cashews, raisins and cranberries.

3. Drop chocolate mixture by teaspoonfuls onto prepared baking sheets. Let stand until hardened, about 2 hours.

Appendix

IT'S AMAZING how fast you can pull together a tasty dinner when you can turn to a well-stocked larder and freezer. Here's a list of the quick-prep items you should always have on hand.

Cupboard Staples

- Canned tuna
- Caponata
- Chutney
- Diced canned green chiles
- Flavored oils (garlic, rosemary and basil)
- Green peppercorns in brine
- Horseradish
- Hot-pepper jelly
- Marinated artichoke hearts
- Mustard (a variety, including Dijon, herbed and spicy brown)
- Pasta (all types and shapes)
- Pesto
- Prepared pizza crusts
- Roasted red peppers
- Salsa (in a variety of flavors)
- Salted cashews
- Spaghetti sauce (marinara, Alfredo)
- Stewed tomatoes (in a variety of flavors)
- Sun-dried tomatoes
- Teriyaki sauce
- Vinegars (a variety, including balsamic and rice-wine)

Freezer Fixin's

- Chopped onions
- Fruit (raspberries, strawberries, blueberries)
- Phyllo dough
- Poultry and meat
- Puff pastry sheets and shells
- Sliced carrots
- Small whole red potatoes
- Sweet pepper stir-fry

Note: Freeze boneless, skinless chicken breast halves on a baking sheet until frozen, then wrap individually for ease of use later; the same method works for pork cutlets or beef strips for stir-fry. Individually wrapped sausages are also quick options.

Pre-Prepped Ingredients

These days, produce and meat counters at many markets can offer a head start on supper. Just be sure to check the dates on the packages to ensure freshness.

- Broccoli flowerets
- Crumbled feta cheese (also in flavored varieties)
- Flavored olives
- Flavored tortillas
- Meat (patties and cut for stir-fry)
- Minced garlic in oil (store in refrigerator)
- Partially cooked new potato slices
- Refrigerated pizza crusts
- Shredded cabbage, carrots and coleslaw mixes
- Shredded mozzarella or taco-flavored cheeses
- Sliced mushrooms (portabella, shiitake, button)

Beyond Basics

OFTEN ALL YOU NEED to transform a plain dish into something special is a dollop of an easy-to-make sauce or a sprinkling of toasted nuts. Here are recipes for these basics and few others as well.

Grilled or Roasted Garlic

Rub 1 whole garlic head with 2 teaspoons olive oil. Loosely wrap in foil. Cook on a hot grill 40 minutes or bake in a heated 350° oven 1 hour or until cloves are soft.

Peanut Sauce

Combine ½ cup smooth peanut butter, ¼ cup water, 2 tablespoons reduced-sodium soy sauce, ½ teaspoon sugar and ¼ teaspoon ground ginger in a small bowl; whisk until well blended. Makes about ¾ cup.

Pesto

Stem, wash and spin-dry enough fresh basil to equal 8 cups (2 to 3 bunches). Working in batches, whirl basil and 1 clove garlic in a food processor or blender until smoothly chopped. Add 2 tablespoons toasted pine nuts (pignoli) or walnuts, 3 tablespoons chicken broth, 2 tablespoons grated Parmesan cheese, ¾ teaspoon salt and ¼ teaspoon black pepper; process until smooth. With processor running, add 3 tablespoons olive oil in a steady stream. To store, refrigerate in a sealed container up to 3 days or freeze up to 3 months. Makes 1 cup.

Toasted Nuts

Place whole or chopped nuts on a baking sheet. Bake in a heated 350° oven 8 minutes or until fragrant and lightly colored, stirring occasionally.

Toasted Pumpkin Seeds or Sesame Seeds

Place pumpkin seeds or sesame seeds in a dry nonstick skillet over low heat and cook several minutes or just until golden, shaking often; do not allow seeds to burn.

Index

Numerals set in bold type indicate
photographs.

Family Circle **Quick & Easy** Recipes

Acknowledgments

THE EDITORS OF *FAMILY CIRCLE* want to thank the members of the food department for their tireless efforts in creating recipes for our speeded-up lifestyles: Diane Mogelever, Julie Miltenberger, Keri Linas, Keisha Davis, Robert Yamarone, Michael Tyrrell, Patty Santelli, JoAnn Brett and Lauren Huber. Thanks also to our frequent contributors: Jean Anderson, Marie Bianco, Sylvia Carter, Bea Cihak, Jim Fobel, Libby Hillman, Michael Krondl and Andrew Schloss. More thanks to the writers, editors and designers who polish and perfect our recipes and photographs: David Ricketts, Jonna M. Gallo and Diane Lamphron. Thanks to the books and licensing team of Tammy Palazzo, Sabeena Lalwani, Tana McPherson and Carla Clark. And kudos to Roundtable Press for bringing this project to life: Marsha Melnick, Susan Meyer, Julie Merberg, Carol Spier, Carrie Glidden, Laura Smyth and Vertigo Design.

Photography Credits

Steve Cohen: pages 3 (bottom), 7 (top), 39, 51, 55, 58, 110, 171, 182, 203 (right) and 207.

Brian Hagiwara: pages 3 (top), 6, 7 (bottom), 11, 19, 35 (left), 42, 63, 67, 75, 79, 83, 90, 91, 99 (all), 107, 115, 123 (all), 135 (left), 139, 147, 159 (all), 163, 167, 170, 178, 187, 191, 199, 203 (left), 206, 210, 211, 215 (all), 222 and 227.

Martin Jacobs: pages 127, 135 (right) and 155.

Michael Luppino: pages 23 and 27.

Steven Mark Needham: pages 46, 102, 131 and 195 (left).

Dean Powell: page 179.

Alan Richardson: pages 7 (left), 14, 35 (right), 47, 95, 119, 195 (right), 219 and 223.

Carin & David Riley: page 82.

Ellen Silverman: pages 2 (right), 18, 31, 43 and 174.

Anne Stratton: pages 87, 146 and 154.

Mark Thomas: pages 2 (left), 71, 138, 143 and 150.